THE ANSWER TO THE LYRE

THE ANSWER TO THE LYRE

Richard Bentley's Illustrations for Thomas Gray's Poems

LOFTUS JESTIN

upp

UNIVERSITY OF PENNSYLVANIA PRESS

Philadelphia

Published with support from the Yale University Library.

FRONTISPIECE: Engraving of Richard Bentley, after Eccardt, by James Heath. (Courtesy of the Print Collection, Lewis Walpole Library, Yale University.)

Printed in the United States of America

Library of Congress Cataloging-in-Publication Data

Jestin, Loftus.
The answer to the lyre: Richard Bentley's illustrations for Thomas Gray's poems / Loftus Jestin.
p. cm.
Includes a facsimile of: Designs by Mr. R. Bentley, for six poems / by Mr. T. Gray.
Includes bibliographical references.
ISBN 0-8122-8184-5
1. Bentley, R. (Richard), 1708–1782—Criticism and interpretation. 2. Gray, Thomas, 1716–1771—Illustrations. I. Bentley, R. (Richard), 1708–1782. II. Gray, Thomas, 1716–1771. Designs by Mr. R. Bentley, for six poems. 1990. III. Title.
NC978.5.B46J47 1990
741.6′4′092—dc20 89-24987
CIP

FOR CHARBRA

Contents

Acknowledgments ix

Facsimile of *Designs by Mr. R. Bentley, for Six Poems by Mr. T. Gray* 1

Introduction 83

I: History of the Publication 91

II: Background for Bentley's Graphic Art 104

III: Title Page Fleuron 131

IV: Designs for *Ode on the Spring* 141

V: Designs for *Ode on the Death of a Favourite Cat* 152

VI: Designs for *Ode on a Distant Prospect of Eton College* 160

VII: Designs for *A Long Story* 175

VIII: Designs for *Hymn to Adversity* 186

IX: Designs for *Elegy Written in a Country Church-Yard* 200

X: Conclusion 211

Appendix I: Designs for *The Bard* 218

Appendix II: Identification of Engravers 222

Appendix III: Illustrations 224

Index 346

Acknowledgments

I owe my deepest debt of gratitude to the late Wilmarth Sheldon Lewis, for without his library this book would never have been written. It was he who sparked my interest in the interplay between Richard Bentley's illustrations and Thomas Gray's poems and who generously invited me to use his unique collection of Walpoliana.

I also give grateful acknowledgment to Ronald Paulson, who taught me to look at book illustrations with critical insight. Valuable help was given to me by Michael McCarthy, Robert Halsband, and two anonymous readers who reviewed my manuscript for the University of Pennsylvania Press. Millicent Abell, Yale University Librarian, and Karin Trainer, Associate University Librarian at Yale, facilitated a subvention from the Yale Libraries for the University of Pennsylvania Press; the Board of Managers for The Lewis Walpole Library have overseen the publication of the illustrations; Joan Sussler, Curator of Prints and Drawings at The Lewis Walpole Library, provided expert assistance with photographic reproductions; and Catherine Jestin helped me in the careful revision of the manuscript. Others who have made contributions include Martin Price, Michael Snodin, Marie Devine, and Karen Peltier.

The following libraries and museums have kindly given me permission to reproduce drawings and prints from their collections: the Boston Museum of Fine Arts, the British Museum, the Hamburger Kunsthalle, the Houghton Library at Harvard, the Kunsthistorisches Museum at Vienna, the Lowe Art Museum of the University of Miami, the Musée du Louvre, and the following departments at Yale University: The Art and Architecture Library, Beinecke Rare Book and Manuscript Library, The Lewis Walpole Library, The Seeley Mudd Library, The Sterling Memorial Library, The Yale Center for British Art, The Yale Medical Historical Library, and the Yale University Art Gallery.

In silent gaze the tuneful choir among,
   Half pleas'd, half blushing let the muse admire,
While Bentley leads her sister-art along,
   And bids the pencil answer to the lyre.

Thomas Gray, *Stanzas to Mr. Bentley*

Poets are liars by profession.

David Hume, *Treatise of Human Nature*, I.iii.10

Facsimile of

Designs by Mr. R. Bentley, for Six Poems by Mr. T. Gray

DRAWINGS, &c.

DESIGNS

BY

Mr. R. BENTLEY,

FOR SIX

POEMS

BY

Mr. T. GRAY.

LONDON:
Printed for R. DODSLEY, in Pall-mall.

MDCCLIII.

Müller Sc.

O D E.

LO! where the roſy-boſom'd Hours,
Fair VENUS' train appear,
Diſcloſe the long-expecting flowers,
And wake the purple year!
The Attic warbler pours her throat,
Reſponſive to the cuckow's note,
The untaught harmony of ſpring:
While whiſp'ring pleaſure as they fly,
Cool Zephyrs thro' the clear blue ſky
Their gather'd fragrance fling.

Where'er

Where'er the oak's thick branches ſtretch
A broader browner ſhade ;
Where'er the rude and moſs-grown beech
O'er-canopies the glade ;
Beſide ſome water's ruſhy brink
With me the Muſe ſhall ſit, and think
(At eaſe reclin'd in ruſtic ſtate)
How vain the ardour of the Crowd,
How low, how little are the Proud,
How indigent the Great !

Still is the toiling hand of Care :
The panting herds repoſe :
Yet hark, how thro' the peopled air
The buſy murmur glows !
The inſect youth are on the wing,
Eager to taſte the honied ſpring,

And float amid the liquid noon:
Some lightly o'er the current ſkim,
Some ſhew their gayly-gilded trim
Quick-glancing to the ſun.

To Contemplation's ſober eye
Such is the race of Man:
And they that creep, and they that fly,
Shall end where they began.
Alike the Buſy and the Gay
But flutter thro' life's little day,
In fortune's varying colours dreſt:
Bruſh'd by the hand of rough Miſchance,
Or chill'd by age, their airy dance
They leave, in duſt to reſt.

Methinks I hear in accents low
The ſportive kind reply:
Poor moraliſt! and what art thou?
A ſolitary fly!

Thy

Thy Joys no glittering female meets,
No hive haſt thou of hoarded ſweets,
No painted plumage to diſplay:
On haſty wings thy youth is flown;
Thy ſun is ſet, thy ſpring is gone ----
We frolick, while 'tis May.

T G
R B

O D E

On the Death of a Favourite CAT,

Drowned in a Tub of Gold Fiſhes.

TWAS on a lofty vaſe's ſide,
Where China's gayeſt art had dy'd
The azure flowers, that blow;
Demureſt of the tabby kind,
The penſive Selima reclin'd,
Gazed on the lake below.

Her conſcious tail her joy declar'd;
The fair round face, the ſnowy beard,
The velvet of her paws,
Her coat, that with the tortoiſe vies,
Her ears of jet, and emerald eyes,
She ſaw; and purr'd applauſe.

Still

Still had ſhe gaz'd: but 'midſt the tide
Two angel forms were ſeen to glide,
   The Genii of the ſtream:
Their ſcaly armour's Tyrian hue
Thro' richeſt purple to the view
   Betray'd a golden gleam.

The hapleſs Nymph with wonder ſaw:
A whiſker firſt and then a claw,
   With many an ardent wiſh,
She ſtretch'd in vain to reach the prize.
What female heart can gold deſpiſe?
   What Cat's averſe to fiſh?

Preſumptuous Maid! with looks intent
Again ſhe ſtretch'd, again ſhe bent,
   Nor knew the gulf between.
(Malignant Fate ſat by, and ſmil'd)
The ſlipp'ry verge her feet beguil'd,
   She tumbled headlong in.

Eight times emerging from the flood
She mew'd to ev'ry watry God,
   Some ſpeedy aid to ſend.

No

No Dolphin came, no Nereid ſtirr'd :
Nor cruel *Tom*, nor *Suſan* heard.
A Fav'rite has no friend !

From hence, ye Beauties, undeceiv'd,
Know, one falſe ſtep is ne'er retriev'd,
And be with caution bold.
Not all that tempts your wand'ring eyes
And heedleſs hearts, is lawful prize ;
Nor all, that gliſters, gold.

AH TELL THEM THEY ARE MEN
J.S. Muller Sc.

O D E

On a Diſtant Proſpect of

ETON COLLEGE.

YE diſtant ſpires, ye antique towers,
That crown the watry glade,
Where grateful Science ſtill adores
Her HENRY's holy Shade;
And ye, that from the ſtately brow
Of WINDSOR's heights th' expanſe below
Of grove, of lawn, of mead ſurvey,
Whoſe turf, whoſe ſhade, whoſe flowers among
Wanders the hoary Thames along
His ſilver-winding way.

Ah

Ah happy hills, ah pleaſing ſhade,
Ah fields belov'd in vain,
Where once my careleſs childhood ſtray'd,
A ſtranger yet to pain!
I feel the gales, that from ye blow,
A momentary bliſs beſtow,
As waving freſh their gladſome wing,
My weary ſoul they ſeem to ſooth,
And, redolent of joy and youth,
To breath a ſecond ſpring.

Say, Father THAMES, for thou haſt ſeen
Full many a ſprightly race
Diſporting on thy margent green
The paths of pleaſure trace,
Who foremoſt now delight to cleave
With pliant arm thy glaſſy wave?
The captive linnet which enthrall?
What idle progeny ſucceed
To chaſe the rolling circle's ſpeed,
Or urge the flying ball?

While

While ſome on earneſt buſineſs bent
Their murm'ring labours ply
'Gainſt graver hours, that bring conſtraint
To ſweeten liberty:
Some bold adventurers diſdain
The limits of their little reign,
And unknown regions dare deſcry:
Still as they run they look behind,
They hear a voice in every wind,
And ſnatch a fearful joy.

Gay hope is theirs by fancy fed,
Leſs pleaſing when poſſeſt;
The tear forgot as ſoon as ſhed,
The ſunſhine of the breaſt:
Theirs buxom health of roſy hue,
Wild wit, invention ever-new,
And lively chear of vigour born;
The thoughtleſs day, the eaſy night,
The ſpirits pure, the ſlumbers light,
That fly th' approach of morn.

Alas,

Alas, regardleſs of their doom,
The little victims play !
No ſenſe have they of ills to come,
Nor care beyond to-day :
Yet ſee how all around 'em wait
The Miniſters of human fate,
And black Misfortune's baleful train !
Ah, ſhew them where in ambuſh ſtand
To ſeize their prey the murth'rous band !
Ah, tell them, they are men !

Theſe ſhall the fury Paſſions tear,
The vulturs of the mind,
Diſdainful Anger, pallid Fear,
And Shame that ſculks behind ;
Or pineing Love ſhall waſte their youth,
Or Jealouſy with rankling tooth,
That inly gnaws the ſecret heart,
And Envy wan, and faded Care,
Grim-viſag'd comfortleſs Deſpair,
And Sorrow's piercing dart.

Ambition

Ambition this ſhall tempt to riſe,
Then whirl the wretch from high,
To bitter Scorn a ſacrifice,
And grinning Infamy.
The ſtings of Falſhood thoſe ſhall try,
And hard Unkindneſs' alter'd eye,
That mocks the tear it forc'd to flow;
And keen Remorſe with blood defil'd,
And moody Madneſs laughing wild
Amid ſevereſt woe.

Lo, in the vale of years beneath
A grieſly troop are ſeen,
The painful family of Death,
More hideous than their Queen:
This racks the joints, this fires the veins,
That every labouring ſinew ſtrains,
Thoſe in the deeper vitals rage:
Lo, Poverty, to fill the band,
That numbs the ſoul with icy hand,
And ſlow-conſuming Age.

To each his suff'rings: all are men,
Condemn'd alike to groan,
The tender for another's pain;
Th' unfeeling for his own.
Yet ah! why should they know their fate?
Since sorrow never comes too late,
And happiness too swiftly flies.
Thought would destroy their paradise.
No more; where ignorance is bliss,
'Tis folly to be wise.

J.S. Müller sc.

A Long STORY.

IN BRITAIN's Isle, no matter where,
An ancient pile of building stands:
The Huntingdons and Hattons there
Employ'd the power of Fairy hands

To raise the cieling's fretted height,
Each pannel in achievements cloathing,
Rich windows that exclude the light,
And passages, that lead to nothing.

Full

Full oft within the ſpatious walls,
When he had fifty winters o'er him,
My grave [a] Lord-Keeper led the Brawls:
The Seal, and Maces, danc'd before him.

His buſhy beard, and ſhoe-ſtrings green,
His high-crown'd hat, and ſattin-doublet,
Mov'd the ſtout heart of England's Queen,
Tho' Pope and Spaniard could not trouble it.

What, in the very firſt beginning!
Shame of the verſifying tribe!
Your Hiſt'ry whither are you ſpinning?
Can you do nothing but deſcribe?

A Houſe there is, (and that's enough)
From whence one fatal morning iſſues
A brace of Warriors, not in buff,
But ruſtling in their ſilks and tiſſues.

[a] Hatton, prefer'd by Queen Elizabeth for his graceful Perſon and fine Dancing.

The firſt came cap-a-pee from France
Her conqu'ring deſtiny fulfilling,
Whom meaner Beauties eye aſkance,
And vainly ape her art of killing.

The other Amazon kind Heaven
Had arm'd with ſpirit, wit, and ſatire :
But COBHAM had the poliſh given,
And tip'd her arrows with good-nature.

To celebrate her eyes, her air - - - - -
Coarſe panegyricks would but teaze her.
Meliſſa is her Nom de Guerre.
Alas, who would not wiſh to pleaſe her!

With bonnet blue and capucine,
And aprons long they hid their armour,
And veil'd their weapons bright and keen
In pity to the country-farmer.

Fame

Fame in the ſhape of Mr. P---t
(By this time all the Pariſh know it)
Had told, that thereabouts there lurk'd
A wicked Imp they call a Poet,

Who prowl'd the country far and near,
Bewitch'd the children of the peaſants,
Dried up the cows, and lam'd the deer,
And ſuck'd the eggs, and kill'd the pheaſants.

My Lady heard their joint petition,
Swore by her coronet and ermine,
She'd iſſue out her high commiſſion
To rid the manour of ſuch vermin.

The Heroines undertook the taſk,
Thro' lanes unknown, o'er ſtiles they ventur'd,
Rap'd at the door, nor ſtay'd to aſk,
But bounce into the parlour enter'd.

The trembling family they daunt,
They flirt, they ſing, they laugh, they tattle,
Rummage his Mother, pinch his Aunt,
And up ſtairs in a whirlwind rattle.

Each hole and cupboard they explore,
Each creek and cranny of his chamber,
Run hurry-ſkurry round the floor,
And o'er the bed and teſter clamber,

Into the Drawers and China pry,
Papers and books, a huge Imbroglio!
Under a tea-cup he might lie,
Or creaſed, like dogs-ears, in a folio.

On the firſt marching of the troops
The Muſes, hopeleſs of his pardon,
Convey'd him underneath their hoops
To a ſmall cloſet in the garden.

So

So Rumor ſays. (Who will, believe.)
But that they left the door a-jarr,
Where, ſafe and laughing in his ſleeve,
He heard the diſtant din of war.

Short was his joy. He little knew,
The power of Magick was no fable.
Out of the window, whiſk, they flew,
But left a ſpell upon the table.

The words too eager to unriddle
The Poet felt a ſtrange diſorder:
Tranſparent birdlime form'd the middle,
And chains inviſible the border.

So cunning was the Apparatus,
The powerful pothooks did ſo move him,
That, will he, nill he, to the Great-houſe
He went, as if the Devil drove him.

Yet

Yet on his way (no ſign of grace,
For folks in fear are apt to pray)
To Phœbus he prefer'd his caſe,
And beg'd his aid that dreadful day.

The Godhead would have back'd his quarrel,
But with a bluſh on recollection
Own'd, that his quiver and his laurel
'Gainſt four ſuch eyes were no protection.

The Court was ſate, the Culprit there,
Forth from their gloomy manſions creeping
The Lady *Janes* and *Joans* repair,
And from the gallery ſtand peeping:

Such as in ſilence of the night
Come (ſweep) along ſome winding entry
([b] *Styack* has often ſeen the ſight)
Or at the chappel-door ſtand ſentry;

[b] The House-Keeper.

In peaked hoods and mantles tarnifh'd,
Sour vifages, enough to fcare ye,
High Dames of honour once, that garnifh'd
The drawing-room of fierce Queen Mary!

The Peerefs comes. The Audience ftare,
And doff their hats with due fubmiffion:
She curtfies, as fhe takes her chair,
To all the People of condition.

The Bard with many an artful fib,
Had in imagination fenc'd him,
Difproved the arguments of [c] *Squib*,
And all that [d] *Groom* could urge againft him.

But foon his rhetorick forfook him,
When he the folemn hall had feen;
A fudden fit of ague fhook him,
He ftood as mute as poor [e] *Macleane*.

[c] *Groom of the Chambers.*
[d] *The Steward.*
[e] *A famous Highwayman hang'd the week before.*

Yet

Yet ſomething he was heard to mutter,
' How in the park beneath an old-tree
' (Without deſign to hurt the butter,
' Or any malice to the poultry,)

' He once or twice had pen'd a ſonnet;
' Yet hoped, that he might ſave his bacon:
' Numbers would give their oaths upon it,
' He ne'er was for a conj'rer taken.

The ghoſtly Prudes with hagged face
Already had condemn'd the ſinner.
My Lady roſe, and with a grace ----
She ſmiled, and bid him come to dinner.

' Jeſu-Maria! Madam Bridget,
' Why, what can the Vicounteſs mean?
(Cried the ſquare Hoods in woful fidget)
' The times are alter'd quite and clean!

'Decorum's turn'd to mere civility;
'Her air and all her manners ſhew it.
'Commend me to her affability!
'Speak to a Commoner and Poet!

[*Here* 500 *Stanza's are loſt.*]

And ſo God ſave our noble King,
And guard us from long-winded Lubbers,
That to eternity would ſing,
And keep my Lady from her Rubbers.

HYMN to ADVERSITY.

DAUGHTER of JOVE, relentless Power,
Thou Tamer of the human breast,
Whose iron scourge and tort'ring hour
The Bad affright, afflict the Best!
Bound in thy adamantine chain
The Proud are taught to taste of pain,
And purple Tyrants vainly groan
With pangs unfelt before, unpitied and alone.

When

When firſt thy Sire to ſend on earth
Virtue, his darling Child, deſign'd,
To thee he gave the heav'nly Birth,
And bad to form her infant mind.
Stern rugged Nurſe! thy rigid lore
With patience many a year ſhe bore:
What ſorrow was, thou bad'ſt her know,
And from her own ſhe learn'd to melt at other's
woe.

Scared at thy frown terrific, fly
Self-pleaſing Folly's idle brood,
Wild Laughter, Noiſe, and thoughtleſs Joy,
And leave us leiſure to be good.
Light they diſperſe, and with them go
The ſummer Friend, the flatt'ring Foe;
By vain Proſperity received,
To her they vow their truth, and are again believed.

Wiſdom

Wisdom in sable garb array'd
Immers'd in rapt'rous thought profound,
And Melancholy, silent maid
With leaden eye, that loves the ground,
Still on thy solemn steps attend :
Warm Charity, the gen'ral friend,
With Justice to herself severe,
And Pity, dropping soft the sadly-pleasing tear.

Oh, gently on thy Suppliant's head,
Dread Goddess, lay thy chast'ning hand!
Not in thy Gorgon terrors clad,
Nor circled with the vengeful Band
(As by the Impious thou art seen)
With thund'ring voice, and threat'ning mien,
With screaming Horror's funeral cry,
Despair, and fell Disease, and ghastly Poverty.

Thy

Thy form benign, oh Goddeſs, wear,
Thy milder influence impart,
Thy philoſophic Train be there
To ſoften, not to wound my heart,
The gen'rous ſpark extinct revive,
Teach me to love and to forgive,
Exact my own defects to ſcan,
What others are, to feel, and know myſelf a Man.

C. Grignion sculp.

E L E G Y

Written in a Country Church Yard.

THE Curfew tolls the knell of parting day,
The lowing herd wind ſlowly o'er the lea,
The plowman homeward plods his weary way,
And leaves the world to darkneſs and to me.

Now

Now fades the glimmering landſcape on the ſight,
And all the air a ſolemn ſtillneſs holds,
Save where the beetle wheels his droning flight,
And drowſy tinklings lull the diſtant folds ;

Save that from yonder ivy-mantled tow'r
The mopeing owl does to the moon complain
Of ſuch, as wand'ring near her ſecret bow'r,
Moleſt her ancient ſolitary reign.

Beneath thoſe rugged elms, that yew-tree's ſhade,
Where heaves the turf in many a mould'ring heap,
Each in his narrow cell for ever laid,
The rude Forefathers of the hamlet ſleep.

The breezy call of incenſe-breathing Morn,
The ſwallow twitt'ring from the ſtraw-built ſhed,
The cock's ſhrill clarion, or the ecchoing horn,
No more ſhall rouſe them from their lowly bed.

For

For them no more the blazing hearth ſhall burn,
Or buſy houſwife ply her evening care:
No children run to liſp their ſire's return,
Or climb his knees the envied kiſs to ſhare.

Oft did the harveſt to their ſickle yield,
Their furrow oft the ſtubborn glebe has broke;
How jocund did they drive their team afield!
How bow'd the woods beneath their ſturdy ſtroke!

Let not Ambition mock their uſeful toil,
Their homely joys, and deſtiny obſcure;
Nor Grandeur hear with a diſdainful ſmile,
The ſhort and ſimple annals of the poor.

The boaſt of heraldry, the pomp of pow'r,
And all that beauty, all that wealth e'er gave,
Awaits alike th' inevitable hour.
The paths of glory lead but to the grave.

Nor

Nor you, ye Proud, impute to Thefe the fault,
If Mem'ry o'er their Tomb no Trophies raife,
Where thro' the long-drawn ifle and fretted vault
The pealing anthem fwells the note of praife.

Can ftoried urn or animated buft
Back to its manfion call the fleeting breath?
Can Honour's voice provoke the filent duft,
Or Flatt'ry footh the dull cold ear of Death!

Perhaps in this neglected fpot is laid
Some heart once pregnant with celeftial fire,
Hands, that the rod of empire might have fway'd,
Or wak'd to extafy the living lyre.

But Knowledge to their eyes her ample page
Rich with the fpoils of time did ne'er unroll;
Chill Penury reprefs'd their noble rage,
And froze the genial current of the foul.

Full many a gem of pureſt ray ſerene,
The dark unfathom'd caves of ocean bear :
Full many a flower is born to bluſh unſeen,
And waſte its ſweetneſs on the deſert air.

Some village-Hampden, that with dauntleſs breaſt
The little Tyrant of his fields withſtood ;
Some mute inglorious Milton here may reſt,
Some Cromwell guiltleſs of his country's blood.

Th' applauſe of liſt'ning ſenates to command,
The threats of pain and ruin to deſpiſe,
To ſcatter plenty o'er a ſmiling land,
And read their hiſt'ry in a nation's eyes

Their lot forbad : nor circumſcrib'd alone
Their growing virtues, but their crimes confin'd ;
Forbad to wade through ſlaughter to a throne,
And ſhut the gates of mercy on mankind,

The

The ſtruggling pangs of conſcious truth to hide,
To quench the bluſhes of ingenuous ſhame,
Or heap the ſhrine of Luxury and Pride
With incenſe kindled at the Muſe's flame.

Far from the madding crowd's ignoble ſtrife,
Their ſober wiſhes never learn'd to ſtray ;
Along the cool ſequeſter'd vale of life
They kept the noiſeleſs tenor of their way.

Yet ev'n theſe bones from inſult to protect
Some frail memorial ſtill erected nigh,
With uncouth rhimes and ſhapeleſs ſculpture [deck'd,
Implores the paſſing tribute of a ſigh.

Their name, their years, ſpelt by th' unletter'd muſe,
The place of fame and elegy ſupply :
And many a holy text around ſhe ſtrews,
That teach the ruſtic moraliſt to dye.

For

For who to dumb Forgetfulneſs a prey,
This pleaſing anxious being e'er reſign'd,
Left the warm precincts of the chearful day,
Nor caſt one longing ling'ring look behind?

On ſome fond breaſt the parting ſoul relies,
Some pious drops the cloſing eye requires;
Ev'n from the tomb the voice of Nature cries,
Ev'n in our Aſhes live their wonted Fires.

For thee, who mindful of th' unhonour'd Dead
Doſt in theſe lines their artleſs tale relate;
If chance, by lonely contemplation led,
Some kindred Spirit ſhall inquire thy fate,

Haply ſome hoary-headed Swain may ſay,
'Oft have we ſeen him at the peep of dawn
'Bruſhing with haſty ſteps the dews away
'To meet the ſun upon the upland lawn.

'There

'There at the foot of yonder nodding beech
'That wreathes its old fantaſtic roots ſo high,
'His liſtleſs length at noontide wou'd he ſtretch,
'And pore upon the brook that babbles by.

'Hard by yon wood, now ſmiling as in ſcorn,
'Mutt'ring his wayward fancies he wou'd rove,
'Now drooping, woeful wan, like one forlorn,
'Or craz'd with care, or croſs'd in hopeleſs love.

'One morn I miſs'd him on the cuſtom'd hill,
'Along the heath and near his fav'rite tree;
'Another came; nor yet beſide the rill,
'Nor up the lawn, nor at the wood was he,

'The next with dirges due in ſad array
'Slow thro' the church-way path we ſaw him born.
'Approach and read (for thou can'ſt read) the lay,
'Grav'd on the ſtone beneath yon aged thorn.

The EPITAPH.

HERE rests his head upon the lap of Earth
A Youth to Fortune and to Fame unknown,
Fair Science frown'd not on his humble birth,
And Melancholy mark'd him for her own.

Large was his bounty, and his soul sincere,
Heav'n did a recompence as largely send:
He gave to Mis'ry all he had, a tear,
He gain'd from Heav'n ('twas all he wish'd) a friend.

No farther seek his merits to disclose,
Or draw his frailties from their dread abode,
(There they alike in trembling hope repose)
The bosom of his Father and his God.

EXPLANATION

OF THE

PRINTS.

ODE on the SPRING.

FRONTISPIECE.

A Figure mufing, &c. The ornaments allude to the chief fubjects of the poems, as the altar, chaplet of flowers and ruftic pipe, to this ode: a boy with a hobby-horfe and a book, to that on Eton: a cat-arion, or a cat with a lyre fitting on a dolphin's back, to that line on the death of a cat

No Dolphin came, no Nereid ftirr'd:

a monkey with a violin and lawyer's wig, to my lord keeper Hatton's dancing, in the Long Story: a Roman fepulchral altar infcribed Diis Manibus Sacrum, with a fpade and fkull, to the elegy. The monkey painting, the lyre, the pen and crayon, are allufive to the poems and drawings.

HEADPIECE.] The Graces and Zephyrs fporting.

INITIAL LETTER.] Flowers.

TAILPIECE.] A landfcape with herds repofing.

ODE

ODE on the Death of a Favourite CAT.

FRONTISPIECE.

THE cat ſtanding on the brim of the tub, and endeavouring to catch a gold fiſh. Two cariatides of a river god ſtopping his ears to her cries, and Deſtiny cutting the nine threads of life, are on each ſide. Above, is a cat's head between two expiring lamps, and over that, two mouſe-traps, between a mandarin-cat ſitting before a Chineſe pagoda, and angling for gold fiſh into a china jar; and another cat drawing up a net. At the bottom are mice enjoying themſelves on the proſpect of the cat's death; a lyre and pallet.

HEADPIECE.] The cat almoſt drowned in the tub. A ſtandiſh on a table to write her elegy. Two cats as mourners with hatbands and ſtaves. Dead birds, mice and fiſh hung up on each ſide.

INITIAL LETTER.] The cat, demureſt of the tabby kind, dozing in an elbow chair.

TAILPIECE.] Charon ferrying over the ghoſt of the deceaſed cat, who ſets up her back on ſeeing Cerberus on the ſhore.

ODE on the diſtant Proſpect of ETON.

FRONTISPIECE.

BOYS at their ſports, near the chapel of Eton, the god of the Thames ſitting by: the paſſions, misfortunes, and diſeaſes, coming down upon them. On either ſide, terms repreſenting Jealouſy and Madneſs. Above is a head of Folly: beneath, are play-things intermixed with thorns, a ſword, a ſerpent and a ſcorpion.

EXPLANATION OF THE PRINTS.

HEADPIECE.] Science adoring the ſhade of Henry VIth. Two angels bearing ſhields inſcribed with that king's name ſupport a Gothic building, in alluſion to his foundations at Eton and Cambridge.

INITIAL LETTER.] Part of Windſor-caſtle.

TAILPIECE.] Two boys dreſt in watermen's cloaths, rowing another. A view of Eton college at a diſtance.

THE LONG STORY.

FRONTISPIECE.

THE Muſes conveying the Poet under their hoops to a ſmall cloſet in the garden. Fame in the ſhape of Mr. P---- is flying before; and after him the two female warriors, as deſcribed in the verſes. On one ſide is my lord keeper Hatton dancing; and among the ornaments are the heads of the Pope and queen Elizabeth nodding at one another; behind him is a papal bull, a phial of ſublimate, a dagger and a crucifix; behind her the cannon called queen Elizabeth's pocket-piſtol.

HEADPIECE.] A view of the houſe which formerly belonged to the earls of Huntingdon and lord keeper Hatton.

INITIAL LETTER.] A coronet, fan, muff and tippet, in the manner of Hollar.

TAILPIECE.] Ghoſts of ancient ladies and old maids, peeping over the gallery.

HYMN

HYMN to ADVERSITY.

FRONTISPIECE.

JUPITER delivering infant Virtue to Adverſity to be educated. Minerva and Hercules on each ſide.

HEADPIECE.] Adverſity diſturbing the Orgies of Folly, Noiſe and Laughter.

INITIAL LETTER.] A Gorgon's head, and inſtruments of puniſhment.

TAILPIECE.] Melancholy.

ELEGY Written in a Country Church-yard.

FRONTISPIECE.

A Gothic gateway in ruins with the emblems of nobility on one ſide; on the other, the implements and employments of the Poor. Thro' the arch appears a church-yard and village-church built out of the remains of an abbey. A countryman ſhowing an epitaph to a paſſenger.

HEADPIECE.] Country-labours.

INITIAL LETTER.] An owl diſturbed and flying from a ruinous tower.

TAILPIECE.] A country burial. At bottom, a torch fallen into an ancient vault.

THE ANSWER TO THE LYRE

Introduction

WHEN *Designs by Mr. R. Bentley, for Six Poems by Mr. T. Gray* was published by Robert Dodsley in 1753, it was an instant success and was followed by six other editions, the last of which appeared in 1789. Although acknowledged as a milestone in the history of book illustration, *Designs* has been out of print for two hundred years and has become so scarce that it is generally to be found only in rare book libraries. The facsimile in this volume provides an opportunity at last for the general reader and specialist in eighteenth-century studies to appreciate the extraordinary collaboration between a great English poet and his illustrator.

Four of the six poems had been published earlier. In 1750 Thomas Gray sent *Elegy Written in a Country Church-Yard* to his friend Horace Walpole, who recognized its importance and in 1751 arranged for its publication. Again it was Horace Walpole who approached Dodsley with the ambitious plan of an illustrated edition of six poems by Gray: *Ode on the Spring, Ode on the Death of a Favourite Cat, Ode on a Distant Prospect of Eton College, Elegy Written in a Country Church-Yard,* and two new poems, *A Long Story* and *Hymn to Adversity.* The artist Walpole had in mind for the illustrations was Richard Bentley, an unknown amateur then and still a minor figure today.

Richard Bentley has inspired little biographical interest, with the result that scant information is now to be found. He was born in 1708, the only surviving son of the renowned classical scholar Dr. Richard Bentley, Master of Trinity College, Cambridge. Unusually precocious, he entered Trinity College at the age of ten, matriculated at eleven, was granted a B.A. as a "Junior Bachelor" at fifteen, and by special favor of his father was simultaneously elected a fellow. At the end of 1724, Dr. Bentley surrendered his position as Keeper of the King's Libraries to his sixteen-year-old son, a lifetime appointment that carried a salary of £200 per annum,[1] an enormous sum at the period. In 1725 the fellows at Trinity College, outraged by Dr. Bentley's nepotism, refused to give young Bentley the Craven scholarship even though his father was one of the judges. In 1727, however, his son having received an M.A. degree at the age of nineteen, Dr. Bentley exerted his influence once more and obtained yet another favor for him, a lay fellowship. On 23 October 1731 a disastrous fire destroyed part of the Cottonian and King's Libraries at Ashburnham House; Dr. Bentley rescued the *Codex Alexandrinus* but valued collections were lost. Young Bentley, in residence at the time,[2] received some of the blame and was eventually forced to resign. He was dependent on his father's influence even after his first marriage in the early 1730s; his continued dependency and the comparisons drawn between father and son made the young Bentley recalcitrant and resentful, although he strongly defended his parent's reputation in later years. Dr. Bentley was so upset by his son's irresponsibility about money that he ultimately disinherited him. When he died in 1742, Dr. Bentley bequeathed the bulk of his estate to his daughters, and his personal library went to a nephew. It had been apparent all along that the younger Bentley's ability was not equal to his father's ambition; his lack of dedication and self-discipline necessary for solid scholarship led eventually to the failure of his academic career, and by 1745 he no longer held any position at Trinity College.

Richard Bentley next lived two or three years in France, probably to escape creditors. In 1750, two years after his return to England, he met Horace Walpole, on whom he made a favorable impression; within a month Walpole remarked to George Montagu that Bentley had "more sense, judgment, and wit, more taste and more misfortunes than sure ever met in any man," and he strongly condemned the cruelty and arrogance of the great Master of Trinity.[3] Remarried by then and penniless, Bentley moved into a small cottage at Teddington in close proximity to Strawberry Hill, where he was invited to join Walpole and John Chute to form a Committee on Taste for the purpose of renovating the house in the gothic style. With Walpole's encouragement, he began his work as an artist in earnest. A burst of energy and creative excitement resulted in his drawings for Strawberry Hill and the rococo illustrations for Gray's poems. Yet, it was not long before Bentley's financial embarrassments angered Walpole too, for he was forced in late 1753 to help Bentley flee once more, this time to the island of Jersey. Returning to Teddington in the summer of 1756, he continued his friendship with Walpole for four more years.

Among Bentley's other works were the illustrations for Walpole's *Memoirs of King George II* and *Fugitive Pieces*; he published at least three poems and a half dozen satires; he contributed to the Strawberry Hill Press a translation into English of Paul Hentzner's *Itinerarium . . . Angliae* and an edition of Lucan's *Pharsalia* with his father's notes. His longer literary pieces—a comedy called *The Wishes, or Harlequin's Mouth Open'd*, a tragedy called *Philodamus*, and a mock-heroic six-canto poem entitled *Patriotism*—were intended to garner the Earl of Bute's and King George III's favor, but they did not bring him either the money or the consequence he hoped for. Even during ten luminous years of friendship with Walpole and Gray, and later during his acquaintance with Lords Melcombe, Halifax, and Bute, in whose exalted circles he hoped to excel, Bentley's writings and drawings drew transitory public attention.[4] Toward the end of the 1760s, neglected, embittered, and poor, he withdrew from society. He died on 23 October 1782 while living in London near New

Palace Yard, Abingdon Street, Westminster, and was buried in the churchyard at Teddington.

Bentley's best and most inspired work consists of the illustrations for Gray's six poems; illustrations for a seventh poem, *The Bard*, are of minor interest for reasons explained in Appendix I. "The most graceful monument to Gothic Rococo," "a barbaric amateurish curiosity," "compelling originality and charm," "timidly decadent"[5]—these quotations represent the mixed feelings of critics in recent years toward *Designs*.[6] Such comments dismiss the illustrations too lightly without adequate recognition of the interplay between poet and artist. Despite their many derivations, the designs represent a giant leap forward in the art of book illustration and were not surpassed until William Blake's work in the 1780s. Bentley did not invent novel forms so much as exploit what he had seen for a new purpose. Instead of pretty embellishment, his pictures were made to dovetail with Gray's poetry in fundamental ways; instead of box-like and mechanical illustration of the text, they develop pictorial themes from the first design to the last. As Gray wrote in *Stanzas to Mr. Bentley*, the artist "fix'd" each "transitory thought" and awakened to "local Symmetry" the idea of each poem.

The sequence of designs, their disposition in relation to the printed page, and their developing imagery show that Walpole and Bentley wanted to make the volume thematically and pictorially coherent, not just a miscellany of odes with attached illustrations. The difficulty lay in assembling six distinct poems to form a single composition, yet without limiting the range of Gray's poetic sensibility. One strategy, to work on the melancholy and self-effacement that generally underlie the poetry, led to a biographical emphasis. Many details are meant to tease the sensitive author. A second, more subtle strategy was to match in picture the poet's ironic use of sources and analogues in verse. Just as Gray's poems imitate, echo, or allude to Virgil or Milton, among other poets, so Bentley's drawings imitate or reflect the work of such artists as Cesare Ripa, Albrecht Dürer, Nicolas Poussin, or William Kent. The interplay of text and design does not result merely in the reflection of images from the verbal to the visual art. Bentley's designs also mirror other graphic works and thereby evolve a unique form of pictorial satire that underscores and embellishes Gray's literary one. They complement and enlarge the meaning.

No admirer of Gray, Dr. Johnson wrote in his *Lives of the Poets* (4 vols., 1781) that the poet's ability to write "but at certain times, or at happy moments" was "a fantastic foppery." The illustrated edition of six poems was damned with faint praise in a single short paragraph, whose damaging effect is increased by the non sequitur of the last sentence:

> Several of his pieces were published (1753), with designs, by Mr. Bentley; and, that they might in some form or other make a book, only one side of each leaf was printed. I believe the poems and the plates

> recommended each other so well, that the whole impression was soon bought. This year he lost his mother. (iv.468)[7]

The words "several of his pieces," and the failure to see that the six brilliant, full-page frontispiece drawings were printed opposite to the verse of the six poems, demonstrate Johnson's blindness to the bonding method and in a more general way to graphic art.[8] The hesitancy in "I believe" and the concession in the penultimate sentence of "recommended each other so well," whose spirit contradicts "that they might in some form or other make a book," trivialize the work and hint a contempt from which it has not recovered until recently.

An appreciation of Bentley's pictorial satire requires a detailed knowledge not merely of the graphic arts popular in mid-eighteenth-century England, but also of the particular aesthetic that was evolving at Strawberry Hill. Bentley had one specific reader in mind, his patron, with the result that many pictorial witticisms are now lost. Private in nature, they were expressly meant for the amusement of Walpole and his friends.[9] The unfurling or unfolding complexity of the designs look typical of rococo ornament, and as Robert Halsband has recently reminded readers in "The rococo in England: book illustrators, mainly Gravelot and Bentley,"[10] the very idea of rococo book illustrations seems contradictory and "self-destructing." "For the rococo is a style of decoration, external and ornamental; book illustration is primarily internal and essential, a pictorial translation of a verbal text" (870). Bentley radically violates expectations. Contemporary reviewers spoke of the book's elegance but failed to record that this elegance is an integral part of his satire.

Horace Walpole brought artist and poet together, initiated their collaboration, and underwrote the publication. His pleasure and pride in the project led to his collection and preservation of the artist's sketches, rough drafts, and final drawings in a variety of lavish scrapbooks and extra-illustrated copies of *Designs*. Years later, after he and Bentley had quarrelled, he directed Thomas Kirgate, his printer at the Strawberry Hill Press, to assemble some of the remaining material in his own copy of the book. These beautiful and fascinating but little-known collections make possible today a thorough study and understanding of the work. They were dispersed in the Strawberry Hill Sale of 1842, and their existence was hardly known until the 1930s and 1940s, when Wilmarth Sheldon Lewis gathered them together again to form part of the Lewis Walpole Library at Farmington, Connecticut. Allowances must be made for Dr. Johnson and later critics who failed to see the significance of Bentley's designs, for the original drawings which they had not been able to study provide the key to interpretation. When Johann Sebastian Müller and Charles Grignion cut the engravings for Robert Dodsley's 1753 edition, lines were softened and subtle changes were made, sacrificing much of Bentley's satire in order to achieve additional rococo charm. The difference between the original drawings and the engravings is not strikingly apparent at first glance, for Bentley's drawings have the appearance of engravings. Their dimensions were not altered by Müller or Grignion, which enabled Walpole to cut out the engravings from one of his printed copies of *Designs*[11] and insert the original drawings into their spaces. A careful comparison of the 1753 edition with Walpole's copy containing the original drawings, as well as a study of their evolution through the preserved drafts, provides the foundation for the analysis and conclusions contained in ensuing chapters.

My purpose is to discover why Walpole was so excited by the drawings that he ranked Bentley with Salvator Rosa and Poussin, and why Gray declared that his odes were not their equal. Gray even hinted in *Stanzas to Mr. Bentley* that his own inspiration had flagged because of the artist's "quick creation" and "unerring line." I shall show that each allegorical frontispiece, headpiece, initial letter, and tailpiece complements and illuminates the verse while subtly and sometimes mischievously adding to Gray's verbal image. Understanding is deepened and broadened by exposure of unexpected contexts; the illustrations and the poems together provide a dimension that either, taken singly, lack. The readers will find themselves fitting word and image into symbiotic relationships, balancing them when pictorial allusion competes with verbal, or reconciling text and illustration when they duel. They will undoubtedly find more puns and more double-entendres than those given as examples and will be struck by self-reflecting details in the drawings.

Bentley includes pictorial comments on his own inventions, on the interaction between text and picture, and on his relationship as artist to Gray the poet. He builds scenes yet undermines the images contained within them in a way that matches Gray's own strategy in irony. When Gray echoes classical sources in the verse, he does so to rebuke his personae who delude themselves in a structure of seductive allusions that foster self-importance; the fictions and sentimental dreams in which they wrap themselves simultaneously undermine or reveal complacency and inertia. Much as the verse surprises the reader by a significant combination of allusions or echoes, so the pictures ignite a reaction in a mock-heroic visual syntax of their own; they join images taken from the words to other visual analogues and invented details. The suggestion of extratextual pictorial analogues undercuts the prettiness of the scenes and helps make visual Gray's verbal exposure of vanity and self-deception. Both poet and artist give rise to a complex contrapuntal effect, partly due to Bentley's contentious and adversarial attitude encouraged by Walpole. When pictorial improprieties distort the meaning of the text, they produce a countercurrent of evaluative satire. The surprising and illuminating fusion of many elements increases the iconographical power of the illustrations as they answer the poems.

A consistent and thorough exploration of Bentley's and Gray's "most graceful monument to Gothic Rococo" has never before been undertaken.

W. S. Lewis, R. W. Ketton-Cremer, Jean Hagstrum, Irene Tayler, John Dixon Hunt, Nobert Miller, Robert Halsband, Ronald Paulson, and Michael McCarthy have provided a glimpse of the unexplored region, including Bentley's place in the rococo movement and his influence on graphic art.[12] Studies of graphic arts by Paulson, in his books on Hogarth and his *Emblem and Expression*,[13] and other studies of the interplay of illustrations and text in Blake's work by recent literary critics[14] have provided a methodology and vocabulary to guide a research of Blake's important precursor. In a review of David Bindman's *The Complete Graphic Works of William Blake*, Joseph Wittreich emphasizes Bindman's recognition of the "mischievous encroachment of design into text" by adding that the "picture augments the work—it both competes with and completes the text."[15] This "first principle of Blake criticism" that "ought now to be accepted," as Wittreich asserts, applies to Bentley. I will attempt to reconstruct the artistic and social environment of the genesis of *Designs* at Strawberry Hill; supply the larger intellectual, historical, and aesthetic background for it; determine the appropriate contexts for its interpretation; and, based upon the study of original drawings, elucidate Bentley's images.

Notes

1. British Library Additional MS 36125 f.232. The appointment was made official by royal decree on 25 January 1724 OS but retroactive to 25 December 1724, evidence of Dr. Bentley's manipulation.

2. *Gentleman's Magazine*, vol. i. 451.

3. Horace Walpole, *Horace Walpole's Correspondence*, ed. W. S. Lewis, et al., 48 vols. (New Haven: Yale University Press, 1937–1983), vol. 9.105. Hereafter referred to as *Corr.* in endnotes, or by volume number and page in text.

4. Here is a brief bibliography of Bentley's written works (all items published were anonymous except for the "Epistle to Lord Melcombe"): *An Apology for his R[oyal] H[ighness] the D[uke]* (London: Printed for R. Webb, 1751); "Epistle to Lord Melcombe," in *The London Chronicle: or, Universal Evening Post*, No. 978 (London, Thursday, March 31, to Saturday, April 2, 1763); *A Full and True Account of the Dreadful and Melancholly Earthquake, Which happened between Twelve and One o'Clock in the Morning, on Thursday the Fifth of April. With an Exact List of such Persons as have hitherto been found in the Rubbish. In a Letter from a Gentleman in Town, to his Friend in the Country* (London: Printed for Tim. Tremor, 1750); *A Journey into England by Paul Hentzner, in the Year M.D.XC.VIII* [tr. Richard Bentley] (Strawberry Hill, 1757); Letter on cruelty to dogs, in *The London Chronicle*, vol. 8 (London, September 18, 1760, 279–280); *M. Annaei Lucani Pharsalia cum Notis Hugonis Grotii, et Richardi Bentleii* [ed. Richard Bentley] (Strawberry Hill, 1760); "On the Sonatas of Bendall Martyn, Esq. Late Secretary of the Excise," *St. James's Magazine*, April, 1763 (ii, 106–108); *Patriotism, A Mock-Heroic in five Cantos* (London: M. Hinxman, 1763); *Patriotism, A Mock-Heroic in Six Cantos* (London: J. Wilkie, 1765); "*A Petition to the Right Hon. Mr. [Pelham], in Favour of Mr.* Maclean. By a Lady" (London: Printed for G. Smith, 1750); *Philodamus. A Tragedy*

(London: J. Dodsley, 1767); *Reflections on the Different Ideas of the French and English, in regard to Cruelty; with Some Hints for improving our Humanity in a particular Branch. By a Man* (London: Printed for J. and R. Tonson, 1759); *To the Printing-Press at Strawberry-Hill* (Strawberry Hill, 1757); *A True and Faithful Account of the Greatest Wonder Produced by Nature these 3000 years, in the Person of Mr. Jehan-Paul-Ernest Christian Lodovick Manpferdt; the Surprizing* CENTAUR, *who will be exhibited to the Publick, on the first of next Month, at the Sign of the Golden Cross at Charing Cross* (London: Printed for M. Cooper, [1751]); *The Wishes* [1782] (never printed. MS Larpent Plays 586. The Huntington Library, San Marino, California); *The Wishes, or Harlequin's Mouth Open'd; a Comedy in the Italian Manner* [1761] (MS Larpent Plays 199. The Huntington Library, San Marino, California. Reproduced in typescript, Jestin, *Richard Bentley the Younger (1708–1782): A Critical Biography* [Ph.D. Dissertation, Yale University, 1985], vol. ii. app. B); "*The World. Number CXC. By Adam Fitz-Adam*" (London, Thursday, August 19, 1756).

5. Kenneth Clark, *The Gothic Revival: An Essay in the History of Taste* (London: Constable, 1928), 67; C. F. Bell, "Thomas Gray and the Fine Arts," *Essays and Studies by Members of the English Association*, vol. xxx (1945), 80; R. W. Ketton-Cremer, *Thomas Gray: A Biography* (Cambridge: Cambridge University Press, 1955), 114; Pat Rogers, "The Involutions of Taste," *TLS* (1 June 1984), 615.

6. A sampling of other comments by recent critics follows: "one of the best of all English picture books," Iolo A. Williams, quoted from W. S. Lewis, *Bentley's Designs for Walpole's Fugitive Pieces* (Farmington: private printing, 1936), 10; "It places Bentley in front of early English book-illustrators, as opposed to book-decorators," W. S. Lewis, *Bentley's Designs for Walpole's Fugitive Pieces*, 10; "a landmark in English book-illustration," A. T. Hazen, *A Bibliography of Horace Walpole* (New Haven: Yale University Press, 1948), 115; "They are the traditional allegorical figures of emblem literature, Gothic themes in a mannerist rendering . . . at once realistic and more elaborately 'arty,' " Irene Tayler, *Blake's Illustrations to the Poems of Gray* (Princeton: Princeton University Press, 1971), 30, 59; "masterpieces of the rococo style in the graphic arts," Michael J. McCarthy, *The Origins of the Gothic Revival* (New Haven and London: Yale University Press, 1987), 67.

7. In fact the demand for the book was so great that seven editions were printed, three in 1753, and the remainder in 1765, 1766, 1775, and 1789. Hazen 117–119.

8. For a reevaluation of Johnson's "supposed half-blindness" to the visual arts, see Robert Folkenflik, "Samuel Johnson and Art," in Paul Alkon and Robert Folkenflik, *Samuel Johnson: Pictures and Words* (Los Angeles: Clark Memorial Library, 1984). Folkenflik argues that Johnson was wary of the inability of polysemic visual art to "fix meanings" (109).

9. In *Thomas Gray: A Biography*, Ketton-Cremer points out that "the drawings were full of private jokes and allusions, some of which must now be lost" (115).

10. *The Burlington Magazine*, cxxvii, no. 993 (Dec. 1985), 870–880.

11. A. T. Hazen, *Catalogue of Horace Walpole's Library*, 3 vols. (New Haven: Yale University Press, 1969), #3698. Hereafter referred to as *Catalogue*.

12. Lewis, *Bentley's Designs for Walpole's Fugitive Pieces*, and *Horace Walpole* (New York: Pantheon Books, 1960), 56ff. Ketton-Cremer, *Horace Walpole*, 2nd ed. (London: Faber and Faber, 1946), 146ff. Jean H. Hagstrum, *The Sister Arts: The Tradition of Literary Pictorialism and English Poetry from Dryden to Gray* (Chicago and London: Uni-

versity of Chicago Press, 1958), 288ff. Irene Tayler, *Blake's Illustration to the Poems of Gray*; "Two Eighteenth-Century Illustrators of Gray," in *Fearful Joy: Papers from the Thomas Gray Bicentenary Conference at Carleton University*, ed. James Downey and Ben Jones (Montreal: McGill-Queen's University Press, 1974), 119–126; and "Bentley Bid the Pencil," in *Women in the 18th Century and Other Essays*, ed. Paul Fritz and Richard Morton (Toronto and Sarasota: Samuel Stevens Hakkert & Co., 1976), 201–215. John Dixon Hunt, *The Figure in the Landscape: Poetry, Painting, and Gardening during the Eighteenth Century* (Baltimore: Johns Hopkins University Press, 1976), 145ff. Norbert Miller, "Richard Bentleys Illustrationen zu den Gedichten von Thomas Gray. Horace Walpole und die ästhetik von Strawberry Hill," *Die Buchillustration im 18. Jahrhundert* (Heidelberg, 1980), 166–188. Robert Halsband, "The rococo in England: book illustrators, mainly Gravelot and Bentley." Michael J. McCarthy, *The Origins of the Gothic Revival*, 63ff., 102ff.

13. Ronald Paulson, *Hogarth's Graphic Works*, rev. ed., 2 vols. (New Haven and London: Yale University Press, 1970); *Hogarth: His Life, Art, and Times*, 2 vols. (New Haven and London: Yale University Press, 1971); and *Emblem and Expression: Meaning in English Art of the Eighteenth Century* (Cambridge: Harvard University Press, 1975).

14. For example, Tayler, *Blake's Illustrations to the Poems of Gray*. Jean H. Hagstrum, *William Blake, Poet and Painter: An Introduction to the Illuminated Verse* (Chicago: University of Chicago Press, 1964). Joseph Anthony Wittreich, Jr., *Angel of Apocalypse: Blake's Idea of Milton* (Madison: University of Wisconsin Press, 1975); and " 'Divine Countenance': Blake's Portrait and Portrayals of Milton," *Huntington Library Quarterly*, vol. 38 (1975), 125–160. David Bindman, *Blake as an Artist* (Oxford: Oxford University Press, 1977); and *The Complete Graphic Works of William Blake* (New York: G. P. Putnam, 1978). Robert F. Gleckner, "Blake, Gray, and the Illustrations," *Criticism*, 19 (1977), 118–140. J. H. Harvey, "Blake's Art," *Cambridge Quarterly*, 7 (1977), 129–150. G. Ingli James, "Blake's Mixed Media; A Mixed Blessing," *Essays and Studies*, n.s. 30 (1977), 61–69. Thomas H. Helmstadler, " 'Bright Visions of Eternity': Blake's Designs for Blair's Grave," *Blake Studies*, 8, no. 1 (1978), 37–64. W. J. T. Mitchell, *Blake's Composite Art: A Study of the Illuminated Poetry* (Princeton: Princeton University Press, 1978).

15. *The Eighteenth Century: A Current Bibliography*, n.s. 4—for 1978 (1981), 282–283.

I
History of the Publication

WHEN in the early summer of 1750 Horace Walpole met Richard Bentley, the namesake and only surviving son of the great Master of Trinity College, Cambridge, he recognized almost at once that Bentley's talents for architectural design, interior decoration, painting, and graphic art were unusual. He persuaded him to join John Chute and himself, forming a committee of three, to decide on matters of taste and design for the remodeling of Strawberry Hill, Walpole's house at Twickenham. As patron of the arts, Walpole self-consciously imitated Richard Boyle, the great Earl of Burlington. Because Burlington and his coterie had dictated taste in the Palladian style, so Walpole assumed for himself and his committee a similar, dictatorial power in the gothic style. In his letter to Horace Mann of 4 March 1753, in which he describes his new hall and staircase designed by Bentley, Walpole gave himself "a Burlington-air," and pronounced "that as Chiswick is a model of Grecian architecture, Strawberry Hill is to be so of Gothic."[1]

In *Anecdotes of Painting* (1762), Walpole wrote that Burlington "was more studious to extend" the fame of William Kent "than his own," even though Burlington's designs were "more chaste and classic." But there was a vital reciprocation. This "Apollo of arts . . . found a proper priest in the person of Mr. Kent."[2] Walpole yearned for a parallel in the person of Mr. Bentley—not Chute, however, for Chute was Walpole's equal in fortune and background. Walpole adopted Bentley, protected him, and was his champion precisely in the fashion that he thought Burlington to have adopted Kent and to have become Kent's champion. Like Kent, Bentley drew buildings, garden houses, chimneypieces, chairs, tables, screens, urns, ornaments, murals, and book illustrations, many of which Walpole pasted into a folio scrapbook with the title page, later printed in 1760 at the Strawberry Hill Press, *Drawings and Designs by Richd. Bentley, only son of Dr. Bentley, Master of Trinity-College Cambridge.*[3] As one might suspect, Walpole influenced much of Bentley's work, which usually reflects something of the complex and often stormy friendship of the two men. This was certainly the case with the designs for Gray's odes, a project that Walpole initiated and paid for.

The first mention he made of Bentley's illustrations for the poems occurs in his letter to George Montagu of 13 June 1751. The subject is introduced with a stricture on Kent's drawings for the new three-volume edition of Spenser's *Faerie Queene*, edited with a life by Thomas Birch (1751): they are "the most execrable performance you ever beheld," Walpole wrote, "the graving not worse than the drawing: awkward knights, scrambling Unas, hills tumbling down themselves, no variety of prospect, and three or four perpetual spruce firs" (*Corr.* 9.116).[4] On the other hand, his own protégé, *his* Kent, would excel. "Our charming Mr Bentley is doing Gray as much more honour as he deserves than Spenser. He is drawing vignettes for his Odes; what a valuable MS I shall have!"

From the letters of Walpole and Gray, we catch glimpses of the work in progress during the next year and a half. It seems Bentley went to Cambridge in September to consult the poet about the designs, for on the twenty-ninth in a cryptic letter Gray said to Walpole that the artist "had cold water thrown upon him, which stunted his growth" (*Corr.* 14.51). On 8 October Gray sent to Walpole *Hymn to Adversity* (as *Ode to Adversity* was called when first published in 1753[5]) "merely to make up half a dozen" items, but because he doubted that this formal ode would "answer your end in furnishing out either a head- or tail-piece," he recommended the substitution of Walpole's own "fable," which he had recently corrected (*Corr.* 14.53)—it was probably "The Funeral of the Lioness," the editors of Gray's correspondence, Toynbee and Whibley, suggest (#161). In their scanty correspondence, Gray makes no other allusion to the project until 28 May 1752, seven and a half months later, when he regrets he cannot go to Strawberry Hill but sends "compliments to Mr Bentley" (*Corr.* 14.58).

These occasional criticisms and oblique remarks about the project contrast sharply with Walpole's more frequent and ebullient references. One is left with the feeling that Gray treated the business casually, even with a superior attitude, yet this impression is false. He soon betrayed a very fragile vanity and an unduly nervous concern about the collaboration. His comments became strident with his growing fear that the odes were becoming subordinate to the drawings, and that he himself in a subtle but increasingly obvious way was an object of ridicule. In fact, during the fall of 1752, as publication became imminent, painter and poet switched roles: if Gray had thrown cold water upon Bentley, now Gray himself came to feel that his was the dampened spirit, as we shall see. Patron and artist, on the other hand, were irrepressible.

Bentley did most of his work at Strawberry Hill. At the height of his powers there were a multitude of projects in hand, not merely illustrations for Gray's poems but also illustrations for Walpole's *Memoirs of King George II* and architectural designs for Chinese summer houses, gothic chimneypieces, and the staircase and hall for Strawberry Hill. On all this work Walpole left his stamp. He encouraged, cajoled, recommended or rejected, and cheered aloud to Montagu and Mann when Bentley got things right. It was all done with competitive gusto and a spirit of adventure.

On 6 June 1752 Walpole wrote to Montagu that Bentley was "finishing the drawings" for the odes: "There are some mandarin-cats fishing for goldfish which will delight you," he said of the frontispiece for *Ode on the Death of a Favourite Cat* (fig. 6). On 8 July in a letter from Stoke Poges where he had gone to visit his ailing mother, Gray exclaimed over the proof print of the *cul-de-lampe* for *Elegy* (fig. 34).[6] The *cul-de-lampe* of a funeral procession approaching a vicar standing before a village church "far surpasses my idea of London graving," he added with a possible pun on "grave":

> The drawing itself was so finished that I suppose it did not require all the art I had imagined to copy it tolerably. My aunts just now, seeing me open your letter, take it to be a burying-ticket enclosed, and ask whether any body has left me a ring? and so they still conceive it to be, even with all their spectacles on. Heaven forbid they should suspect it to belong to any verses of mine: they would burn me for a poet. (*Corr.* 14.59)

In the same letter Gray enclosed a rough outline of Stoke Manor House (fig. 17) to be redrawn as the headpiece for *A Long Story*. "Mr Bentley . . . will catch a better idea of Stoke House from any old barn he sees, than from my sketch," he wrote. (It is likely that the thought of being burned for a poet and the name of the house suggested another pun.) Bentley's transformation of Gray's sketch (fig. 18) shows something of the artist's abilities. Walpole was so impressed that two years later when he asked the then exiled Bentley[7] to submit a plan for the chapel at The Vyne, Chute's house in Hampshire, he said: "I have enclosed a scratch of mine, which you are to draw out better, and try if you can give yourself a perfect idea of the place. All I can say is, that my sketch is at least more intelligible than Gray's was of Stoke, from which you made so like a picture" (35.185).

"The Poemata Grayo-Bentleiana, or Gray's Odes better illustrated than ever were by a Bentley, are in great forwardness, and I trust will appear this winter," Walpole crowed to Montagu on 28 August 1752. The eager tone and indirect reference to Bentley's father by the words "a Bentley," as with his earlier derision of Kent, betrays Walpole's combative nature.[8] Moreover, in the same letter, when he next describes Gray's "love to distraction" of Bentley's tailpiece for *Hymn to Adversity*, he is actually triumphant: the poet had doubted that "either a head- or tail-piece" could be drawn for it; now his pleasure over the tailpiece is excessive. The picture of Melancholy is shown as a forlorn woman sitting on a rocky crag (fig. 29), not as in Ripa's emblem (fig. 78) or Dürer's portrait (fig. 83), but as a stoically beautiful creature. The gloating Walpole, remarking the poet's pleasure in misery, told Montagu that Gray asked Bentley for something else from his pencil: "Mr Bentley desired him to choose a subject:—he chose *Theodore and Honoria*—don't mention this, for we are shocked—it is loving *Melancholy*, till it is not strong enough, and he grows to dram with Horror!" (9.143–144), words implying that he imbibed horror much as a drunk might liquor.

Clearly Bentley was now the favorite at Twickenham, a matter the poet sensed. The change of tone in Gray's letters reveals irritation and insecurity; his distrust of Walpole's moods had never been far beneath the surface since their quarrel on the Grand Tour ten years before.[9] Walpole was aggressive; his wit and raillery were a challenge to his friends; unlike Bentley, Gray was no match.[10] When Walpole fomented competition between poet and artist, Gray lost his nerve. Walpole teased, Gray withdrew, and he rightly suspected that the two in Twickenham were laughing at him behind his back, even though they ostensibly tried to include him in their jokes. These jokes were to them irresistible. However gentle the mockery, it increased Gray's anxiety about the forthcoming book, an emotion deepened by worry over his mother who in fact died on 11 March, eighteen days before the publication. At the same time, with Walpole's encouragement, Bentley's designs became more spirited. By the beginning of 1753, the poet demanded that the artist's name be raised above his own on the title page.

Gray's sensitivity, lack of humor, and serious turn of thought put him at a disadvantage before Bentley's and Walpole's wit. In each poem Gray united an incident or occasional meditation with a universal theme; in the illustrations Bentley introduced topical satire, often with unpleasant implications. But before anger and embarrassment got the better of Gray, he expressed the hope that *Designs* would be a significant publication, much more than a meager collection of odes prettily adorned. This is proved by *Stanzas to Mr. Richard Bentley* written by Gray in 1752[11] to commemorate the joint endeavor:

In silent gaze the tuneful choir among,
   Half pleas'd, half blushing let the muse admire,
While Bentley leads her sister-art along,
   And bids the pencil answer to the lyre.
See, in their course, each transitory thought
   Fix'd by his touch a lasting essence take;
Each dream, in fancy's airy colouring wrought,
   To local Symmetry and life awake!
The tardy rhymes that us'd to linger on,
   To censure cold, and negligent of fame,
In swifter measures animated run,
   And catch a lustre from his genuine flame.
Ah! could they catch his strength, his easy grace,
   His quick creation, his unerring line;
The energy of Pope they might efface,

And Dryden's harmony submit to mine.
But not to one in this benighted age
Is that diviner inspiration giv'n,
That burns in Shakespear's or in Milton's page,
The pomp and prodigality of heav'n.
As when conspiring in the diamond's blaze,
The meaner gems, that singly charm the sight,
Together dart their intermingled rays,
And dazzle with a luxury of light.
Enough for me, if to some feeling breast
My lines a secret sympathy *impart;*
And as their pleasing influence *flows confest,*
A sigh of soft reflection *heave the heart.*

Half-pleased, half-blushing, Gray humbled himself. Notwithstanding his resort to the convention of declaring himself inadequate as a poet and suggesting that he lived in a benighted age, as Collins had recently done in *Ode on the Poetical Character* (1747), his admiration of Bentley was genuine. The echo of Dryden's *Epistle to Kneller* and Pope's *Epistle to Mr. Jervas* aptly suits Gray's purpose of praising the sister art, yet if exaggerated praise is typical of this genre, as Jean Hagstrum has said in *The Sister Arts*, the "longer and better" poems of Dryden and Pope have not made "so handsome" a compliment.[12] Gray was also influenced by Charles Du Fresnoy's well-known book *De Arte Graphica* (1695), translated into English by Dryden, and by the treatises of the painter Jonathan Richardson. Du Fresnoy expanded the formula that originated with Simonides and Horace, "Ut pictura poesis erit," with the corollary "similisque poesi sit pictura" (a picture and a poem are like one another, one a silent poem, the other a speaking picture); Richardson went further by advocating the superiority of the artist who, he argued, had to be historian, poet, and "curious Artificer" at once.[13] Hagstrum shows that likewise Gray thought painting possessed "the power of enargeia in even greater measure than poetry, the power of rendering the animation and luster of life itself" (289). Walpole would certainly have agreed with the idea; he himself had implicitly made such an assertion in his own praise of the sister art when he wrote *The Beauties. An Epistle to Mr. Eckardt the Painter* (1746), one of his *Fugitive Pieces (Wks.* i.19).

The way William Mason finished *Stanzas*[14] (his words are in italics above) implies that he, Mason, saw a connection between the poem and the sonnet on Richard West's death. Gray's failing inspiration and lack of confidence increased with his depression; Gray seemed as powerless to revive his muse in the tribute to Bentley, as he is in the sonnet before his schoolmate's bones. He cannot resuscitate either. He feared for the loss of his own youth, idealism, and creative power. Henceforth, his work and letters are filled with complaints, while Bentley's "quick creation" suggested the vitality of Virgil, Milton, Dryden, and Pope. Bentley's animation in the sister art was disclosing to him his threatening languor.

In the sonnet on West's death, Gray echoes the classical poets to assuage his grief, but as Patricia Meyer Spacks has explained in *The Poetry of Vision*, the attempt fails.[15] Rather, because artificial, the imitations heighten, instead of diminish, his sorrow, a matter stressed by the contrast of the poet's direct and simple expression of loss in the middle quatrain and final couplet. The counterpoint of artifice and simple sincerity gives the sonnet its power.

Similarly, when Gray in *Stanzas* refers to Dryden and Pope or echoes their lines, he does not merely allude to his difference from them and from the painter but compensates for his avowed deficiency by using this contrast to invigorate his theme. The literary exploitation amounts to a personal and clever irony against himself. His suggestion that his ambition as a poet has eluded him or proved impossible to fulfill, and that he cannot rise to the level of his antecedents in poetry or of Bentley in the sister art, redeems his verse in a new, unexpected way. In other words, when an exposure of his own inadequacy is his subject, he writes an inspired poetry. He even echoes his own successful *Elegy*, both in its "Epitaph" and in the lines, "Full many a gem of purest ray serene / The dark unfathom'd caves of ocean bear . . . ," but in *Stanzas*, unlike the mute rustics, he underscores the opportunity for success that he has had and they have not, thus producing the essential pathos of the poem despite coming close to self-pity. If the "diviner inspiration" in the "benighted age" has been withheld from him, as he adds in this gracious compliment to Bentley, then the sister art has made him shine more brightly—or at least more publicly.

The illustrator in Gray's tribute has played antithetical roles: he has exposed the poet's weakness, even as in *Designs* he has embellished and expanded the meaning of the poetry. His vitality has jeopardized the poet's own, yet it has also stimulated him. This is the universal sympathy Gray imparts, for who would not feel awed or humbled by the pomp and prodigality of heaven? *Stanzas*, in short, effectively uses the strategy of his great poems.

It must be confessed that much of Gray's achievement depends on his personal mortification, or that of the speakers or protagonists in the odes. This is the theme that Bentley develops from picture to picture. He repeatedly depicts the ambition of the poet (or of his personae in the odes), yet then exposes it as an unreal hope, a vanity, or a self-delusion. Gray's transitory thought or aspiration is fixed by the artist's touch, but as that touch found a vital theme in a portrait of mortification, so inevitably it accentuated a more personal satire.

Gray says in *Stanzas* that his relationship to the artist inspired a run of swifter, animated measures,[16] but in fact, the luster and power of this poem springs less from what is caught from Bentley's genuine flame than from the familiar play on his own disillusionment or inadequacy. His confession gives depth to *Stanzas*, yet, one asks, if this is true, why did Gray suppress the poem? Moreover, if Bentley's illustrations in part satirize the odes and poet in *Designs*, why did he make no particular mention of the satire?

I believe the answer lies in chronology. The tone of *Stanzas* implies that he wrote it when excited by the drawings of Stoke Manor House, the funeral cortege for *Elegy*, and the tailpiece showing Melancholy. He had not yet been hurt by the latent ridicule in the drawings, more personal than he might at first have understood and undeniable by the time the sequence was completed. At the end of 1752, the jauntiness of his letters turned to irritation and petulance, a change of mind that also, possibly, drove him to suppress *Stanzas*. Not a single word about the poem ever occurs anywhere in his own or in Walpole's correspondence, or for that matter in any of Bentley's preserved writings. This absence is remarkable, especially given the poet's apology for his failure to write more verse and his fears for his own creative power, not to mention Walpole's encouragement and promotion of *Designs*. Had Bentley or Walpole ever heard of *Stanzas*? The reference in it to Dryden and Pope hints that Gray had originally intended to make a contribution to an established genre.

Gray neglected to write out *Stanzas* in his Commonplace Book, an omission later rectified by Mason, his literary executor, who entered the poem after the poet's death. Had Mason not preserved the single, damaged manuscript copy found among the poet's papers, it would have been lost. Whereas he called the poem "masterful," saying that many of its verses "are equal in merit to his [Gray's] best in his most finished poems" (*The Poems of Mr. Gray* i.226–227), Mason was less sure about the drawings, an ambivalence that might recall something of Gray's own later reaction. Mason's equivocal comments artfully avoided giving Walpole offense:

> Many readers will perhaps think the panegyric carried too far; as I own I did when he [Gray] first shewed it me. Yet it is but justice to declare, that the original drawings . . . are so infinitely superior to the published engravings of them, that a person, who has only seen the latter, can by no means judge of the excellencies of the former: Besides, there is so much of grotesque fancy in the Designs themselves, that it can be no great matter of wonder (even if the engravers had done justice to them) that they failed to please universally. (226)

Mason went on to say that what he had previously written about *A Long Story* "might easily be applied to these productions of the sister art." The adjectives that recur in his condemnation of that poem are "extravagant," "unnatural," and "grotesque" (212ff.).

Bentley's rapid pencil made Gray's diffidence and chagrin over his own small production worse. Gray feared a volume with only six short poems would be a "fantastic foppery" (to use Dr. Johnson's phrase of thirty years later), especially as Bentley's large and lavish designs seemed to usurp the predominance of the poetry. As early as August 1752, he told Walpole that Dodsley's own reservations did not surprise him: "You have talked . . . of six *odes*, for so you are pleased to call everything I write, though it be but a receipt to make apple-dumplings. He [Dodsley] has reason to gulp when he finds one of them only 'a long story'. I don't know but I may send him very soon (by your hands) an ode to his own tooth, a high Pindaric upon stilts" (*Corr.* 14.60). This was *The Progress of Poesy*, but as Gray already knew, it was too late for the collaboration with Bentley, and it was not published until 1757. On 17 December he wrote again that he had sent "what little alterations I had to make" to the publisher and asked if Walpole "thought them for the better or the worse." Then, as the proofs from London arrived just as he was finishing the letter, he complained in a postscript that the quarto had changed into "a little folio" and that the stanzas were numbered, "which I do not like" (14.61–62). Walpole deleted the numbers. By 12 February 1753 the agitated, exasperated poet pleaded with Dodsley to change the title:

> To have it conceived, that I publish a Collection of *Poems* (half a dozen little Matters, four of wch too have already been printed again & again) thus pompously adorned would make me appear very justly ridiculous. I desire it may be understood (wch is the truth) that the Verses are only subordinate, & explanatory to the Drawings, & suffer'd by me to come out thus only for that reason. (Toynbee and Whibley, #172)

On the next day, 13 February, an explosion occurred. Gray heard that Johann Sebastian Müller was to cut an engraving after his portrait by Eccardt for the edition: "Sure You are not out of your Wits!" he screamed at Walpole; "to appear in proper Person at the head of my works consisting of half a dozen Ballads in 30 pages, would be worse than the Pillory. I do assure you, if I had received such a book with such a frontispiece without any warning, I believe it would have given me a palsy." He offered to make up the loss to Dodsley if he were at the expense of engraving the portrait, and added that "the thing," as he referred to the book, "will make me ridiculous enough" (*Corr.* 14.63).[17] On 20 February Walpole, now uneasy, answered that Dodsley "feared the price of half a guinea would seem too high to most purchasers" without further embellishment, so he, Dodsley, had the portrait engraved against Walpole's opinion, "as I concluded it would be against yours" (14.65). According to Walpole Gray destroyed the plate; if true Müller must first have struck off a number of prints, for several survive (14.63 n.1). Walpole pasted one in his own copy of the poems.[18]

In his letter of 13 February, Gray suggested petulantly that if Walpole thought it necessary "to print . . . explanations" for the designs, "for the use of people that have no eyes," he wished them "a little alter'd."[19] Although agreeing with Gray, Walpole published what he had written for the explanations anyway. He next tried to bully the poet into having his name printed as plain Thomas Gray instead of Mr. T. Gray: "*Mr* is one of the Gothicisms I abominate." But *Mr.*, as Bertrand H. Bronson has written, was "a significant gesture of self-depreciation" for Gray; it modestly announced his social status, "a nuance" he further refined "when he omitted his first name."[20] Finally, Walpole rebuked Gray for the fuss he was making over the title with what should appear unassailable logic: "The title I think will be wrong, and not answer your purpose, for as the drawings are evidently calculated for the poems, why will the improper disposition of the word *Designs* before *Poems*, make the edition less yours?" But on this point nothing could dissuade the humiliated poet, not even the conciliatory end to Walpole's letter: "I praise and scold Mr Bentley immoderately as I think he draws well or ill; I never think it worth my while to do either, especially to blame, where there are not generally vast excellencies. Good night—don't suspect me when I have no fault but impatience to make you easy" (14.65–66). Of obdurate temper, the poet could hardly have found consolation in the tell-tale clause "the drawings are evidently calculated for the poems," where the adverb signaled perhaps a too evident compunction. Walpole seemed arrogant. The argument must have struck Gray as lacking in candor.

In an impish mood Bentley wanted to suggest, however untrue, that the poems were as much calculated for the drawings as the reverse. Gray's letter to Dodsley of 12 February, in which he said the verses are explanatory to the drawings, makes this supposition credible, as does the published work itself. What is more, the odes, including *Death of a Favourite Cat* and *A Long Story*, might have looked explanatory to the topical and sometimes impertinent illustrations, for in emblem books of the period it was common practice for verses to explain visual allegories.[21] In 1753 Walpole commissioned John Giles Eccardt to paint portraits of himself and Bentley to complement one he had already asked Eccardt to paint of Gray in 1748; he hung them all together in the blue bedchamber for which a chimneypiece had been designed by Bentley (*Corr.* 35.174). All three portraits in black and gold frames, showing the sitters in Van Dyck dress, confirm the pride Walpole took in their friendship and collaboration; Gray holds a copy of the Eton ode and Bentley holds his portrait of Melancholy for *Hymn to Adversity* (see frontispiece), as Walpole notes in his *Description of the Villa* (*Wks.* ii.436).[22]

Bentley's designs were engraved and printed to look like reproductions of established works of art from Italy and France. Vignettes, the word Walpole initially used in his letter to Montagu, inadequately describe the illustrations for *Designs*. The imperial or royal quarto, as handsome as a folio, contained twenty-five illustrations including one large fleuron for the title page. Of the six frontispiece drawings, one each for the six poems, the largest is 8¾ by 11¼ inches in size, a full two inches taller than the type-page, and each frontispiece is followed by a large headpiece, an enormous initial letter wrapped up in an allegorical scene, and a big tailpiece. Each drawing engraved on copper plate by Müller and Charles Grignion, together with the engraved text, makes the publication unique. The initial letters were made to fit the poetical context; this is just one of the novelties that make the edition a landmark in English publishing.

Dodsley's placement of Bentley's name before Gray's, and Gray's insistence that it be put first, had a genuine artistic basis. In fact, only *Drawings, &c.* is printed on the half-title,[23] the very first heading the reader sees. For the titlepage itself, *Designs by Mr. R. Bentley, for Six Poems by Mr. T. Gray* was settled upon, although in *The Daily Advertiser* for 27 March the title still reads *Poems by Mr. T. Gray, with Designs by Mr. R. Bentley*, evidence of struggle to the last moment. In the actual title, "Poems" is printed in larger type than "Designs,"[24] one last attempt to mollify Gray. The book was published on 29 March 1753. In the *Monthly Review* for July 1753, the founder and editor Ralph Griffiths wrote:

> We have now before us one of the most elegant publications that our country hath produced for some years past: whether we consider the beauty of the printing, the genius that appears in the designs for the cuts, or the masterly execution of most of the engravings. Nor will the connoisseur in prints, we are persuaded, think the price . . . too high: whatever may be the judgment of the mere poetical purchaser, to whom it may appear somewhat rare to pay half a guinea for thirty-six pages of verse.[25]

The high cost did not deter buyers. In his *Bibliography of Horace Walpole*, Allen Hazen has shown that Dodsley printed three distinct editions in 1753 and four others in 1765, 1766, 1775, and 1789 (116–119). The last four editions also included *The Progress of Poesy* and *The Bard*; although *The Progress of Poesy* was published without illustrations, *The Bard* was given a tailpiece in 1766 (fig. 43), probably by Bentley but without Walpole's collaboration, for the two men had quarreled and parted ways six years previously.

Bentley's concern that picture and print be integrated can be seen by looking at one of four drafts for the tailpiece to *A Long Story* (fig. 23), luckily preserved in Thomas Kirgate's extra-illustrated edition of the volume.[26] The verse has actually been copied out just as it was to be printed above the drawing; the proportion of the lines on the page and their relationship to the design were obviously vital to Bentley. Pictures and text make an aesthetic whole, and as each sheet was printed only on one side, the volume of thirty-six leaves looks more like a work of art than an illustrated volume of poetry.

Despite the popularity of the book, Gray, it seems, never recovered from humiliation. Many years later, on 24 December 1767, he wrote to James Beattie of James Dodsley's desire to print a new edition in smaller size. Agreeing to the proposal but without illustrations, the poet disingenuously added that *A Long Story* was to be omitted as it "was never meant for the publick, & only suffer'd to appear in that pompous edition because of Mr Bentley's designs, wch were not intelligible without it" (Toynbee and Whibley #457). On 25 February 1768 he told Walpole[27] that he had dissuaded Dodsley from "so silly an expense" of re-engraving the plates and "desired he would put in no ornaments at all." He would supply the publisher with a substitute for *A Long Story*: "lest *my works* should be mistaken for the works of a flea or pismire, I promised to send him an equal weight of poetry or prose" (*Corr.* 14.172).

Dodsley's request to issue an octavo with illustrations was eminently reasonable, given the contemporary sale of the quarto, yet he bowed to Gray's wish. The octavo of 1768 was published without new plates. Gray also arranged, through Beattie, for R. and A. Foulis of Glasgow to print in the same year a quarto without illustrations at five shillings. This act, and his refusal to let Dodsley cut new plates, which would have made his octavo special, threatened Dodsley's potential profit. He might well have been irritated. Dodsley countered by publishing in early May two editions at 2s. 6d. before the issuance of the Glasgow volume; Gray complained to Beattie that Dodsley had "contrived to glut the Town" with an inferior, cheaper product.[28]

Worse still for Dodsley that year was the appearance of a pirated edition in Dublin, published by William Sleater, with engravings. There were three illustrations: one after Bentley's frontispiece to *Elegy* (fig. 37); the second, a tailpiece for *Elegy* taken, not from the tailpiece published in 1753, but from Bentley's earlier, simpler draft with double line margins (figs. 35a and 38), and the third for *The Bard* after the tailpiece first published by Dodsley in his fifth edition of *Designs* in 1766 (figs. 43, 44). I suspect that these illustrations (including the new tailpiece for *Elegy* that had not been previously published) were supplied by Bentley himself, possibly through the unidentified friend in Dublin who had arranged a performance of *The Wishes* there in 1762.

Sleater published a second edition of Gray's poems with illustrations in 1775 to coincide with Dodsley's sixth edition of *Designs* in the same year. Gray was dead; although Dodsley had a free hand, he decided after all not to have the tired plates newly engraved for an octavo, but to reissue the book as it was. He reprinted it one more time in 1789. Since this final edition, Gray's poems with Bentley's illustrations have never again appeared.[29]

Notes

1. *Corr.* 20.361–362. See also *Corr.* 21. 120, and the preface to the second edition (1784) of Walpole's *Description of the Villa . . . at Strawberry-Hill near Twickenham, Mid-*

dlesex, reprinted in *The Works of Horatio Walpole, Earl of Orford*, 5 vols. (London, 1798), ii.395. Hereafter referred to as *Wks*.

2. *Anecdotes of Painting*, in *Wks*. iii.488. See also 483, and ii.395.

3. This book is presently part of the collection at the Lewis Walpole Library. The fleuron on the title page was designed by Bentley. It shows Strawberry Hill in the background surrounded by vines, strawberry flowers, and Walpole's shield and motto. The book is listed in A. T. Hazen, *Catalogue* #3585.

4. In *Anecdotes of Painting* Walpole decried "the wretchedness of drawing, the total ignorance of perspective, the want of variety, the disproportion of the buildings, and the awkwardness of the attitudes. . . . There are figures issuing from cottages not so high as their shoulders, castles in which the towers could not contain an infant, and knights who hold their spears as men do who are lifting a load sideways. The landscapes are the only tolerable parts, and yet the trees are seldom other than young beeches, to which Kent as a planter was accustomed" (*Wks*. iii.490–491).

5. *Correspondence of Thomas Gray*, ed. Paget Toynbee and Leonard Whibley, revised by H. W. Starr, 3 vols. (Oxford: Oxford University Press, 1971), #465.

6. Possibly Gray received an earlier version. See figure 35a.

7. Because of debt, Bentley fled to Jersey in December 1753, and could not return to Strawberry Hill until the summer of 1756.

8. Walpole's and Bentley's sympathy for one another came in part of their both having powerful and autocratic fathers. Walpole rarely attacked his parent in print or letter but often displaced his anger or jealousy in criticism of Dr. Bentley; likewise, Bentley satirized Sir Robert in his mock-heroic epic *Patriotism* (1765) (canto v. 159).

9. See Ketton-Cremer, *Thomas Gray*, 44–50, 72–75. Ketton-Cremer remarks that "slight and momentary friction" between the two subsequent to their quarrel was produced by their contrasting temperaments, "Gray's reticence against Walpole's exuberance" (75).

10. George Hardinge, a friend of Walpole's in the 1780s, judged that Walpole was not really well-bred: "He demanded a full stretch of admiring homage to his *bon mots*, and rather lectured in a series of prose epigrams than conversed playfully and so as to put the hearer quite at his ease" (*Corr*. 35.647). Unlike Gray, Bentley apparently presented an exciting challenge that could simultaneously be understood as homage.

11. William Mason gave *Stanzas* this date, rightly, as the evidence of Gray's change of heart confirms. He added that the poet "greatly admired not only the elegance of his [Bentley's] fancy, but also the neatness as well as the facility of his execution." *The Complete Poems of Thomas Gray*, ed. H. W. Starr and J. R. Hendrickson (Oxford: Oxford University Press, 1972), 247.

12. Hagstrum, *The Sister Arts*, 289.

13. Ronald Paulson writes a lucid essay on the sister arts in eighteenth-century England, in *Hogarth: His Life, Art, and Times*, to which I am indebted.

14. Reverend J. Mitford's alternative version for the words torn from the original manuscript emphasizes the echo of Dryden's *Epistle to Kneller* and Pope's *Epistle to Mr. Jervas*. His terminal words are "convey," "is exprest," and "dies away." *The Complete Poems of Thomas Gray*, 98, 247. Mason's version seems preferable thematically. Although Mason remarks that he is "not quite satisfied with the words which I have inserted in the third line" and that he should "be much pleased if any reader finds

a better supplement to this imperfect stanza," he might nevertheless have had a memory of the original. Gray had shown him the poem at an earlier time. William Mason, *The Poems of Mr. Gray. To Which are Prefixed Memoirs of his Life and Writings*, 2nd ed. (London, 1775), section i. 226–228.

15. Patricia Meyer Spacks, *The Poetry of Vision: Five Eighteenth-Century Poets* (Cambridge: Harvard University Press, 1967), 95ff.

16. The phrase "animated measures" may refer both to *Stanzas* itself and to *The Progress of Poesy*, begun in 1752.

17. Although quoting from *Corr.*, I have preserved Gray's capital letters, as printed in Toynbee and Whibley #173.

18. Hazen, *Catalogue* #2044. As for the cost of the book, *The Daily Advertizer* for 27 March 1753 advertised *Designs* as "Elegantly printed in royal quarto, priced sewed 10s. 6d."

19. Gray's reticence to include explanations for the designs also suggests that, as in emblem books, the meaning of the drawings, like orphic or mystical arcana, could be understood only by the wise. The epigraph he chose from Pindar for *The Progress of Poesy* just at this time perhaps expresses the same idea.

20. Bertrand Harris Bronson, *Facets of the Englightenment: Studies in English Literature and Its Contexts* (Berkeley and Los Angeles: University of California Press, 1968), 343–344.

21. For a description of popular emblem books, see Rosemary Freeman, *English Emblem Books* (London: Chatto & Windus, 1948); Hagstrum, *The Sister Arts*; and Paulson, *Emblem and Expression*.

22. All three portraits are now in the National Portrait Gallery, London. The engraving of Bentley reproduced in the frontispiece is by James Heath after Eccardt.

23. In all the other editions, the half-title reads *Designs, &c.*

24. Tayler also notes the difference in type size in "Bentley Bid the Pencil," 201.

25. Quoted from Hazen, *A Bibliography of Horace Walpole*, 116.

26. Part of the collection at the Lewis Walpole Library. In a footnote Kirgate says that this draft was the first sketch. More likely it was the third. See figure 22 for two earlier sketches.

27. Walpole had registered his annoyance to Gray about not being told of Dodsley's plans to print a new edition. *Corr.* 14. 166–167.

28. See Toynbee and Whibley #457, 465, 466, 471, 487.

29. A facsimile of the titlepage of *Designs* was published in Austin Lane Poole's *Poems of Gray* (1926, 1937) and A. F. Bell's edition of Gray's *Poems* (1915). Hazen, *A Bibliography of Horace Walpole*, 117ff.

II
Background for Bentley's Graphic Art

THE designs for Gray's poems were an integral part of the developing aesthetics at Strawberry Hill. The Committee on Taste, composed of Walpole, Chute, and Bentley, was deeply serious in its admiration of early English gothic; it was Walpole in particular who wished to revive a patriotic English style in defiance of the rage for Palladian architecture. The committee's aim was to incorporate details of gothic cathedrals and the romance of ruined castles into domestic buildings; however, what Walpole called gothic "gloomth" was not to preclude the comforts of a modern house. When Walpole gave himself a Burlington-air and asserted that as Chiswick was a model for Grecian architecture, so Strawberry Hill was to be of gothic, he avowed but half his purpose, for he also perceived the house in theatrical terms.

It was designed as a stage set. It contained an oratory, chapel (later called the Tribune), refectory (later called the Great Parlour), long gallery, armory, cloisters, and a prior's garden, none of which had any real relationship to their names. More than architecture, renovations and additions evoked the fashionable melancholy as expressed in Pope's *Eloisa to Abelard,* Blair's *Grave,* and Gray's *Elegy*; they conjured up the heraldic romance of Spenser's Renaissance. "One only wants passion to feel Gothic" architecture, Walpole wrote in *Anecdotes of Painting (Wks.* iii.94). He confessed to Montagu that "Visions, you know, have always been my pasture" (*Corr.* 10.192) and declared in the preface to his *Description of the Villa . . . at Strawberry-Hill* that the house was built "to realize my own visions" (*Wks.* ii.398).

Although Walpole went about the countryside to inspect historic monuments, he used as his chief source for designs the beautiful engravings of cathedrals and tombs in folios by the Reverend John Dart, Sir William Dugdale, and Francis Sandford, books he recommended to Bentley as source material for his drawings.[1] Walpole was deeply concerned that the detail be correct, yet the two men embodied their derived architectural features in improper materials and in strange, incongruous contexts, a matter of no surprise given their predilection for dreams; the romantic enchantment inspired by engravings was more powerful than the science of archeology. They imitated stone in plaster, or even in paper and gilt; they turned designs for tombs into chimneypieces; they thought of chapel screens when they made a bedroom screen. Their rooms appear sometimes to honor the sources from which their details were taken, and sometimes to burlesque them. Walpole was an allusionist who emphasized formal (if not material) accuracy, largely because he wanted gothic models to create a convincing atmosphere in which one could receive a kind of literary pleasure, akin to that given by echoes and allusions in poetry. The house became a reliquary, like contemporary allegorical gardens.

The achievement inside the house is nowhere better illustrated when Bentley was working on *Designs* than by his hall and staircase (fig. 63). As can be seen in his watercolor, it is a whimsey of gothic and rococo ideas. The balustrade is a dramatic reduction of staircases like those at Hatfield House and Knoll; the Strawberry Hill structure ascends in a lilliputian play of delicate fretwork. Called the Paraclete after Eloisa's cloister in *Eloisa to Abelard* (*Corr.* 20.372), the hall was dimly lit by "lean windows fattened with rich saints in painted glass," as Walpole described it to Horace Mann (20.381), and at night by a one-candle lantern of japanned tin and stained glass, also of Bentley's design, that hung in the well of the staircase on a black and yellow cord. On the landing outside the library, Bentley included an Armory for trophies that everyone was to pretend were taken by Sir Terry Robsart during the Crusades (fig. 64); atop each newel post was placed an antelope, one of Lord Orford's supporters on his coat of arms, holding a shield. The floor was paved with hexagonal tiles and the walls were covered with paper painted to look like gothic fretwork from the screen of Prince Arthur's tomb as shown in Sandford's *Kings of England* (442).

When finished the addition appeared so tiny and neat that Montagu "was in raptures, and screamed, and whooped, and hollaed, and danced, and crossed himself a thousand times over." Walpole imagined William Augustus, Duke of Cumberland, when he came to visit, to be like Gulliver having to cut "down some of the largest oaks in Windsor Forest to make jointstools, in order to straddle over the battlements and peep in at the windows of Lilliput" (35.161). Walpole declared to Mann that his gothic staircase "is so pretty and small . . . I am inclined to wrap it up and send it you in my letter" (20.361), like a toy, perhaps, from the shop owned by Mrs. Chenevix, the woman from whom Walpole had first rented and then bought his cottage.[2] Bentley's entry hall might be compared to a frontispiece illustration, one in three dimensions, with Walpole at its center, like the embowered Gray in the frontispiece to *Designs*. Its contrived gloom succeeded so well that later it inspired the setting for Walpole's *Castle of Otranto*.

The work for the house and for the illustrations in *Designs* was governed by the same mentality. Strawberry Hill was conceived in romantic terms with details that were allusive in a literary manner; Bentley's drawings for the poems were enriched with pictorial analogues recognizable at least to the members of Walpole's set. By the gothic villa, Bentley helped his patron to stage a mythology, or a kind of masque; by his illustrations for the six poems, Bentley provided a challenging visual context for the verse and the poet. The designs form an architecture to contain the poems, and Bentley placed nearly every scene inside a scaffolding of suggestive shapes and figures. The result was intended to amuse Walpole, who referred to Strawberry Hill in monastic terms with himself as high priest and who considered the Bentley-Gray text its first major literary product.[3]

It is impossible to tell in every case which drawings Bentley used for models or analogues as he plotted the illustrations for the odes, but it is certain that he and Walpole studied a multitude of pictures, just as they did for their architectural sketches. Walpole's approach to building was so novel an experiment he wrote in due course a *Description of the Villa* with detailed lists of paintings and objects in each of his gothic rooms, many of which were reproduced in his own extra-illustrated copy of the book in elephant folio size. He carefully identified sources of his architecture and interior decoration; the book had a polemical purpose in the establishment of the gothic revival.

He did not, however, provide a similar key to Bentley's illustrations in *Designs*, but gave explanations that tell us little more than what is plainly shown. They do not so much confirm a basic agreement with Gray's stricture that "Explanations" are "for the use of people who have no eyes" (*Corr.* 14.64) as reveal a decision not to explain them. This is uncharacteristic of Walpole. Yet it was proper for him to bow to the poet's wishes in a publication of his work, and he knew Gray was sincere. When Gray admitted of his "high Pindaric upon stilts," *The Progress of Poesy*, that "the very best scholars will understand but a little matter here and there" (*Corr.* 14.60), he nevertheless refused at first to include notes about his allusions or echoes, and when the poem was finished, he gave it an epigraph from Aeschylus that said, in effect, this is not for the common reader.[4] But I believe the overriding reason for Walpole's lack of an explanation of Bentley's designs, even in the margins of his own copies, was due to his collaboration in pictorial allusions that were often personal and wounding to Gray.

To identify and explain the particulars in each illustration (an analysis that will be the subject of the following chapters) requires first a brief review of both European graphics that influenced *Designs* and English work of such artists as William Kent, John Pine, and William Hogarth.

Upon receipt of the tailpiece for *Elegy*, Gray said to Walpole that illustrations of the kind were not to be found in England; in fact the influence of European design can be detected in them. John Summerson has proposed that they "derive . . . from Jean Berain,"[5] and Irene Tayler has agreed that "one can see parallels in certain of the details, . . . the comic grotesques, or the interlaced strapwork" of the borders ("Bentley Bid the Pencil" 204), such as that of the bottom rim in the frontispiece to *A Long Story* (fig. 16). But much of the detail and general architecture or framing of Bentley's designs seems closer in spirit to Watteau, especially engravings taken from his *singeries*, decorations, and pictures; Walpole owned a collection of 595 of them published in four volumes by Julienne (1734–1740) (Hazen, *Catalogue* #3635) to which Bentley would have had access. Their more precise parallelism can be seen, for example, in Gabriel Huquier's engraving of *La Pèllerine altérée* (1715) (fig. 68), whose borders are like the top rim for *A Long Story*, and whose details remind one of Bentley's treatment of trees, rocks, water, and figures.

The evidence of the drawings further reveals borrowings from rococo pattern books such as *Livre d'ornemens* (ca. 1734), with rocaille decorations by Juste Aurèle Meissonier, and *Livre nouveau de divers morceaux de fantaisie* (1736), with decorations by Jacques de la Joue—the engravings for both books were made by Huquier.[6] Bentley's headpiece and tailpiece designs for Walpole's *Memoirs of King George II* drawn from 1752–1760 show this influence, perhaps more exotically than the designs for Gray: an escutcheon melts in the headpiece for Henry Fox (fig. 52); architectural shapes break, curl, and wrinkle in the tailpieces showing the Duke of Argyle and William Pitt (figs. 50 and 53); or more amazingly the shell cartouche containing the gorgon Faction and her Hydra asleep in a bed of poppies twists and writhes as do the monstrous serpents in the tailpiece for Henry Pelham (fig. 51). The water falling from a shell on the left side of the frontispiece for *Ode on the Death of a Favourite Cat* (fig. 6) can be traced directly to de la Joue. In all the drawings the balance of irregular, zoomorphic shapes appearing just ready to turn into something else makes them, as we shall see, a medium for pictorial satire.

Illustrated texts in Holland, France, and Italy in the early eighteenth century show a more sophisticated integration of words and pictures with superior engraving and printing than in England. Many of these works were available to Bentley in Walpole's well-stocked library. Tayler suggests that he might have looked at Molière's *Oeuvres* (1739) published with engravings by François Boucher, who was one of Watteau's engravers, and he might also have seen the sumptuous edition of Tasso's *Jerusalem Delivered* printed by the Venetian Albrizzi in 1745 with engravings after Piazzetta whose head and tailpieces were "tossed on the page with a casual airiness that had never before been seen in book illustration."[7] Although these books were not at Strawberry Hill, the illustrated folio of Tasso printed by Girolama Mainardi in 1735 at Urbino was there. It had lavish designs by the influential Pier Ghezzi (1674–1755), whose work in this case, engraved by Francesco F. Aquila, anticipated Piazzetta (fig. 73). Their general technique prepares the eye for Bentley's tailpieces.

Walpole owned at least the first volume of J. F. Bernard's *Céremonies et coutumes religieuses de tous les peuples du monde* (1732–1738) with designs by Bernard Picart, called by Frederick Antal "far and away the most important contemporary engraver in Holland."[8] His wiry curves and sense of scale influenced the graphic art of Hogarth and others at the Academy, St. Martin's

Lane, work which Walpole collected and assessed. The fifth volume (1738) "Qui contient les Cérémonies des Mohametans &c." inspired Bentley's exotic drawings, such, for example, as his *Turkish Bath* showing an opium smoker, a bathing houri, columns sprouting vegetation, and anthropomorphic draperies (fig. 61). The difference between this drawing and Hogarth's comparatively severe *Turkish Bath*[9] results from Picart's influence. The sixth and seventh volumes of *Cérémonies* (1728), *Des peuples idolâtres*, with grotesques of orgies, initiation rites, Chinese magicians, penitent fakirs, pagoda of apes, and anthropomorphic landscapes, were probably sources for Bentley's *Prospect of Vapourland* (fig. 62).

One of Bentley's inspirations for *Designs* came from a Picart print (not in *Cérémonies*), a satire on the John Law scandal; it was copied by Bernard Baron for an English audience (1720) with the title *A Monument Dedicated to Posterity in Commemoration of ye Incredible Folly Transacted in the year 1720* (fig. 97).[10] The flying angel blowing on two trumpets appears as Fame who soars before the glamorously clothed Lady Schaub and Henrietta Jane Speed at the top of the frontispiece for *A Long Story* (fig. 16); the use he makes of this design points to another incredible folly. This time the poet is the central figure; the sexually suggestive details of the composition threaten to expose another kind of "scandal."

Not only was Bentley's herbamorphic and zoomorphic idea prompted by contemporary European work, it was almost certainly nourished by the lush mythography and gothic complexity of early English woodcuts for which Walpole had a fondness. The frontispiece for volume two of Holinshed's *Chronicles* (folio ed., 1586–1587) (Hazen, *Catalogue* #597) (fig. 66), to take one of many possible examples,[11] resembles in some particulars the frontispiece to the Eton ode (fig. 11). There are similarities in both between the terms with their folded arms and draperies. Folly at the top of Bentley's illustration is like the grotesques at the bottom of the design for Holinshed, and Bentley's distorted figures (including the boys themselves, especially evident in the original drawing) are like the priapuses, pans, and satyrs drawn for Holinshed. Recognition of such sources intensifies the satire on Eton College. In this case, embraced by representations of Jealousy and Madness, the boys become part of a visual chronicle of English history, that is (to use Holinshed's words printed between his terms) their "conquest" and "inhabitation" of the garden of Eton.

Of course it would be a mistake to assert that Bentley wanted his readers (other than Walpole with whom he shared many a private joke) to make an explicit connection with Holinshed, and hardly possible to prove that he took this obscure source from Walpole's shelf. It is not a mistake or gratuitous, however, to assert that the satirical theme of the Eton-ode frontispiece is set off by the counterpoint of rude, gothic fecundity and the polite decoration derived from contemporary European art. Illustrations such as those in Holinshed were commonplace and can be seen as generic; because of their fascination with things gothic, Bentley and Walpole would have looked at them.

The designs by Francis Barlow, Wenceslaus Hollar, and Francis Cleyn in John Ogilby's translation of the *Aeneid* printed in 1654 (later reissued in folio for Dryden's more famous translation in 1697) and Ogilby's translation of *Aesop's Fables* (1665–1668) had a deservedly high reputation. Walpole admired them; he owned the *Fables* and mentioned the *Aeneid* in the *Catalogue of Engravers* (*Wks.* iv.42). In the explanation of the prints for *Designs*, he wrote that the initial letter for *A Long Story* is in Hollar's style, a style, he said in his *Catalogue*, that advances "to perfection" the nearer it approaches "to wanting a magnifying glass" (38). In *Anecdotes of Painting*, Barlow, Walpole said, excelled in pictures of animals but, because an indifferent colorist, "the prints from his works did him more honour" than the originals, especially those Hollar engraved (*Wks.* iii.248–249). Cleyn received emphatic commendation for his "designs . . . in grotesque" (252).[12]

Bentley's penchant for animals and grotesques was not incidental but encouraged by Walpole. In his drawings a bestiary of monkeys, lions, toads, hares, cocks, cats, dogs, horses, insects, worms, and lizards are subject to an anthropormorphic pressure, or rather, in the context of gothic-revival architecture, a gargoylish one. On two notable occasions Bentley portrayed himself as a monkey, first holding a paintbrush and palette before an easel in the titlepage fleuron for *Designs*, and second, when in exile in Jersey a year later. Here he is seen muzzled like a bear with a monkey's tail and crouching in a trefoil arch before Bentley's gigantic monogram above the arms of Jersey, and surrounded by strawberry fruits or flowers, and by bunches of grapes (fig. 57), signifying that exile from the fruitful "monastery" at Twickenham had isolated and stifled the artist in him.

Having studied "all your drawings," Walpole wrote to Bentley, "I determine that you succeed in nothing better than animals" (*Corr.* 35.243). At an unspecified date Walpole showed Bentley his quarto of Giovanni Battista Bracelli's *Bizarie di varie figure*, in which human figures are (in Walpole's words) "formed by the strangest materials, as diamonds, hoops, bladders, pieces of carpentry, battledoors, kitchen-stuff" (*Wks.* ii.448); in this "composition of a madman" Walpole inserted seven of Bentley's imitations. He frequently indulged in what he called his "Vasari-hood" (*Corr.* 35.207), suggesting ways to Bentley to improve his allegorical pictures and landscapes—"you . . . paint with more melancholy, than ever anybody did: your woody mountains hang down *somewhat so poetical* . . . that your own poet Gray will scarce keep tune with you" (35.157). The pictures are often grotesque, monstrous, and melancholy, just as Walpole liked them to be. A vaulted bridge, the muzzled ape, a scene in Jersey, an illustration of the "Cave of Care" in Spenser's *Faerie Queene* (Book IV, canto v, stanzas 32–46), the *Temptation of St. Antony*, the *Turkish Bath*, and

A Prospect of Vapourland are samples reproduced in figures 56 to 62 that show the tendency from which Mason recoiled when he used the phrase "grotesque fancy" to describe the illustrations for Gray.

* * *

From the very start at Strawberry Hill, Bentley's satires involved the grotesque. Its most pronounced expression early on occurs in the *Centaur*,[13] which was published just prior to 1 April 1751, as an April Fool's Day hoax, nearly three months before the first known reference to the publication of *Designs*. In this twenty-two page pamphlet, Bentley ridicules hypocrisy, preciosity, and sexual perversity. War profiteers, the politically ambitious (with emphasis on the Jacobites), the socially pretentious, the virtuosi, and fraudulent scholars make up a corrupt gentry who, like Ixion on Juno's cloud, beget or foal monsters. The centaur becomes the representative emblem; its name, Manpferdt, derived from the German *pferd* for horse yet also, with the added *t*, suggesting the English word *fart*, is one of many cross-language puns with obscene or scatological inference. In this satire, when the polite are overly delicate, politicians overly ambitious, or scholars unduly presumptuous, all are hypocrites who search out secretly ever more lurid ways to satisfy the fundamental appetites they pretend to deny. Refinement paradoxically begets an equal and opposite crudity.

The *Centaur* is a study in teratology. Bentley's narrator, who "with the greatest satisfaction" will show Manpferdt to the public, warns that "Reasoning, Persuasion, or Terror" cannot prevail upon Manpferdt "to forebear Dunging or Staling." He is barely able to resist "lewd and indecent talk" unless one of the proprietors is by "with a Whip in Hand," at which time he will say "nothing but what the nicest Lady may hear without blushing, even tho' her Father or Husband were present." Yet it is clear that the nicest ladies in this fiction secretly enjoy lewdness. Unbridled bestial appetite, particularly gambling at Newmarket, or drinking, or lechery that hints of unnatural longings, is thematic.

Reverend George Whitefield's "remonstrance" against showing Manpferdt, a creature that will encourage "the most horrid Vices, among the fine Gentlemen of the Age, to which . . . they are already only too much addicted," the narrator answers by asserting that despite the "near Approach of *Newmarket* Meeting" he believes "the present Mode of Vice" cannot actually be increased or "any Kind of it can be introduc'd new." It is not true, the narrator says further on, that the centaur is an intemperate drinker, although it might have seemed so, because he relied upon a promise made to him by "a Right Honourable as well as Right Learned Person" [Lord Granville], who visited and drank with him, and was known to drink too much claret. As to the complaints about "Dunging and Staling," no one has "expressed any remarkable Dislike . . . except a *Scotch* Gentleman [Alexander Murray], and a *Dutch*

Merchant from the City [Sir George Vandeput], the two People upon Earth, who, after having made Cleanliness a Plague to themselves and every body that comes nigh them, remain dirtier than their Neighbours." Certain women [Ladies Hardwicke and Townshend are alluded to] desire a morning ride on Manpferdt; the narrator promises that men of the City need not be jealous of the centaur on this account, for this privilege will be extended only to "People of Quality," and further, he hopes this privilege "will raise no new Objection in the City, to the Naturalization Act."

Although city men, corrupt politicians, and affected ladies are ridiculed, the virtuosi, prelates, and scholars like William Whiston and William Warburton, men who wrote tracts such as *The Divine Legation of Moses* or folios about the origins of the Earth after Burnet's *Sacred Theory*, receive the brunt of Bentley's attack. Because of unnatural isolation or celibacy, seminarially arrogant men become pestilential windbags and either father centaurs (which like mules are sterile, we are told) or make horse's asses of themselves.[14] In other words they become liars, and Bentley has made it his business to expose their pretention. Walpole made many marginal notes in his copy of the *Centaur*; they identify allusions, show approval, and make additions or corrections in the text, evidence of collaboration.

The literary is complemented by the pictorial satire of the *Centaur*'s prefatory print. Its legend and iconography suggest the unpleasant themes (fig. 46). Described as "finely engraved" in *The Gentleman's Magazine* (xxi.153), the illustration shows the human torso and head of the centaur clothed and groomed like a fine gentleman. The exaggerated equine hindquarters are complete with bushy tail and exposed parts, the angle and shape of which are mirrored by the beast's long sword whose hilt hangs down over his left front leg and whose blade by a trick of perspective rises above the tail to pierce the steeple of a monastery. In the middle distance to the left is the Roman gate of the monastery at "wild Schwein-Bergen" or hills of swine. Sitting bolt upright and riding through the gate is the Provincial of the Order, "R. P. *de Sales*" (French for foul or obscene), who according to one rumor recorded in the pamphlet begot the monster on a mare owned by "Holtzbawer" (German for woodsman). Bentley wanted his reader to infer from de Sales and Holtzbawer the opposition between the Stuarts and Hanoverians. In the Schwein-Bergen neighborhood, by which Scotland seems meant, everyone believed the birth of the centaur to be a divine judgment on Holtzbawer (the Duke of Cumberland) for refusing one day to lend his filly (England) to de Sales (Bonnie Prince Charles). Behind Manpferdt in the picture is a view of the mountain meadow where he was foaled. The inscription tells us that the frontispiece was designed and engraved by "Hermannus Freidlieben ad vivum." This was not the only picture Bentley drew of a centaur. In a letter to Bentley of 15 August 1755, Walpole criticizes a drawing, now lost, of Hercules and Nessus that the artist had sent him from Jersey: "The figures are too large . . . ; the centaur, though he dies as well as Garrick can, is outrageous" (*Corr.* 35.243). Walpole probably had a hand in the drawing of Manpferdt too.

The design for the *Centaur* shows that the artist had already discovered the secret of pictorial satire. However similar it appears to the legion of unexciting book illustrations of the time, it has an affinity with the frontispiece for Swift's *Battle of the Books* (fig. 96) and the pictures Pope drew or perhaps suggested for his *Rape of the Lock* (1714) and *The Dunciad* (1734). These books Bentley must have examined, especially as the drawings and the texts (excluding the *Rape*) ridiculed his father.[15] Moreover, Kent designed for *The Dunciad* at least three of the illustrations, which Walpole admired, in part perhaps because he suspected that Pope had guided the artist and that Peter Fourdrinier, originally one of Picart's students, had engraved them.[16] In his article "The *Dunciad* Illustrations" (*Eighteenth Century Studies*, 7, 1973–1974) Elias Mengel explains the contributory role of the designs:

> all the prints reflect the mock-heroic style of the poem by pictorial confrontation of the high with the low. The visual equivalents . . . of the poem's epic background are the mock-heraldic, the decorated initial letter, the ornate picture frame, and, in one instance, the framelike use of a line of Latin. The low subjects of the illustrations are those of the poem itself: the owl and ass, the dunces and their works, the poem's second hero Colley Cibber. (161–162)[17]

These designs add to the fun of the text. Similarly, the drawing for the *Centaur* sharpens its nasty revelations.

Yet one need only set the illustrations for *Designs* beside the crude, flat frontispiece Bentley drew for the *Centaur* to see that his study of prints in Walpole's library was teaching him two basic principles that dramatically changed the quality of his work, namely, to make the decorative detail of the illustration expressive and to use the space provided on the page more effectively for each drawing. Rococo curves and gothic vaults stretching into the white space become significant. Moreover, the illustrations for Gray often contrast neoclassical and rococo elegance on one hand and gargoylish inelegance on the other, an opposition Bentley uses to good satirical effect. From European works he was learning to make his designs graceful and polite, yet both European and English prints also showed him how to oppose the pretty against the coarse.

Walpole's criticism of illustrated books, European and English, was part of Bentley's education; he emphasized in particular the integration of picture and text. Of the many emblem books the two men must have known since boyhood, Walpole had a particular fondness for those by Francis Quarles. Rosemary Freeman has shown in *English Emblem Books* that Quarles did not simply hang a verse off an image "to describe and interpret" it, but tried "to base varieties of poetic effect" on it; he strove for a truer balance of the sister arts than his predecessors had achieved. Moreover, Quarles's emblems are "concerned with action" in their adoption of "the single personified figure or the single emblematic object of the earlier emblem books only to make them part of an episode symbolizing some experience of the soul" (114, 121). If by 1750 the Horatian ideal of *ut pictura poesis* had often retrogressed to texts only with extraneous ornament, Walpole and Bentley wanted to restore the ideal, obviously not in the manner of Quarles per se but as the Earl of Shaftesbury had recommended in *A Notion of the Historical Draught or Tablature of the Judgment of Hercules* (1713) where the artist is told to depict the crucial moment for a soul. He must avoid enigmatic emblems, which ruin "natural simplicity and grace"; rather he should use but natural and simple ones that do not violate verisimilitude, that follow "the rule of consistency" and credibility, yet that still serve a didactic, moral purpose.[18] Walpole and Bentley used natural and simple emblems in their designs not only to illustrate crucial moments from Gray's poetry, but also to make the poetry, by its varied effects, seem interpretations of the images.

Bentley's small watercolor illustrating a scene from Book IV of Spenser's *Faerie Queene* is a case in point. Finished in 1754, it depicts the interior of the blacksmith's cottage, which Bentley called the "Cave of Care" possibly because of the "darksome cave" of Despair in Book I (fig. 59), or its connection with the cave of the Cyclops in the *Aeneid* (VIII.424ff.). The grim interior is painted in smoky browns, yellows, and reds. The abject Scudamour sitting in the foreground recalls the figure of the poet in the frontispiece for *Ode on the Spring* and of Melancholy in the tailpiece for *Hymn to Adversity*; he is the image of a supine, exhausted spirit. His breast plate, lance, and sword are propped against the wall in shadow behind him, useless. With tongs in hand Care bends over his shoulder to place a burning cinder at his heart. At the far end of the room, a figure works the bellows; the dirty fire casts a lurid glow over a grid of ceiling beams and angular walls that make an effective, Piranesian evocation of imprisoning geometry. Three twisted men, seeming to have stepped out of El Greco's *Laocoön*, and possibly inspired by Giordano's *The Cyclops at their Forge* that hung in the Salon at Houghton Hall, work at the anvil. Their writhing, elongated shadows on the wall multiply them into Care's six monstrous servants.

As close inspection shows, Care is not drawn "with hollow eyes and rawbone cheeks" as if he had been pent up in prison; instead he is a satyr, and as such must add to the torment of the hero. Similarly, the servant at the bellows is not a character in Spenser, but a woman, representative perhaps of both Belphoebe and Amoret. The heavily ribbed room with wheezing bellows and pounding hammers shows itself to be merely a projection of Scudamour's breast. The figures are emanations of his nightmare. Bentley compresses, interprets, and transforms Spenser in an exciting way by using natural and simple emblems, as Shaftesbury recommended. This illustration contrasts sharply with Kent's comparatively dull design for the Cave of Despair (fig. 82), which condenses the details of the episode from Book I into a single picture, but does little more than represent them.

Simon Gribelin contributed the illustrations to Pope's *Works* of 1717; Walpole judged him to have no "greatness in his manner"—his prints "have no more merit than finicalness" and "at best are neat memorandums" (*Wks.* iv.101). For the frontispiece and headpiece to Gray's *Ode on the Spring* Bentley copied images from two of the tailpieces that Gribelin scattered indiscriminately through the volume of Pope's poetry, an artist seated under a tree with buildings in the distance and a zephyr tossing flowers (fig. 98). Whereas Gribelin's recurring vignettes decorate the pages but connect to the items they embellish only in the loosest way, Bentley's pictures are uniquely suited to the poetry they delineate. His artist poring over the brook from under the beech tree may recall Gribelin's figure, as well as traditional depictions of Melancholy, yet at the same time he is Gray's speaker in both *Spring* and *Elegy*. The zephyrs in the headpiece for *Spring* are the zephyrs of the poem who fling petals before rosy-bosom'd hours.

Under Walpole's guidance Bentley probably examined the folio of Prior's *Poems on Several Occasions*—the edition at Strawberry Hill, published in 1718, belonged to Walpole's mother and is inscribed in her own hand. Louis Cheron designed the prints.[19] Unlike Pope's *Works* of 1717 and a multitude of other contemporary collections, the frontispiece does not show a portrait of the author, but a river goddess (her profile is surprisingly like Pope's) from whose urn flows the Pierian Spring; the scene of which she is part, depicting the initial four lines of Horace's Ode xxvi, Book III,[20] obliquely alludes to Prior's service to his country as a diplomat and treaty maker, and to his service as a poet on the battlefield of love. Cheron inserted biographically significant detail into a design that has the primary purpose of introducing the poetry contained in the anthology.[21] This innovation anticipated Bentley's introductory frontispiece, in which the figure sitting under the beech is not only the speaker in *Spring* and *Elegy*, the first and last poem in the volume, but also the poet Gray himself. Gray's large nose, unmistakable in the original drawing (fig. 2), was changed to anonymity by Müller for the engraving.

Cheron's subsequent headpieces, initial letters, and tailpieces suit the verse; with a single exception of an initial letter, they are not stock or repeated embellishments. For some of the poems, they are unique and purposeful, such as for the Hudibrastic satire *Alma, or the Progress of the Mind* (figs. 94 to 95). In accordance with the satirical description spoken by the character Matthew, the headpiece shows the stages of developing intelligence: children dance, wear masks, worship idols, march like military troops, and make love. Each child or group of children represents Alma's placement in the body, whether she rests in the feet, legs, groin, or breast. In the next design, behind the initial letter, Alma "sits Cock-horse on her throne, the Brain," with a captive bird that flutters at the end of a string to signify the brain's tenuous grasp on reality, an idea loosely derived from Matthew's imagery in canto iii. (In this context the cypher M might also signify Mind.) Topped with a wreathed death's head between two dying branches from which pears still hang, the tailpiece portrays the aftermath of life and its fruits: grief and elegy beside the bones of the dead, memorial sacrifice, and the settling of accounts.

The progression from headpiece to tailpiece is from youth to death, yet curiously, Cheron begins and ends the sequence with children. Adults and grown-up activities are not shown, but only those of posturing children; first they mimic adult behavior and then grieve over those who predecease them, while counting their money. Cheron underscores the tiresome preoccupations that exhaust men or render them childish. By this sequence he reveals the satiric contribution pictures can make to a poem, even though he never thoroughly developed the verbal-visual interplay as Bentley and Walpole did later in 1752.[22]

More important than Bentley's examination of Cheron, however, was his study of Kent and the artists of St. Martin's Lane. Together they showed Bentley how to change pinched, stiff lines to a flowing, open rococo that in fact became more irregular, exotic, and exciting, if technically less skillful, than Gravelot's. Moreover, the work of Kent, Pine, and Hogarth taught Bentley how to fill drawings to bursting with commentary on the poems they illustrate, as well as with complementary satire.

Bentley learned to juxtapose significant detail and to use pictorial analogues as demonstrated by a single example, Wootton's headpiece to Gay's Fable XX, "The Old Hen and the Cock" (fig. 106), an analogue for the frontispiece to *Ode on the Death of a Favourite Cat.* The headpiece is found in the first volume (1727) of Gay's *Fables* illustrated by Wootton and Kent; Bentley's extensive use of these illustrations as well as those by Gravelot in the second volume (1738) will be proved in later chapters. The analogue prompts us to read Gray's poems as a beast fable and brings into neat coincidence mock-heroic and Aesopian genres. Bentley wanted his design to reflect the mock-elegiac tone of the poem "by pictorial confrontation of the high and the low" (to return to Mengel's words describing Kent's *Dunciad* illustrations), a "visual equivalent" that in this case is strengthened by the referent external to the ode. Expansive finery of a rococo European framework is wrapped round the chinoiserie bowl, yet balanced on the edge of the tub, Bentley's cat is hardly better than a barnyard animal. She is utterly unadorned, unlike the costumed cats fishing with lines and nets on either side of the elaborate frame. Because she recalls the humble cock at the well, she extends and intensifies Gray's own satire on a tabby with delusions of grandeur.

Bentley paid particular attention to Kent's work because of Walpole's preoccupation with the Burlington-Kent model. I have already mentioned the contempt Walpole felt for the illustrations in *The Faerie Queene*, yet suggested the appeal *The Dunciad* illustrations had for him.

Kent's designs for Thomson's *Seasons* (1730) (figs. 101 to 104) also left an impression on Walpole and Bentley. Evidence of influence from this volume is shown not merely by Bentley's establishment of a seasonal progression from Gray's *Ode on the Spring* (Bentley exploits the pun) to the winterscape of the cortege that ends *Elegy* (no mention of winter is made in the poem), but by many other derived details in the drawings that enrich the interplay of Bentley's and Gray's coincident media. Bentley's descending "angels"—the zephyrs in the headpiece for *Spring*, Miss Speed and Lady Schaub in *A Long Story*, the furies of the frontispiece for *Eton*, and Adversity in the headpiece for *Hymn*—are meant to recall Kent's more typical ethereal forms, so that the difference in Bentley's figures, which might be called anti-Tiepolonian, stand out. In this way Bentley stressed their special function. To burlesque the swimming boys in the Eton ode frontispiece, as well as perhaps the Graces in the headpiece for *Spring*, he may have wanted to remind readers of pictures showing bathing Venuses by Boucher, and also, more particularly, Kent's women in the frontispiece for "Summer" (fig. 102). The parallel between Damon who spies on the women and the Etonian who stares at the behind of his schoolmate suggests a consequence of the celibate environment at a boy's school.

Bentley could have learned much from Kent's personal and sophisticated procedure that in some measure changes the content of Thomson's verse. In *The Unfolding of The Seasons* (London: Routledge & Kegan Paul, 1970), Ralph Cohen finds that the mock-heroic narrative of Damon and Musidora alludes to the legends of Paris and the birth of Venus (161ff.). As one can see from the activities of the women in the illustration, Kent does not evoke a memory of these myths. Rather, latent in his illustration of Damon behind "a secret waving shade" spying on Musidora, Sacharissa, Amoret, and a fourth woman not mentioned in the poem, there is an invocation of the myth of Actaeon, whose metamorphosis into a stag and pursuit by huntsmen seem implied by the illustration for "Autumn."[23]

In English literature the popular precedent for linking this myth to lovers occurs in *Twelfth Night*. Orsino complains, just after he has said, "if music be the food of love, play on," that he was "transformed into a hart" at the sight of Olivia and then chased by the "cruel and fell hounds" of desire. Kent establishes the hidden Actaeon motif in "Summer" and "Autumn" by a parallel placement of figures in each of the illustrations: in "Summer" the voyeur at the center and the bathers below him correspond in "Autumn" to the stag at the center and the huntsmen below it.

This parallel placement recalls the parallel love stories in the verse; according to Cohen (155ff.), a proper understanding of each romantic episode must involve comparison with the others: Celadon and Amelia with Damon and Musidora, and later with Palemon and Lavinia. The tragic history of Celadon and Amelia immediately precedes and contrasts with the happy tale of Damon and Musidora; Kent's portrayal of Palemon and Lavinia in "Autumn" brings to mind and accents the earlier stories. With the huge stag bounding above them, Palemon and Lavinia seem to reach out beyond the text, beyond the other two couples, to the implied fourth pair, Actaeon and Diana. Palemon's sickle underscores the implicit violence—sudden death or potential calamity—touching all of these lovers, first by reflecting the harvesters' sickles and huntsman's horn below the fleeing deer, and second by its further more ominous reflection of Time's scythe depicted in "Summer."

Thomson may not have thought of the myth in the 1730 version, or he may have wished to reverse it. He wrote that the sight of the women put Damon's

> harsh philosophy to flight,
> The joyless search of long-deluded years;
> And Musidora fixing in his heart
> Informed and humanized him into man.

By inspiring a memory of Actaeon, the artist suggests a reversal of this description, a possible dehumanizing of Damon, a change that may have spurred the poet in 1738 to rework the episode of the "soul-distracted" lover into something closer to Shakespeare's description of Orsino. Moreover Kent hints pictorially that Damon is Thomson himself, an idea fostered by the verse with the naming of Musidora and the others after well-known love goddesses in literature. Damon's harsh philosophy was put to flight by personifications of poetry, a circumstance befitting the writer, not the character. That, I believe, is why Kent shows Damon leaning on a book. No such thing is mentioned in the poem.

Kent also intrudes autobiographical material into his illustration for "Autumn" with the display of Burlington's house at Chiswick in the left distance. The Actaeon myth must have struck the members of Burlington's circle as an apposite, classical allusion. Leaping toward Chiswick house, the stag is like Thomson himself who, having been touched by a Diana-like fame in some measure because of Burlington, was now pursued by the literati of the day. The design for "Autumn," hints that he is about to be brought down and carried to Chiswick as part of its artistic harvest.

Similarly Walpole and Bentley hunted their game for the Strawberry Hill harvest. By intruding biographical material and aesthetic detail peculiar to Strawberry Hill upon visual representations of Gray's poems, they gave the interplay of design and text the hint of a chase. Gray originally wrote his poems without thought of illustrations. But when Bentley gave the poems a particular arrangement and then enveloped, challenged, and encroached upon them with foreign and not always coincident ideas, he captured the text within the pale of a completely new and personal theme.

Careful inspection not only of Kent's illustrations, but also of Pine's, helped Bentley to sharpen the technique he and Walpole were developing. Pine was a student of Picart and Hogarth; Hogarth admired him so much he painted him in the attitude of Rembrandt. Among Pine's most beautiful accomplishments was his illustrated edition of Horace's works, *Quinti Horatii Flacci Opera* (London, 1733); this modest octavo published in two volumes with verse and illustrations printed from engraved copper plates rivaled European work. Walpole himself noted that "the whole text" of this "fair" edition "with ancient bas-reliefs and gems illustrating the subjects" was "engraven" (*Wks.* iv.113). Picture and text join to make a single graphical composition; in headpieces and tailpieces Pine skillfully integrated his own play of pictorial allusions and Horatian themes.

Pine's achievement can be shown at a glance by a single set of drawings, the head and tailpiece for Ode ix, "Ad Thaliarchum," of Horace's first book (fig. 113). He abstracted from the verse scenes of merriment and love. In the headpiece only the dance, the jar of four-year-old Sabine wine, and the lovers on a couch in pleasing conversation are drawn; in the tailpiece, only the chase of the lovers is shown. Horace's ominous undercurrent of doom conveyed by sharp images of winter, necessary to the carpe diem theme, was completely ignored by Pine. Moreover, he changed the love scene: the tailpiece does not show a maiden lurking in a secret corner yet giggling to reveal her location as described in the last four lines:

> Nunc et latentis proditor intimo
> Gratus puellae risus ab angulo,
> Pignusque dereptum lacertis,
> Aut digito male pertinaci.[24]

Rather it appears that Pine has depicted the English game of "course-a-park," a country frolic in which "a girl called out one of the other sex to chase her" (*OED*), as mentioned for example in Suckling's "Ballad upon a Wedding" and memorably incorporated in Pope's "Spring":

> Strephon: Me gentle *Delia* beckons from the Plain,
> Then hid in Shades, eludes her eager Swain;
> But feigns a Laugh, to see me search around,
> And by that Laugh the willing Fair is found.
> Daphnis: The sprightly Sylvia trips along the Green,
> She runs, but hopes she does not run unseen,
> While a kind Glance at her Pursuer flies,
> How much at variance are her Feet and Eyes!
> (53–60)

It appears that Pine remembered Strephon's speech when he read Horace's ode; in fact he did not draw what Horace described, but reproduced the image in Daphnis's lines. By duplicating graphically this link of Horace and the contemporary game that rural lovers play, Pine revitalized Horace, as Pope had done in verse, and made him current. The picture sweetens the carpe diem theme of the ode. At the end of a poem about the end of joy, the inclusion of a rococo border blooming with flowers honors life and dispels gloom.

Pine worked with Gravelot and Hayman at the St. Martin's Lane Academy. Gravelot left France for London in 1732 to make engravings for the English edition of *Cérémonies Religieuses* and is said in Walpole's *Catalogue* to have as neat a manner as Picart and to be superior "in composition and design" to "his favorite Hollar" (*Wks.* iv.112). Influential at Old Slaughter's Coffee House, he helped give shape to Hayman's art, and both men employed Grignion and Müller as engravers. Hogarth taught his disciples to shift the emphasis of the rococo away from the elegance of Watteau to the wiry realism more appropriate to satire; book illustrations by Gravelot or Hayman, or both together, were plentiful and could be found in Dryden's plays (1735), Gay's *Fables* (1738), Richardson's *Pamela* (1742), Hammer's edition of Shakespeare (1744), editions of *The Tatler* and *The Spectator*, and Milton's *Works* (1749). In 1754 at Strawberry Hill many of these volumes stood in the same case or in close proximity to one another, near also to Kent's Thomson and Spenser, Jonathan Richardson's *Discourses* (1719), and Dryden's translation of Du Fresnoy (1695).

Hogarth cleared the path that the other artists were to follow. Although Bentley did not naively imitate their work, or Hogarth's prints and illustrations which were collected and first catalogued by Walpole, he learned from the artists of St. Martin's Lane to make designs speak. Paulson has discussed the evolution of Hogarth's method, its difference from C. A. Coypel's inspirational illustrations for the popular English edition of *Don Quixote* (1725), and its relationship to the work of Picart, Gravelot, and Hayman. More effectively than his predecessors or disciples, Hogarth made rococo form a narrative and satirical tool. The reading of his illustrations for *Hudibras* (second series, 1726), for example, or his cycles such as *The Harlot's Progress* (1732) is a complicated and subtle business; to understand them one must perceive the interpictorial commentary of analogues, emblems, and tricks of perspective, as in plate 2 of *The Harlot's Progress* where the Old Testament pictures, the collapsing table and dressed-up monkey, the apparent stabbing of the Jew by the sword of the escaping lover, and the wallpaper design that turns into horns on the Jew's head supply information essential for an understanding of the satire.

Walpole called Hogarth in *Anecdotes of Painting* a "great and original genius, . . . a writer of comedy with a pencil," who did not imitate the works of others but caught "the manners and follies of an age living as they rise"

(*Wks.* iii.453). Because Hogarth observed life rather than books he did not condescend "to explain his moral lessons by the trite poverty of allegory. If he had an emblematic thought, he expressed it with wit, rather than by symbol" (456). This somewhat confusing statement means, I think, that Hogarth resorted less frequently than his contemporaries to received emblems, and that the standard symbols he used, such as a cuckold's horns, he placed in unique contexts that enriched or focused their meanings.

Bentley in like manner did not compile in his drawings for Gray merely received emblems. He too staged sets to be read by building them out of allusions, witty images, surprising juxtapositions, and optical puns that hold many meanings, as for example in the impertinent tailpiece to *Ode on the Spring* with its visual play on tail/tale ends. His strategy here is reminiscent of Gay's literary one in the *Shepherd's Week,* for which Louis du Guernier made illustrations published in the editions of 1714; although they translate Gay's incongruities into picture, they do not interpret them and are not nearly as clever or refined as Bentley's for Gray. Like Hogarth Bentley uses analogues and pictorial puns to stress his mischievous themes, yet as directed by Shaftesbury, he avoids monkish and enigmatic emblems in this case and includes only "natural and simple" ones.

Paulson writes that three forms pervade Hogarth's work from early in his career, "the emblematic, the reportorial, and the droll" (*Hogarth* i.69). Because Walpole wanted "nature methodiz'd"[25] and was strongly attached to the delicacy of rococo art, he censured the reportorial depictions of Hogarth by placing him "between the Italians, whom we may consider as epic poets and tragedians, and the Flemish painters, who are as writers of farce and editors of burlesque nature" (*Anecdotes of Painting, Wks.* iii.454). Hogarth, Walpole said, pleased his "vulgar customers" when he "stooped to low images and national satire" as in his print *The Gate of Calais* (456).[26] But if in book illustrations Hogarth sacrificed the decorative to textual elucidation, and beauty to burlesque, Bentley tried harder to combine the two approaches. To please his patron he subordinated reportorial or literal renderings in favor of elegant comedy and satire, but not in the manner of Gravelot and Hayman who also managed more successfully than Hogarth to combine a greater degree of rococo prettiness in meaningful design. Their illustrations for Richardson's *Pamela,* for example, disclose the characters' emotions by skillfully compressing episodic details into a single scene "without sacrificing the rococo texture of costumes and background."[27] Bentley, who can be said to stand between them and Hogarth as Hogarth stands between the Italian and Flemish painters, uses a pretty rococo design to depict the verse, yet he extends it by a contribution of his own that usually offers an unseemly and often unpleasant satirical counterpoint. In other words the decoration in his scenes becomes a vital part of the visual-verbal relationship in unexpected Hogarthian ways.

To sum up, Bentley's strategy corresponds to Gray's in the poems, the ironic effect of which is often based on echoes and imitations. Like Gray, Bentley demarcates the Apollonian or sentimental affectation of the protagonists in the odes but does so in the graphic medium by using rococo elegance to set off his satirical revelation. He even extends the satire to Gray himself. The effect of Bentley's illustrations relies on distortions of the verbal scene within a play of reflections and imitations from extratextual sources, as well as from biographical allusions. One peers, as it were, through analogical layers. The illustrations recall the mock-heroic/heraldic methodology of the Augustans, an influence also evident in Walpole's and Bentley's gothic revival architecture at Strawberry Hill.

* * *

The evolving drawings for Gray's poems so excited Walpole that some time in 1752 he asked Bentley to illustrate his own *Memoirs of King George II*. Those made for the chronicle for 1751 (figs. 47 to 49) were finished in 1753,[28] and the result, a frontispiece, headpiece, initial letter, and tailpiece, impish in tone and style, superceded simple collaboration and surprised Walpole with a satire upon himself. The connection of these drawings to the prose duplicated the strategy of Bentley's *Designs* more completely than Walpole had bargained for. A brief examination of them will help to prepare the eye for the illustrations of Gray's odes.

In his explanation for the headpiece for Book I of the *Memoirs*, Walpole said that the portrait of King George II (fig. 48) was taken from a miniature by James Deacon.[29] Bentley pasted his little oval copy in the space provided within the background scene he had carefully drawn on the manuscript page, and then added a frame of leaves to disguise the edges. George II's armor makes an allusion to his prowess in war at Dettingen; the placement of the King between "St. James's house" and "the Gate in St. James's park that leads into the Garden of Carleton house" alludes pictorially to the feud with his son Frederick Prince of Wales, whose campaign against his father was conducted from Carlton House.[30]

Their quarrel began over money: "The King had refused to pay what debts he [the prince] had left at Hanover" where he was educated, Walpole wrote, "and it ran a little in the blood of the family to hate the eldest son."[31] Indeed George II was himself a recalcitrant son banished from his father's house, a fact that might have sent Bentley to Hogarth's print of George II when Prince of Wales, engraved in ca. 1720, during the time of his painful opposition to George I.[32] Bentley's emblematic borders and their similarity in size and method recall Hogarth's work, as no doubt they were intended to do; moreover, the king's philosophic smile and open countenance show a righteous yet wise self-confidence that appears to combine the attributes of Hogarth's Hercules and Athena. Bentley's initial letter on Walpole's manuscript page, with a view "of the house of Commons, taken from the garden of the Auditor of the Exchequer" (according to the manuscript explanation[33]), points to the cause of the quarrel as well as to the battleground, for it was in Parliament that the prince tried to direct political opposition to the king as well as to Sir Robert Walpole. Bentley's illustration puts Walpole's chronicle into perspective.

The tailpiece (fig. 49) identifies a second but related cause of faction, the rivalry between the royal brothers. Their father, King George II, doted on his younger son as much as he despised the Prince of Wales. The military glory of the Duke of Cumberland, not to mention his simpler, more forthright character, made a sharp contrast to Frederick's effeminacy. Walpole makes much of their difference. After speaking of the death of the prince, he writes with cruel irony:

> Frederick, Prince of Wales . . . resembled his pattern the Black Prince in nothing but in dying before his father. Indeed it was not his fault if he had not distinguished himself by any warlike achievements: he had solicited the command of the army in Scotland during the last rebellion; though that ambition was ascribed rather to his jealousy of his brother, than to his courage. (50–51)

Walpole confirms this judgment with an anecdote about the prince who threw sugar plums at a "representation of the citadel of Carlisle in paste" (51) on the eve of the Duke's great siege, the very night his wife, Princess Augusta, was in labor. He "was really childish" (54). The satire of the drawing enriches Walpole's theme and is also reminiscent in some ways of Bentley's own ridicule of the Duke of Cumberland's enemies in a pamphlet entitled *An Attempt towards an Apology for his R*[oyal] *H*[ighness] *the D*[uke] (1751). Walpole says of the drawing: the "feathers, a caduceus to represent his [Prince Frederick's] patronage of arts, and a mourning mantle, point out [his] rank, character, and death." With pretty hair and ostrich feathers, an emblem of his royal title, he is placed with simpering smile opposite a serpent of the caduceus. Bentley suggests a vacuous mind capable of the impropriety displayed at the banquet.

By contrast the Duke wears armor; it establishes his connection with his father depicted as a warrior in the headpiece. The Duke looks upright and stolid, even though we are reminded of his obesity. He is surrounded by the symbols of his accomplishment: "a Helmet, Sabre, and palm-branch describe the military genius and victory . . . at Culloden." Yet it appears in the drawing that his eyes are closed in contrast to his wide-eyed brother. The Duke, an obstinate authoritarian for whom military discipline was important, seemed blind to the prince's jealousy and never deviated from "his maxim to bear anything from his brother" in order to preserve "the dignity of the blood royal" (69).

The placement of Bentley's design emphasizes another contrast between the brothers. Directly above Bentley's illustration in the manuscript, Walpole compares Sir Robert and his brother Horatio Walpole (created Baron of Wolterton in 1756) with Pelham and his brother the Duke of Newcastle:

> Both were fortunate in Themselves, Unhappy in their Brothers. With unbounded Thirst for Politics, the Duke of Newcastle and Horace Walpole[34] were wretched Politicians: Each inferior to their Brothers in every thing laudable; Each assuming and jealous of their own Credit, tho the Duke nor Horace could ever have been considerable, but by the Fortune of their Brothers. The One childish and extravagant; the Other a Buffoon and Avaricious; Horace sunk into Contempt when His Brother fell with honour; The Duke was often on the point of dragging his Brother down, and was the Object of all Contempt, even where his Brother had still Power and Honour. Mr Pelham maintained his Inferiority to Sr Robert Walpole even in the Worthlesness of his Brother.

Bentley's scene makes a third and more pointed parallel.

In Lord Holland's two-volume edition of the *Memoirs* published in 1822, the engraver James Thomson softened Bentley's depiction, and Holland removed it to the front of the volume. The unspoken but intended satire is lost.[35]

Bentley completed drawings only for the first five years of the chronicle. In the printed *Memoirs* of 1822, nearly all of them have been displaced, one reason for which was the editor's decision to intersperse them throughout the history. But there is no doubt that Walpole and Bentley had carefully planned the position of every drawing.[36] Even when Bentley drew the final portraits after returning from Jersey in 1756, Walpole pasted them, including a satire on Holland's ancestor Henry Fox, in the appropriate spots on his manuscript pages. In the first book, however, he and Bentley actually coordinated their fair drafts of text and drawings on the page, in the same way that Bentley had written out the final stanzas of *A Long Story* above his tailpiece design (fig. 23). The displacement in Holland's 1822 edition mars the interplay of word and picture nowhere more sharply than in the first book where what should have been revealed about Walpole's and Bentley's collaboration is not.

The frontispiece showing Walpole standing between Heraclitus and Democritus with Strawberry Hill in the background (fig. 47) was correctly placed. Yet Thomson did not engrave the emblematic scene of the arms, motto, caduceus, and mask, even though Murray printed the explanation for them. The omission in the engraving impairs the satire.

Walpole's explanation for the frontispiece provides only a hint of Bentley's theme:

> The Author, leaning on a globe of the World, between Heraclitus and Democritus, presents his book to the latter. In the Landscape is a view of the Author's Villa at Strawberry-hill, near Twickenham, where the Memoires were chiefly written. At bottom is the Date of the year, with emblems, and the Author's arms and motto. The Ivy over the mantle that is lifted up, and discovers a mask and caduceus, imply that Time and History reveal what has been concealed.

Typical of his artistic strategy, Bentley wanted his frontispiece to recall certain elements of high European art, particularly in this case, I believe, Giorgione's *The Three Philosophers* (fig. 74). This is suggested by the similar disposition of the three figures before the trees, the building in the background, and the dark line of the trunk along the left border. Rudolf Wittkower has described the "sweet and gently swinging rhythms" and "melancholic mood" of Giorgione's allegories. They "resuscitate by purely visual means the sadness, dreamed about by the poets and the philosophers"; his art descends directly, Wittkower further asserts, to Claude Lorrain's work and English landscape gardening of the eighteenth century, both of which promise "peace of mind in this world rather than the hereafter."[37] Bentley evokes this arcadian melancholy by his background scene.

During the eighteenth century Giorgione's unidentified figures were thought to represent the three wise men.[38] In Bentley's drawing the intimation of religious overtones is supported by the surprising similarity of Heraclitus to many depictions of Joseph, such as those drawn by Battista (or Dosso) Dossi in *Flight into Egypt* (fig. 75).[39] The details of the portrait could have been borrowed from Leonardo's *St. Jerome*, especially in the modeling of the sinews and muscles. Bentley may also have remembered large pictures like Raphael's *School of Athens* (Heraclitus sits in the foreground); he undoubtedly thought of the famous cartoons of Apostolic acts that hung at Hampton Court and that were recommended for study by Steele in *Spectator* #226 both in the originals and in the engravings of Nicholas Dorigny who was invited to England by Queen Anne to make prints of them. The cartoons were frequently copied, engraved, or imitated, for they supplied a language of gestures.

The allegorical frontispiece shows the contemplative and devotional life at Walpole's back, represented first by a Heraclitus meant to recall St. Jerome or St. Joseph, or perhaps the wise man on the lookout for the star in the Giorgione; and second by the "abbey" that was not yet finished, the arcadian haven of its owner's future hopes. Yet Walpole leans on the World with his back to Heraclitus. His preoccupation is the record of mundane affairs which he casually hands to the atomist and realist portrayed like Peter in Raphael's cartoon of the miraculous draught of fishes. In fact the composition of Walpole and Democritus may even recall the cartoon of Christ delivering the keys to St. Peter. Whether Bentley had Raphael in mind cannot of course be proved, yet still the essential point that he intended to tease his patron in a mock-heroic way, at least by the surer analogue of the Giorgione, duplicates the same tactical device used in the drawings for Gray's poems.

The picture then is more than an assertion of order and clarity by which his patron is paid a compliment, as I imagine Bentley wanted him to perceive at first glance. Among all those prominent legs Walpole and the two philosophers recall the poet under the skirts of the Muses in the frontispiece for *A Long Story* (fig. 16). Walpole and Gray are pretty and boyish in their respective pictures. If the two Greek thinkers were to stand, they would dwarf the historian, much as the poet is dwarfed by the mock Olympian muses who in *A Long Story* are meant to emphasize his captivity by women. The philosophers emphasize the incongruity between themselves as rugged Italian giants and the dandified Walpole. He is ridiculed in a mock-heroic setting that relies for its effect on its imitation of the high Italian style.

Reminiscent of a Hogarthian trick,[40] a detail causes a moment of confusion and almost seems an accident of bad drawing; it would have amused Walpole, although it might further have ruffled his complacency. One consequence of the gothic jumble of legs makes the front leg of the stand supporting the World appear to be Walpole's, or the reverse. When Walpole's leg doubles as a support, there is the suggestion that he holds up the "world," namely the powerful and great whose reputations, good and bad, are conveyed to posterity. A still more immediate and personally amusing allusion might be to Walpole's authorship of essays for *The World*, which were being written concurrently (1753): opposite the title page, the picture seems to announce, "by the author of essays in *The World*."[41] Bentley teased this Herodotus with a pun, by giving legs to the magazine and its proprietor "Mr. Fitz-Adam."

Such visual confusion also embodies sharper ridicule: when the leg of the stand becomes Walpole's, he is changed from a polished gentleman into a pigeon-toed, knock-kneed fop about to palm off his precious gossip on Democritus who, upon closer view, now looks reluctant, even groaning in protest. Perhaps out of revenge, he points at the leg in order to direct our attention to the satire, or the satyr Walpole, which the drawing seems to unveil. The placement of the philosopher's hands like a hieroglyph implies something underhanded.

Similarly ambiguous is Heraclitus who no longer is absorbed by obscurities but actually squints up at Walpole out of a surprised, contemptuous eye, as careful scrutiny of the original drawing will show. Bentley may have intended the opposition of high and low ideas in the frontispiece, a scene of multiple perspectives, to correspond to the contrast in the tailpiece for 1751 between the Prince of Wales and the Duke of Cumberland, one that could even insinuate a link between Walpole and Prince Frederick. From the caduceus below, the serpent looks up at Walpole, just as in the tailpiece it stares at the prince. The placement of the mask (implying the many different roles Walpole liked to play as politician, historian, architect, and patron of the arts) over the end of the caduceus and the conjunction of the royal lion with Walpole's escutcheon, whose motto *Fari Quae Sentiat* now has ironic overtones, seem to betoken their association. If again these possibilities cannot be proven, they nonetheless suggest themselves, for Bentley has purposely filled his drawing with intriguing, enigmatic references. The ivy and raised curtain disclose, if nothing else, a strategy of pictorial satire.[42]

* * *

The Hogarthian irony of Bentley's pictures for Walpole and Gray is discovered by strangeness, ambiguity, and curious detail that prompts "reading," not in terms of received emblems, but of composition and analogues. One is led from visual complexity and confusion through visual puns, allusions, and structural relationships that are not always derived from the text and that ask to be interpreted separately. Bentley's is a form of "literary" painting with metaphorical and metonymical landscapes. These "verbal-conceptual" structures aspire to the ideal of *ut pictura poesis.*

The elaborate framing for the Gray illustrations helps to maintain order within them. The technique might have been derived in three ways: first from the title pages of architectural folios, such as Kent's frontispiece to Isaac Ware's *Four Books of Andrea Palladio's Architecture* (1738) (fig. 67). Second, as Irene Tayler has suggested, it may have come from a comparatively mundane source, simple tradesmen cards that Bentley and Walpole must have received when they fitted out Strawberry Hill. Among the multitude of cards printed in the early 1750s, a few examples nicely show the connection: cards of Mary Hooker, milliner and seller of fans; Richard Lyford, leatherseller; Edward Ashworth, sadler; and Benjamin Whitton, copper and brass platemaker (figs. 69 to 72).[43] The frames show the objects of their art; the borders on Bentley's designs contain pictorial allusions to the poems that suggest by the parallel his trade as illustrator. The greeting cards Bentley drew for Lady Northumberland with Chinese or picturesque borders and for Lady Ailesbury in the rococo style (fig. 65) similarly reflect the particular charm of their houses. A third source for the technique might have been looking-glass frames frequently shown in the pattern books of furniture makers. In the role of architect and decorator, Bentley could well have thought that as trade cards hold up a mirror to their maker's affairs, so his designs for Gray might reflect the lines of the verse, and lineaments of the poet and artist themselves.

Like the edges of a stage these frames bring to mind the simile of life as a play, as was suggested by the motto *Veluti in Speculum* above the actors in Hogarth's final painting of the *Beggar's Opera.* Bentley's architecture is theatrical; his designs for Gray present pantomimic stills of key moments in the poems. The scenes appear framed by proscenium arches with the curtains drawn to reveal dramatic frontispieces like that for *Elegy* or the ode about

Selima (figs. 6 and 31), or for *Spring* (fig. 2). Even in the tailpiece for *A Long Story* (fig. 20), a curtain is pulled up above the ladies sitting in a box as if at the theater. The initial letters become theatrical set pieces too, as for example the "T" of *Elegy* where the "moping owl" flies from the ivy-mantled tower (fig. 33). An emblem of death, it opposes the scene of vigorous rustic life in the headpiece.[44] Such opposition between drawings is typical, and it repeats the strategy observed in the *Memoirs*. But to see the analogical and witty theater that operates throughout the book on public and private levels, one must examine each drawing in sequence.

Notes

1. Dart, *History and Antiquities of the Cathedral Church of Canterbury* (London, 1726) and *Westmonasterium* (London, 1723); Dugdale, *History of St. Paul's Cathedral* (London, 1716) and *Antiquities of Warwickshire Illustrated* (London, 1730); Sandford, *Genealogical History of the Kings of England* (London, 1677).

2. "It is a little play-thing-house that I got out of Mrs. Chenevix's shop, and is the prettiest bauble you ever saw." Walpole to Henry Seymour Conway, 8 June 1747. *Corr.* 37.269. See also Walpole to Mann, 5 June 1747. *Corr.* 19.414.

3. Walpole sanctioned his view of himself as a successor to Burlington (the "Apollo of arts, [who] found a proper priest in the person of Mr. Kent") by the example of Matthew Parker (1504–1575), Archbishop of Canterbury. On the inside of Walpole's *Journal of the Printing Office* (1757) is written: the churchman "kept in his House [Lambeth Palace] a Painter, Engraver, and Printer." *Journal of the Printing Office at Strawberry Hill*, ed. Paget Toynbee (London, 1923), 1. See also *Wks.* iii.139, iv.5 and *Corr.* 21.120.

4. When Gray found that fewer readers understood *The Progress of Poesy* and *The Bard* than he had expected, he was upset. See Starr and Hendrikson, *The Complete Poems of Thomas Gray*, 205.

5. John Summerson, *Architecture in Britain 1530 to 1830* (London: Penguin Books, 1953), 242.

6. See Peter Ward-Jackson, "Some Main Streams and Tributaries in European Ornament from 1550–1750," *Victoria and Albert Museum Bulletin Reprints*, III (1969); Paulson, *Emblem and Expression: Meaning in English Art in the Eighteenth Century* (Cambridge: Harvard University Press, 1975), 226ff.; and *Rococo: Art and Design in Hogarth's England*, ed. Michael Snodin (London: Trefoil Books/Victoria and Albert Museum, 1984).

7. A. Hyatt Mayor, "Italian XVIII Century Book Illustration," *Metropolitan Museum of Art Bulletin*, n.s. 8 (1950), 140. Quoted from Tayler, "Two Eighteenth-Century Illustrators," 124.

8. Frederick Antal, *Hogarth and his Place in European Art* (New York: Basic Books, 1962), 80.

9. Reproduced in Ronald Paulson, *Hogarth's Graphic Works*, rev. ed., 2 vols. (New Haven: Yale University Press, 1970), cat. 21, Plate 24.

10. *Monument Consacré à la Postérité en Mémoire de Folie Incroyable de la XX. Année du XVIII. Siècle.*

11. I will give other examples where applicable; the illustration of Holinshed is a representative work that Bentley had available for research in Walpole's library.

12. Cleyn's chairs with large shell backs, also described in *Anecdotes of Painting*, could have inspired Bentley's shell seat that was carved out of oak and placed in the garden at Strawberry Hill in 1754.

13. *A True and Faithful Account of the Greatest Wonder Produced by Nature these 3000 years, in the Person of Mr. Jehan-Paul-Ernest Christian Lodovick Manpferdt; the Surprizing* CENTAUR, *who will be exhibited to the Publick, on the first of next Month, at the Sign of the Golden Cross at Charing-Cross* (London: M. Cooper, [March 1751]).

14. In *The Snarling Muse: Verbal and Visual Political Satire from Pope to Churchill* (Philadelphia: University of Pennsylvania Press, 1983), Vincent Carretta writes that "as the 1750s drew to a close, satires of diminution became satires of dehumanization" (186) and that during the early years of the Seven Years' War the targets were portrayed as animals (208ff.). With Manpferdt in 1751, half man, half beast, the metamorphosis had already happened.

15. Dr. Bentley is depicted as the spider in the upper corner of the window in the drawing for Swift. It came from the studio of Bernard Lens and John Sturt (1710). In the initial design for *The Dunciad* (1734), Dr. Bentley is portrayed as an ass laden with books.

16. In a footnote, just before he condemned the drawings for Spenser, which by contrast he thought added little beauty or meaning to the text, Walpole wrote that the "vignettes to the large edition of Pope's works are in good taste." *Anecdotes of Painting, Wks.* iii.490n.

17. See also James Sambrook, "The *Dunciad* Illustrations," *ECS*, 8 (1974–1975), 211–212. Bentley probably examined Kent's other early designs in editions of Gay's *Poems* (1720) and *Fables* (1727), the quarto of Thomson's *Seasons* (1730), the second volume of Pope's *Works* (1734), and fifty designs for Pope's *Odyssey*. See W. K. Wimsatt, *The Portraits of Alexander Pope* (New Haven: Yale University Press, 1965), 125–127.

18. Quoted from the facsimile in *Cebes in England: English Translations of the Tablet of Cebes from Three Centuries, with Related Materials*, ed. Stephen Orgel (New York and London: Garland Press, 1980), 318, 215. Shaftesbury in his *Second Characters* (1713) calls enigmatic emblems "magical, mystical, monkish, and Gothic" in a more forceful argument against their use. *Shaftesbury's Second Characters or the Language of Forms*, ed. Benjamin Rand (Cambridge: Harvard University Press, 1914), 91. See Freeman, 9–18.

19. Engraved by Bernard Baron and Nicholas-Dauphin de Beauvais. Walpole's feelings about Cheron's work were ambivalent. See *Anecdotes of Painting, Wks.* iii.371.

20. Vixi puellis nuper idoneus / Et militavi non sine gloria; / Nunc arma defunctumque bello / Barbiton his paries habebit.

21. Cheron elaborates the frontispiece to Prior's *Poems on Several Occasions* (London, 1709), designed by H. Howard and engraved by du Guernier.

22. In his designs for John Dart's translation of *The Works of Tibullus* (London, 1720), Cheron used headpieces of children many times over but abandoned the innovation that Bentley exploits.

23. In *The Judgment of Hercules* Shaftesbury says of the subject of Actaeon, "one of the commonest in painting," that "hardly is there any where seen a design of this poetical history, without a ridiculous anticipation of the *metamorphosis*." He advises

instead "truth and credibility" and "unity and simplicity of design" as part of an aesthetic theory that, in Paulson's words, was "a clarion call to action which Burlington was to heed" (*Hogarth* i.104). There is a notable and suggestive similarity between Kent's design for "Autumn" and the illustration for *Acteon* in Michel de Marolles's *Tableaux du Temple des Muses* (Paris: Nicholas L'Anglois, 1655) (*Livre* III.xix. 147).

24. ". . . now, too, the delightful laugh, the betrayer of the lurking damsel from some secret corner, and the token ravished from her arms or fingers, pretendingly tenacious of it." *The Works of Horace*, tr. C. Smart (New York: Harper & Brothers, 1855), 11.

25. Alexander Pope, *An Essay on Criticism*, I. 89.

26. This artistic judgment contradicts Walpole's own evident pleasure in low satire and obscene material, as in his *Memoirs of King George II* and *Judgment of Solomon*; Bentley drew illustrations for both works. Walpole's antipathy for Hogarth's politics was the chief reason for his strictures.

27. Halsband, "The rococo in England," 876.

28. Walpole identified Bentley as the artist "for all these drawings" at the bottom of the manuscript explanation for the initial designs. The date of composition for the headpiece, initial letter, and tailpiece is 1752, as indicated by the medal for Prince Frederick: the date of the frontispiece can be determined as no later than 1753 by the theoretical drawing of the library wing at Strawberry Hill, quite different from the final plan decided upon early in 1754.

29. In the Strawberry Hill Sale Catalogue of 1842 (xic.20) the oval is described as a "Curious miniature portrait . . . (1749)." Walpole in an oblique comment said that Deacon "had a great genius for Drawing" (*Book of Materials*, ms.218) and "painted portraits in miniature in a very masterly manner" (*Wks.* iii.477). The miniature was kept in the cabinet in the Tribune (*Wks.* ii.475).

30. The prince purchased Carlton House from Lord Burlington in 1732.

31. *Memoirs of King George II*, ed. John Brooke, 3 vols. (New Haven and London: Yale University Press, 1985), i.51.

32. Derek Jarrett, *The Ingenious Mr. Hogarth* (London: Michael Joseph, 1976), 56ff.

33. This part of the manuscript and Bentley's drawings for the *Memoirs* are presently at the Lewis Walpole Library.

34. Earlier Walpole described his uncle in terms that could be applied to the prince: "He knew something of everything but how to hold his tongue, or how to apply his knowledge. . . . interest was in all his actions" (Brooke i.93).

35. Although reproduced in Brooke's edition of the *Memoirs*, Bentley's illustrations have been placed in an appendix (#12). As a result they have again lost their apposite satire. For Holland's dislike of Horace Walpole and his editorial practice, see Brooke, i.xvi–xvii.

36. Hazen wrote that Walpole's "final copy of the earlier part [of the *Memoirs*] was carefully prepared for the printer, with head- and tail-pieces . . . pasted at the proper places" (*A Bibliography of Horace Walpole* 93), but failed to say that the position of the drawings was changed in the edition of 1822.

37. Rudolf Wittkower, *Idea and Image: Studies in the Italian Renaissance* (London: Thames and Hudson, 1978), 166, 173.

38. A. Richard Turner, *The Vision of Landscape in Renaissance Italy* (Princeton: Princeton University Press, 1966), 87.

39. In the Ante-Chapel of the Vyne (for which Bentley submitted a plan) was hung *The Holy Family*, possibly by Agostino Masucci; the head of Joseph is similar to Bentley's portrait of Heraclitus.

40. For example, the horns that appear in the wallpaper behind the cuckold's head in plate 2 of *The Harlot's Progress*, or the horns of the cow behind the husband's head in plate 3, "Evening," of *Four Times of the Day*.

41. The headpiece for each essay in *The World* shows a scribe, feather pen in hand, seated at a desk peering over his shoulder at a globe of the World.

42. With what is discovered in the first four illustrations for the *Memoirs*, one can expect the subsequent drawings to be satirical. After returning from Jersey in 1756, Bentley sketched the allegorical backgrounds, which are of a simpler, less private nature than the work completed in 1753. The portraits themselves in these later pictures were drawn by Johann Heinrich Müntz.

43. Chosen from the scrapbook collection entitled *Token and Trades Cards* at the Lewis Walpole Library.

44. Noted by Tayler in "Bentley Bid the Pencil," 202.

III
Title Page Fleuron

THE title page fleuron and the initial frontispiece announce Bentley's intention for the designs. They hold up a mirror to the poems and poet and reveal the counterpoised shadows of other texts and pictures. The drawings are labyrinthine in complexity; they operate on several coincidental levels at once, presenting layer upon layer to be mined. As analogues change, so the meanings of the images change, with the result that the illustrations seem almost too contrived and too obscure. Hermeneutics is bound to be impressionistic at the remove of over two hundred years, yet Bentley's drawings, whether literal or imaginative reflections of the text, cannot be fully understood without interpretation. Evidence shows that details are not accidents of decoration. Bentley wanted his public, particularly members of Walpole's set, to "read" the drawings as they would the poetry.

Bentley's illustrations are a personal response to the verse, to the poet, and to the creative energy unleashed by Walpole at Strawberry Hill. Each exaggeration of an image subtly enhances or mocks or provides a darker side to the meaning of the poet's lines and records the artist's perception of the poet's insinuation of himself into the verse.

When Richard Cumberland, Bentley's nephew, wrote a description of the fleuron (fig. 1) in his *Memoirs,* it is clear that he had not understood his uncle's intentions:

> Bentley had those powers in embryo, that would have enabled him to excel, but submitted to be the projector of Gothic embellishments for Strawberry Hill, and humble designer of drawings to ornament a thin folio of a meagre collection of odes by Gray, the most costive of poets, edited at the Walpolian press.[1] In one of these designs Bentley has personified himself as a monkey, sitting under a withered tree with his pallet in his hand, while Gray reposes under the shade of a flourishing laurel in all the dignity of learned ease. Such a design, with figures so contrasted, might flatter Gray, and gratify the trivial taste of Walpole; but in my poor opinion, it is a satire in copperplate, and my uncle has most completely libelled both his poet and his patron without intending so to do.[2]

Cumberland's "without intending so to do" is wrong. The tone of Bentley's early letters to Walpole (who, it should be remembered, was nine years younger than Bentley) do not suggest the subservience Cumberland had in mind, though it is true that Bentley increasingly resented Walpole's attempt to make him his priest. To be possessed as an artist on the model of Kent in the household of Lord Burlington was to be low, lower than Walpole anyway, and Walpole's teasing, even bullying to this effect late in the decade, led to their separation and also to Bentley's ostentatious dress and behavior in London when he made a bid for Lord Bute's patronage in the early 1760s. In the frontispiece for the *Memoirs of King George II* and in the fleuron for the title page of *Designs*, the satire may be animated by revenge, but it is without real asperity, and the evidence of the work shows that his compliance to Walpole's wishes inspired rather than deflated his genius.

Bentley's ridicule is purposeful and pungent; its challenge and impertinence infused the relationship of artist, poet, and patron with the excitement of emotional tension. Irene Tayler has observed that Bentley used the classical topoi of the artist as ape of God and the poet as Arcadian singer, or more particularly Apollo with his laurel crown and lyre: "he pictures Gray as Apollo at the lyre and himself (with witty deference) as a busy ape at the canvas . . . imitating Nature, the Art of God" ("Two Eighteenth-Century Illustrators" 125–126). The interplay of poetry and drawing was encouraged by Walpole whose wit and psychological thrust-and-parry with Bentley at Strawberry Hill suggested the "figures so contrasted" in the fleuron.

The fleuron evokes emblems of high classical art, one model for which might have been Cheron's headpiece for Prior's occasional poems that shows Apollo surrounded by the nine muses (fig. 93). Secure within the Augustan tradition but in the mode Walpole approved, Bentley's monkey "methodizes" nature: he sits in a waste under a dead tree—perhaps like those Kent "planted" in Kensington Gardens "to give a greater air of truth to the scene"[3]—and against Alpine scenery, no doubt the twin peaks of Mount Parnassus, which in this instance, Halsband suggests, represent the sister arts ("The rococo in England" 879). The idealized portrait of Gray sitting on a ledge has been drawn to look superimposed on the background as if it had been cut out and pasted on; Bentley wants us to know that this is the scene on the monkey's canvas.

His pencil transforms the barren wilderness into the picturesque, into the "flourishing laurel" of cross-pollinating arts. In a play of words and images, Bentley makes a visual pun on *fleuron*. The contrast of the barren tree accentuates the flowering of the canopy surrounding the poet; the laurel literally flowers into a fleuron, not simply to announce the purpose of the design, but to show visually the creative action of both painter and writer. The ape fills the tree with the flowers of his art. The flowers and leaves surrounding the bard also represent poetry; flowers are threaded through the strings of the lyre (a detail Müller, the engraver, has omitted in his comparatively awkward rendition) to suggest a double play on the use of poetical flowers (i.e., figures) and on posy and poesy, an idea, by the way, that is carried over to the lyre placed inside a wreath of flowers at the lower left of the frontispiece. Painter and poet, the fleuron tells us, will foliate bare ruined choirs and blank quires.

"Nature methodiz'd" here is not simply more beautiful but more dramatic. The dead tree and counterpoint of doleful poet evoke Cesare Ripa's emblem for "Malinconia" (fig. 78).[4] This analogue establishes pictorially the pervasive melancholy in the poems and pictures, especially as the configuration also reflects a second analogue, "Muta Poesis," a traditional depiction of Simonides' idea of painting as a "silent poem" in, for example, Giovanni Pietro Bellori's *Le vite de' pittori, scultori et architetti moderni* (Rome, 1672, p. 19) (fig. 79). In this sequence of associations, Melancholy is subsumed in a broader Apollonian context. The development of associations, enriching at each stage the quality of the scene, reveals a Lockean epistemology suggestively parallel to Addison's famous description of the primary and secondary characteristics of things in *Spectator* #413, where the "poor appearance" of the world, seen in its "proper figures and motions" without secondary attributes, is described as a "barren heath" and "solitary desert." The contrast between untouched, barren nature on the left of the fleuron and the "flourishing laurel" on the right—literally, *fleuron*—tells us that Bentley's subject is artistic creation. The landscape viewed by the sprightly monkey is being thoroughly transformed by his hand. What the artist-ape creates is shown; we "read" from left to right, first about the maker and then about what he makes. The effect of art is a secondary characteristic, Bentley suggests, an idea implicit in *Spectator* #413 when Addison's observer feels like an "enchanted hero of romance" after the sensuous beauty of the world has been restored to him.

By making the picture of the youth with the lyre look superimposed on the background (just as the secondary qualities are superimposed on the primary), and then retaining his own figure as an ape painting the very scene (in part to emphasize the play on *fleuron*), Bentley focuses our attention on the process of his art. One cannot help thinking that the suggestion of a range and play of associations was as attractive to him as the clever readjustment of canonical emblems. To draw attention to the method of his work is to multiply opportunities for wit and ridicule; representation of melancholic or Apollonian figures is thus distanced yet invigorated.

The palette, brushes, and easel so carefully displayed are the tools by which perceptions are wrought; these tools are necessary for the illusion of Arcadia. Overweight, round shouldered, effeminate, and with a large nose about which he was unusually sensitive, Gray undergoes a metamorphosis at the tip of the brush into a paragon of muscular form. Bentley wants this drawing to reveal the magic power of art, and at the same time to intimate that the poet with his lyre in hand actually produces the same kind of alchemy by making ordinary language musical. The ape represents man without art; his nose is like Gray's in real life. The Greek youth, whose posture is staged to look natural, is man transformed by art. The two figures mirror one another: the turn of their heads, the placement of arms, their relationship to lyre and easel with line of strings reflecting line of brushes, stress the connection between them, even as the foliage covering the bard's private parts is removed from the ape. The paradigmatic enchantment that the fleuron spreads over the poet dissolves with the thought that an erasure might reveal his original form beneath. Both ape and singer recall the pose of Melancholy.

The establishment of an Arcadian context on the high Apollonian level is accentuated by a low, homely parallel; Bentley's composition roughly recalls Kent's design for the introductory fable "The Shepherd and the Philosopher" in Gay's *Fables* of 1727 (fig. 105). It is the first item of a pattern, for as we shall see, Bentley recurs throughout the edition to Kent's designs in order to counterpoise analogues from "low" and "high" genres. His two figures correspond to Kent's shepherd and philosopher in deep discourse under a tree with flocks, pastures, and mountains receding into the distance. The philosopher, "whose rules of moral life were drawn from schools," learns from the shepherd that a pastoral existence and study of "nature's laws" have taught him truth. The philosopher must concede two points: first, the shepherd's virtue proves him wise, and second, "Pride often guides the author's pen," with the result that books are as affected as their authors.

Kent's typical, pastoral image shows a wayfarer who, staff in hand, learns truth from a rustic moralist. It is the theme of Poussin's *Arcadian Shepherds* (fig. 77); Bentley returns to the image in his frontispiece to *Elegy*, and even in his *Temptation of St. Antony* (fig. 60). By reminding us of the analogy in the fleuron, he suggests that meditation on particulars in Gray's verse, from the stream in *Ode on the Spring* to the sequestered vale in *Elegy*, will disclose not just the simple morality learned by a shepherd-fabulist but the consequences of pride and affectation for a quintessentially cultured bard contemplating nature. The artist-ape shows that Gray's odes together with Bentley's pictures will, despite their evocation of a pastoral scene and high golden age, expose the complexities and ambiguities of sophistication.

If by the picture Bentley linked the sister arts as Pope had done in the *Epistle to Mr. Jervas* ("images reflect from art to art"), he also implies by the artist-ape, placed lower on the page than the poet, that his role is subordinate, such for example as it was conceived by Edward Topsell in the *Historie of the Foure Footed Beastes* (1607): "The Poets (with their apes, the painters, limners, and carvers)."[5] This is the view taken by Tayler when she writes that Bentley has pictured "himself (with witty deference) as a busy ape at the canvas." But more than witty deference, the pert expression, the mischievous, wide-eyed look and soulful demeanor (which Müller changes into a broad grin), the parody of the poet's posture and attitude, and the play on fleuron with all that it implies, tell us that this self-portrait simultaneously mocks the poet.

Insubordination rather than subordination becomes the ape's objective. Reinforcing the meaning of the analogue of "The Shepherd and the Philosopher," he makes a monkey of the bard, if only to remind us that by our pretentions we make monkeys of ourselves. The equivalent theme is forcefully articulated in the first poem of the volume, *Ode on the Spring*, and in a more muted way by the following odes. Bentley's reflecting images of the ape and Apollonian youth hint that they are variant forms of one another, or interchangeable states of being, and by prompting satiric reversal make visual a complementary, cross-language pun in the nearly homonymous link of singer and *singe*. Such paronomastic tricks in Bentley's work are common, as, for example, the visual play on *fleuron* and *tailpiece*, and the verbal one on *Manpferdt* in the *Centaur*. Indeed, the idea of the *singe* in the first place might have come from Bentley's work at Walpole's "monastery" where he was the "key monk" in the preparation of its first "sacred" text, the designs for Gray's odes, although the more likely origin was his use of Watteau's *singeries*. In the fleuron the monkey serves a similar purpose to the monkeys in Gay's Fables XIV and XL (1727) and in plate 2 of *The Harlot's Progress*.[6]

We have seen that Bentley has toyed with the classical topos (as artist he is the ape of God) and that, as ape, he is subordinate to the poet. Now he gets the better of the poet by making him his ape. In contrast to Topsell, Bentley's wily creature acquires mastery. Jonathan Richardson had argued for the superiority of the artist. Moreover, Bentley perhaps remembered that the artist-ape was described as nature's consummate imitator in *The Winter's Tale*, where Shakespeare says of Giulio Romano (whose architecture influenced Bentley's own[7]) that could he "put breath into his work," he "would beguile Nature of her custom, so perfectly he is her ape" (V.ii.102ff.).

Walpole's interest in Stowe, Richard Grenville Temple's house in Buckinghamshire, probably introduced Bentley to the Congreve Monument designed by Kent and erected there in 1736. This memorial to William Congreve consists of a pyramid with a blunted top on which squats an ape peering into a mirror. According to iconographical commentators, as explained by Paulson in *Emblem and Expression* (explanation to the frontispiece), the wide base of the pyramid signifies matter or man's mortality and the taper rising to a point, the immortality of the soul and its heavenly aspirations. But Kent undermines the traditional purpose by sculpturally punning on apex. Blunted by an ape holding a mirror in the traditional attitude of *vanitas*, this pyramid explodes man's pretense and folly, a favorite theme of Congreve's comedies. The monument is inscribed with the motto, *Vitae imitatio, Consuetudinis speculum, Comoedia*, Comedy is the imitation of life and mirror of fashion.

Bentley similarly undermines his Apollonian topos. It may be coincidence that the easel in Bentley's fleuron makes a pyramid and that its apex seems blunted by the withered limbs of the tree. Indeed, the saucy little monkey holds a palette that looks suspiciously like a mirror, and in fact it is the tool by which a mirror of reality is produced. When the ape looks to his palette, he sees the poet in classical, human form. This is the reflection conveyed to the canvas. On the other hand, were the singer-poet to look to the palette-glass, the rule of reversal established by the satire suggests that he would see his image as *un singe*.

Bentley deliberately shows a range of pyramids in his fleuron. Centrally placed, the Parnassian sisters provide the governing pattern for the interplay of reflecting images on the two sides of the drawing. The stark forms to the left, of the monkey, easel, and dead tree, reveal the skeletal structure of the lush scene to the right, of the poet, lyre, ledge, and laurel. The two sides of the picture, the monkey and easel to the left and the poet and lyre to the right, work as one: together they invert the pyramidal shapes by forming a single wedge or funnel whose striking dominance, far more emphatic in the drawing than in the engraving, iconographically turns the poet's immortal aspirations upside down and returns them to the clay from which they have sprung.

This consuming wedge establishes the fundamental theme. Beneath the poet's handsome, god-like skin, the artist reveals a mortal ape. When in effect he strips the flourishing laurel of its leaves to expose its hidden structure (a defoliation of the Apollonian text, one might say), he shows that the lyre held by the bard has become an instrument of Apollonian delusions. It has made him a liar.

The play on lyre/liar contributes to the contemporary debate over the reliability of poets, a debate later joined by Richard Hurd, one of Gray's friends at Cambridge, in Letter X of *Letters on Chilvalry and Romance* (1762). Hurd challenged the controversial statement that poets are "liars by profession" made by Hume in 1739 in his *Treatise of Human Nature* (I.iii.10).[8] Poets do not expect to be believed, Hurd asserted: "a legend, a tale, a tradition, a rumour, a superstition; in short, any thing is enough to be the basis of their air-formed visions. . . . The poet has a world of his own, where experience has less to do than consistent imagination."[9] Although in agreement, Gray himself reacted against the "consistent imagination" that had betrayed him into vanity, especially in *Spring*, where he described the self-deception that accompanied the exuberant imitations of his youthful verse. Experience forced truth upon him in a painful irony that led to disenchantment. Gray recorded the paradox that a lie often reveals truth.

Bentley's pictorial answer to Gray conveys the same melancholic idea. As in the thematic development of the six odes, the pictorial satire on bardic vanity and immortal aspiration helps to purge the poet of pretense and folly. Bentley's pictures and Gray's poems oppose, compete with, and yet complement one another. In the fleuron, the painter sits in the shape of a double-*v* on a hard square bench before his easel. The picture bristles with double meanings; like a *w*-easel the artist completes a rebus.

Melancholy is produced by reversals of meaning—an unmasking, as it were, at each step of analysis.[10] Yet if it is implied that beneath the Apollonian skin there is to be found an all-too human form, so in turn, deeper than the truth of vanity and self-delusion, there must underlie another Apollo who expresses the pathos of the discovery. Forming one side of the downward sloping wedge, the bard represents the sorrow of the verse.

One of the themes extending through the drawings is the contrast between idealism and reality, or of man before and after the Fall. Undoubtedly Bentley examined the new *Paradise Lost* (1749) with Hayman's illustrations, which Walpole bought in the expensive, three-volume quarto. Hayman's frontispiece for Book IV, also engraved by Müller, shows Adam reclining against the double trunk of a flourishing laurel in which perch two cockatoos; Eve is sitting beside him. At their feet a dog, lamb, goat, and lion frolic together, while behind the tree Satan leers at the couple. Gray's posture in the fleuron is similar to Adam's, implying that the poet's fate is human, analogous to Adam's.

Better suited to the idea of the Fall is Orpheus, who joins Adam to Apollo. He becomes a type of Adam when he falls. He is aptly described by Ovid in the *Metamorphoses* (xi.8) as *Vates Apollineus*, Apollo's bard, in part because like the god he sings of unrequited love. Apollo, it may be remembered, wears the laurel taken from Daphne, who was changed into laurel to escape him; his song is about his loss. But Orphean verse expresses the perplexities and inner torment of fallen man as Apollonian song cannot, which despite its subject generally remains serene, detached, and appropriate for a god. The speakers for the first and last of Gray's odes in Bentley's volume, *Spring* and *Elegy*, are both thwarted lovers, "cross'd in hopeless love." They recall Spenser's Collin Clout in "June" and "December" and Pope's Alexis in "Summer," the setting of which is the bank of a stream at noon; the central allusion to Orpheus is particularly echoed in *Spring*, which Mason has informed us (*The Poems of Mr. Gray* ii.73) was originally called *Noontide*.

If the poet in the fleuron is meant to remind us of Ripa's Melancholy (fig. 78), Bellori's "Muta Poesis" (fig. 79), and even, say, Cheron's mourning figure in the frontispiece for Tibullus's *Love-Elegies* (fig. 80), it is also similar in appearance to typical portraits of Orpheus, such as that used as the first emblem in P. Agustino Chesneav's *Orpheus Eucharisticus* (Paris, 1657) (fig. 92). Like Chesneav's animals, Bentley's monkey appears captivated and inspired by the sorrowful music.

Yet Bentley intended, I believe, that we should be reminded not merely of Orpheus's astonishing powers with the lyre, but of his unpleasant death. With some frequency, the fatal moment was depicted by artists such as Mantegna, in a fresco in the Camera degli Sposi at Mantua, or the unknown engraver at Ferrar at the end of the fifteenth century, who made the prototype for Dürer's more disturbing and emphatic drawing *The Death of Orpheus* (fig. 86).[11] It is hardly likely that Walpole or Bentley actually saw this drawing, although they, as thorough students of the graphic arts, may well have seen either the Ferrarese engraving, in which the figures are depicted precisely as in the Dürer, or others like it.[12] The placement of the withering oak above the fleeing child in opposition to the rich tangle of leaves and trunks above the poet in Dürer's *Death of Orpheus* serves a similar purpose to the parallel contrast in the fleuron. Above the boy running from the center, the ruined branches tell us something of the sterility revealed, just as barren branches reveal impotence in prints of Melancholy. According to the story taken from Ovid's *Metamorphoses* (x.78–85), Orpheus's pederasty inflamed the jealousy and wrath of the already spurned Thracian women; revengeful Maenads, they destroy the poet. They "are clad in billowing draperies which accentuate the vigourous beauty of their bodies," Erwin Panofsky has written, whereas Orpheus on his knees vainly trying to protect himself displays "that beautiful *contrapposto* which classical art had employed for the countless heroes and warriors dying in battle" (32). The hero's adoption of a heroic posture at the extremity of violent death is a measure of the distance he has placed between himself and ordinary mortals. To this poet a heroic attitude had become more important than life itself.

The posture of the ape is similar to that of the escaping boy in the Ferrarese engraving as well as in Dürer's drawing; the relationship of the ape and bard in Bentley's fleuron may imply a similar play of emotions. This Orphean analogue complicates the theme already developed from Topsell. Overtly, of course, no sexuality is suggested, although Bentley is not inhibited in other illustrations. The beautiful attitude he has given the bard shows the isolation that attends elegant posing. *Ode on the Spring* effectively makes the same point: the insects, quick glancing to the sun, frolic in the May warmth, whereas the solitary poet merely observes them, having himself turned away from any active connection with life. In the ode about Selima, the averted faces and deafened ears of the common cats and even of the bemused gods at the drowning of the narcissistic tabby surprise the poet with the same theme. He is not simply portrayed as Melancholy in the fleuron. Bentley shows the artist-ape painting a picture of him striking a pose; his affectation, his undue absorption in the very process of art that causes his fall, is thus emphasized.

Hercules, like Orpheus, was another mythic hero who descended into Hell and also returned, but with the crucial difference of fulfilling his quest. Orpheus and Hercules are a contrasted pair, the one effeminate and devoted to music and poetry, the other manly, muscular, and courageous; one never redeems his loss, the other succeeds in his labors; Orpheus succumbs to pleasure, Hercules prefers virtue. Hercules was the more popular subject in eighteenth-century iconography, perhaps the most popular of all, according to Paulson (*Emblem and Expression* 30, 38ff.). Dürer's sixteenth-century version in *Der Hercules* (fig. 87) can be fully understood only in its relationship to, and contrast with, *The Death of Orpheus*: the hero is astonished not simply by the orgy of Pleasure, the Satyr, and the child, but by the violent reaction of Virtue; although he remains a "supporting witness" (as Panofsky calls him) of the figural duplicate of the Maenads in *The Death of Orpheus*, he stops Virtue from destroying the couple. The panic-stricken child flees just as the boy flees from Orpheus. George Wither's emblem for the Choice of Hercules, "When *Vice* and *Virtue* Youth shall wooe, / Tis hard to say which way 'twill goe" (fig. 90), is much more typical. He links the musical instrument, a lute in this case, with artifice, pleasure, and death—as for that matter, did Holbein in his illustration of Adam and Eve's expulsion from Paradise (fig. 89).

The counterpoised figures of ape and bard, and the play that underlies their composition, are intended to prompt these associations. The beauty of the poet with lyre in hand conveys the latent meaning that prepares for his unmasking just as Pleasure is unmasked in Wither's emblem.

Bentley's portrayal of the sister arts is thus complicated by analogues and parallels, and by the process of art he self-consciously displays. Not only does he pun on the idea of *fleuron*, undermine and change the Apollonian topos, initiate satirical reversals, and funnel the action down the wedge in order to accomplish a cathartic purpose, but he also emphasizes the difficulty of the process because of the ambivalence of signs. The ape represents an affectation just as much as the bard, and because of the principle of reversal invoked by the mirroring images, it is hard to decide which of the two will have the last laugh—or sigh.

Notes

1. *Designs* was not printed at the Strawberry Hill Press; the Press was set up in 1757.

2. Richard Cumberland, *Memoirs of Richard Cumberland written by himself*... (London: Lackington, Allen, 1806), 17. Cumberland was the son of Bentley's elder sister Joanna and Dr. Denison Cumberland, Bishop of Clonfert and Kilmore. Cumberland very strongly took the part of his uncle after he, Bentley, had irreconcilably quarreled with Walpole in November 1760.

3. Kent "was soon laughed out of this excess," Walpole wrote in *On Modern Gardening* (*Wks.* ii.539). Walpole championed Kent's new mode of gardening, except for this extreme. See his essay for *The World*, vi., 8 February 1753, 34.

4. In the 1709 English translation of Ripa's *Iconologia: or, Moral Emblems*, "By the Care and at the Charge of P. Tempest" (London: Benj. Motte, 1709), the image of Melancholy is split between two representations, "Malenconico, per la Terre" (translated as Melancholy) (p. 15, fig. 59) and "Malinconia" (translated as Pensiveness) (p. 55, fig. 217). Bentley uses the latter.

5. Edward Topsell, *History of the Four Footed Beasts* (1673), 10. Quoted from the *OED*.

6. See Paulson, *Emblem and Expression*, 43.

7. For example, Bentley's use of Romano's house at Mantua as a model for "The Cöhue or Town House at St. Helier in Jersey," designed in 1755.

8. This often repeated idea, that poets are liars, is derived ultimately from Hesiod's *Theogony*, i.22–28; it should be remembered that irony, essential to poetry, derives from the Greek *eiron*, meaning liar.

9. *Literary Criticism in England, 1660–1800*, ed. Gerald Wester Chapman (New York: Alfred A. Knopf, 1966), 384.

10. Bentley's strategy partly derives from Hogarth's burlesques of his own work. At the beginning of the 1750s, Hogarth was commissioned by the Honourable Society of Lincoln's Inn to paint *Paul Pleading Against His Accuser Tertullus Before Felix, Governor of Judea*; the important model was Raphael's cartoon *Paul and Elymas Before Sergius Paulus*. Having completed the monumental and classically balanced composition, he then in 1751 caricatured his own work in the engraved subscription ticket that showed the same scene, but in the "vulgar manner" and unsuitable style of "the true Dutch taste." Whereas Hogarth espoused the official view as expressed, say, by G. de Lairesse in *Het Groot Schilderboek* (English trans. 1738) and Lord Shaftesbury, not to mention Walpole (whose later criticism of Hogarth in *Anecdotes of Painting* was that he "stooped to low images"), he simultaneously mocked academic pomposity and hypocrisy. Beginning *Designs* just at this time, Bentley adopts a similar tactic by subjecting formal imitation to caricature in a single picture.

11. Erwin Panofsky, *The Life and Art of Albrecht Dürer* (Princeton: Princeton University Press, 1955), 32.

12. Many details in Bentley's illustrations recall Dürer's work; it would be surprising had he not carefully studied the prints Walpole assembled and Chute mounted at the Vyne. Dürer's influence seems the stronger in retrospect when one reviews the whole of *Designs*.

IV
Designs for *Ode on the Spring*

THE frontispiece for *Ode on the Spring* (fig. 2) serves to introduce all six poems in the volume. The placement of Gray's poet under a tree, reminiscent of Pope's Alexis, links him with the bard of the fleuron; his pose suggests the deepening associations and sadness of *Spring* as well as the melancholy of the *Elegy*. The details of the design framing him allude to each ode in turn, thus bringing them together. Walpole's explanation is simple and brief:

> A Figure musing, &c. The ornaments allude to the chief subjects of the poems, as the altar, chaplet of flowers and rustic pipe, to this ode: a boy with a hobby-horse and a book, to that on Eton: a cat-arion, or a cat with a lyre sitting on a dolphin's back, to that line on the death of a cat
>
> *No Dolphin came, no Nereid stirr'd:*
>
> a monkey with a violin and lawyer's wig, to my lord keeper Hatton's dancing, in the Long Story: a Roman sepulchral altar inscribed Diis Manibus Sacrum, with a spade and skull, to the elegy. The monkey painting, the lyre, the pen and crayon, are allusive to the poems and drawings.

In the fleuron, by means of the ape Bentley ridicules the poet in the ode for his classical affectation, his false pretense, his lie on the lyre. In the frontispiece he conveys the same idea through contrasted images, reflections, and associations, much as Gray ridicules the poet in *Spring* through echoes and contrasted diction. Bentley uses classical symbols to conceal his satire; Gray's revelation follows Apollonian language in the ode. According to P. M. Spacks, "the poem creates its highly individualistic effect through its exploitation of 'classical pretense,' its deliberate avoidance of personal observation, in conjunction with its ironic self-revelation."[1]

Bentley's bard of the fleuron is now, in the frontispiece, no longer young. He ponders his loss, "On hasty wings thy youth is flown." The flourishing laurel behind him in the fleuron has turned into the moss-grown beech, or rather the "nodding beech That wreathes its old fantastic roots so high" above the listless figure of *Elegy*,[2] and even the dead tree behind the easel in the fleuron is now made huge and broken. Inspection of the original drawing for the frontispiece shows that Bentley, by means of a large distinctive nose, has actually turned the Apollo of the fleuron into Gray himself, a little joke that Müller expunged, no doubt after the poet's outcry over the engraving of his portrait.

The relationship between poet and ape has changed: with easel, palette, and brushes, the monkey has clambered up the rococo frame. His smaller size symbolizes his diminished role as a figure in the designs, and suggests that Bentley will be less concerned with the process of art than with the illustration and illumination of the text. Although the drawings by the artist-ape will answer the poems, they are no less consecrated to its mocking gods (to echo the latent but improper play in the sepulchral formula *Diis Manibus Sacrum*). On the opposite side of the frame, the second monkey, whose mace, wig, and fiddle allude to Sir Christopher Hatton, looks over his shoulder to see what the first will make of him as well as to imply that art will answer art. The two monkeys recall Watteau's *singeries*; the setting is reminiscent of Claude Lorrain's landscapes; and the citadel in the background looks as if it were lifted straight from Bernard Lens's *A New and Compleat Drawing-Book... Being the Close Study of the late Mr. Lens* (1751).[3] The imitation of an elegant, academic style used as a foil to the reality of death and its harbingers of frustration, bewilderment, and despair corresponds to Gray's echo of Virgil in *Spring*. The portrait of Gray, plain and with a receding hairline, is contrasted not merely to the Apollo of the fleuron, but to the stylized, classical idealizations of the boy with a hobby horse and the Arion-like cat opposite him.

The frontispiece appears to be governed by the circle. Each serpentine curve (recalling Walpole's aphorism that nature abhors a straight line[4]) seems to unfurl toward the laurel crown inside a star at the zenith representing the immortal aspirations of the poet. Yet his dispirited vision of mankind conveyed by his melancholic posture initiates an opposite movement marked by his rounded back and downward looking head. The smooth, stylized, star-like canopy drops through palm leaves to the altar tombs at the right and left; the shape of the frame is reflected by the musing figure and by nearly every other item around and above him. Things unfold upward; simultaneously, they seem pressed downward. The circles or swirls repeat or invert one another like the spiralling thoughts of frustrated dreams. They are answered by the squared bottom and foundation covered with emblems of mortality. The opposition of hope and doom is nicely defined by the skull under the gravestone, whose rounded, rising brow curves down, back to a flat base in earth, making a representative hieroglyph.

The very different effect of the frontispiece from that of the fleuron results from the intricate, scrolling framework. The poet is wrapped in rich design, a thick cover of leaves and branches, apes, musical instruments, swags, whorls, the boy and cat-Arion, star, wreath, palm leaves, and the overarching dome plate of the empyrean. The extraordinary busyness bewilders and encumbers; it represents the convolutions of a generative fancy that has been distracted and crazed with care. The figure is not simply embowered, but entombed in a deep shadow anticipating the vault of the crypt shown in the tailpiece to *Elegy*. Even the lyre and counterpoised spade appear to reach up to enclose him.

The lyre, positioned at the bottom of the page, seems to intone a dirge. It reflects the spade on the opposite side. It is made of ram's horns and leans against a burning, sacrificial altar decorated with ram's skulls that is itself mirrored by the "Roman sepulchral altar." If the "altar, chaplet of flowers and rustic pipe" refer to *Spring*, as Walpole says, Bentley shows pictorially that this poem also anticipates winter, the season depicted in the tailpiece for *Elegy*. The chaplet, enclosing the lyre as the trees enclose the poet, is like a funereal garland.

From top to bottom and side to side and crosswise in a pictorial chiasmus, elements of the frame reflect or answer one another. The wreath inside the incandescent star is answered by the crossed quill and crayon caught in the strapwork at the bottom; they are tools by which both artists yearn to achieve glory. The poet sitting between these emblems is placed on an isthmus of a middle state, while extremes above and below him appear to distil his ambitions and the means to achieve them. These things are allegorical disembodiments: within the star the laurel wreath is a spiritual symbol; beneath the sepulchral altars, like the taper buried beneath the church at the end of *Elegy*, the ape and bard of the fleuron are respresented by inanimate objects, the quill and crayon.

At the upper left and right, the boy and Selima balance one another. Both anticipate the affectations or delusions to be undermined in their respective odes, a mortification suggested here by the sepulchral altars below them. At the top of the frame, both have undergone an apotheosis. The boy looks secure in his youthful innocence. The placement of the bard between the boy and the skull at the lower right suggests the ambivalence of the bard's middle age. The child turns his back to the scene below; the poet turns his back to the tree of life and the star above. Saved from drowning by Apollo's dolphin like Arion in myth, the cat-Arion embodies the mythographic power of pastoral elegy that can raise the dead from oblivion, as in the case of the drowned Lycidas. Bentley invents a suitable complement to Gray's mock-elegy: the cat has died for a fish, and so here she is rescued by one; her lyre is connected with the garlanded lyre diagonally below, suggesting death and rebirth. The poet seated between the boy and the skull and between the two lyres, as at the center of an *X*, ponders the cycle.

The artist-ape answers the musical ape across the page like a reflecting image in paint, or echo in song. Both apes carry emblems of worldly vanity, interest, and accomplishment: the canvas, violin, wig, and mace. The fiddle of the one on the right brings the merriment of the dance, intrigue, and escape from duties, as described in *A Long Story*.[5] So too both suggest the entanglements of life intimated in all the poems. Below them the rustic pipes of the *Spring* ode and the tamborine and mouth organ of the country folk of *Elegy* hang above their respective altars to left and right, which mark the beginning and end of the volume as well as of life. By their reflection of one another they recall the line from *Spring* that all creeping and flying things "Shall end where they began."

According to John Sitter in *Literary Loneliness in Mid-Eighteenth-Century England*, Gray believed that " 'pure poetry' should be about a lonely poet surrounded by 'nature' ";[6] it is not surprising, therefore, that Bentley has isolated the figure in the frontispiece to *Spring*. But the "nature" that surrounds this figure is of a complex kind, a natural scene infused with social significance that suggests at once hopelessness and melancholy. In the six poems, man is betrayed by temptation and ambition; in negative mood he contemplates despair and certain death. The circumambient emblems encasing the bard fall round him like a printed shroud.

On the right Bentley traces the general fall from innocence by illustrating Selima above, *A Long Story* in the center, and the grave of *Elegy* below. The serpentine curve of this fall, matching the shape of the poet's back and cape in the middle of the picture, tells us that he broods over the paradigm. The eye drops from simplicity to complexity, from Selima's pastoral elegy, to the sprightly Manor-House dance, to the sober georgics of the plowman and swain, and finally to the meditative, epic-like trial at the grave where the poet moulders in "the bosom of his Father and his God."

Yet Bentley counters this fall with a movement on the left side of the picture that unfolds upward with the ascending smoke and emblems suggestive of the odes *Spring*, *Eton*, and *Hymn to Adversity*.

In his explanation Walpole makes no mention of *Hymn*, but because three poems are alluded to on the right side of the frame, we should expect the other three to be represented on the left. *Hymn* is indeed represented there. Its emblem is the very same altar that stands for *Spring* as well as the boulder behind it, a coincidence I will return to in a moment. Walpole begins his explanation with this altar and moves round the frame in clockwise fashion, up the left side and down the right, to the opposite altar of *Elegy*, the last poem in the volume, as though to suggest the sequence of the odes. His omission of *Hymn* possibly occurred because reference to it would have upset the logic of his own progression. We must remind ourselves that Bentley and Gray have not arranged the odes in this sequence, yet also that the accident of seeming disorder gives emphasis to the idea that the poems share a theme, explicit or implicit, of self-deception against a painful recognition of truth.

Overlaid images of *Spring* and *Hymn* join the specific torment of the one to the more general suffering of the other. In fact, the three odes alluded to on the left side of the frame deal explicitly with the problem of youth by invoking false, self-enamored innocence about to be destroyed. Their speakers recoil from the mortifying discovery that must humble and sober them; the poet in *Hymn*, who has the most fully developed consciousness, prays for fortitude. The fall on the right, therefore, followed by the ascent on the left, suggests that humiliation may lead to salvation or even apotheosis, but not necessarily according to a particular sequence. In the volume the odes are organized in complementary pairs; each ode finds its meaning reflected in the succeeding one: *Spring* in *Favourite Cat, Eton* in *A Long Story*, and *Hymn* in *Elegy*. It is also true that the essential idea of the final poem, whose evolving meditation finds its reflection in every mind but whose speaker ponders his own fate, is clarified for us by reference to all the other poems. In the introductory frontispiece Bentley divides the two sets of three, yet the emblems, because they do not exclusively replicate the details of their particular poems, impress us with the interconnection of all six, each of which contains in germinal form the idea of the others.

The protagonists of the poems on the right side of the picture actually do fall: Selima into the tub, the poet-speaker of *A Long Story* into the clutches of the women, and the speaker of *Elegy* into the grave. Episodic and eventful, these odes are less intensely introspective and painfully personal than the other three on the left side, where the cycle of mortification and redemption is an essential part of their meaning. The upward curve on the left is launched by the implements at the bottom center, which, after the fall to the grave on the right, seem washed clean at the "rushy brink" as though from a kind of baptism; water from the spring leads to renewal as in spring. The play of sister arts (the pen holds the crayon to the strapwork to signify that the poet restrains the painter) reincarnates the process, first with the immolation of the poet corresponding to the suggestion in *Spring* and *Hymn*. The smoke of this sacrifice rises from the altar through rustic pipes to the artist-ape who makes the music visual and produces *Designs . . . for Six Poems*. The studious boy with hobbyhorse signifies youth; thus, the cycle reaches completion before descending again.

The moralist in *Spring* describes the sacrifice of youthful arrogance necessary for redemption. The setting into which the first lines of the ode are placed, including the Virgilian phraseology and the allusion to the "Hours of Venus," leads us eventually and in retrospect to connect the "Attic warbler" with the poet himself; Gray's strategy depends upon our initial blindness. When the warbler answers the "cuckow's note" it augurs the discovery of the speaker's self-delusion. The phrase "untaught harmony of spring" acquires a double implication, a reference to the birds whose song is beautiful in spite of their ignorance of prosody and to the poet who may know the rules of prosody but is ignorant of the real meaning of his language of life.

The speaker's arrogance in his phrase "With me the Muse shall sit" is stressed by the word order that places "with me" at the beginning of the line. When he identifies himself with the Muse, he makes her think with him of the ardor of the crowd. His exclamation "How low, how little are the Proud,

How indigent the Great!" becomes a judgment on himself. The speaker's artifice and his echo of Virgil, Shakespeare, and Milton, which so pleased him at first, inadvertantly exaggerate his fall; his sophomoric grandiloquence reveals his youthful narcissism. Ultimately, it forces upon him the humility and despair of age.

Gray has parodied the pompous diction of his own juvenilia (and other false poets who merely echo the classics) in order to rid himself of his undue and unhealthful fascination for earlier poets. Not only have the classics removed him from direct experience of life, he seems to confess, but they have made him conceited. This the insects show his persona in the ode when they intimate that he is no better than they; their rebuke purges the smug self-importance and clarifies the mind of the speaker. Bentley's distinct portrait of Gray in the original drawing for the frontispiece connects him and his invented narrator.

Maynard Mack has recently remarked in his *Alexander Pope, A Life* that the insect metaphor for human arrogance was typical in theological arguments of the day,[7] and Gray admitted to Walpole that he had unwittingly taken the idea from Matthew Green (*Corr.* 14.39ff.). As Gay's illustrated fables provided analogues for other pictures, Bentley when he drew the initial letter might also in this case have thought of Fable XLIX from the 1727 edition, "The Man and the Flea," in which a flea rebukes the speaker for presuming that creation was made for him, when in fact human beings were bred for insects "that more important Fleas might feed." The elegance of Kent's illustration for this fable (fig. 109) exaggerates the posturing of the moralist who stands smartly dressed in front of ledge, roots, and tree trunks, but with a fly on his nose. Bentley omitted the insects in the frontispiece for *Spring* because they would not have been to the purpose of his larger, more philosophic theme. Kent's humor was out of place and too reductive. Bentley's melancholic bard accurately represents the idea in *Spring* and anticipates the serious mood of *Elegy*.

The overlaid allusions to *Hymn* and *Spring* further emphasize the extension of the poet-speaker's isolation and melancholy. The ram's skulls on the left-hand altar reappear on the altar depicted in the headpiece for *Hymn* (fig. 26), which is also placed beneath musical pipes. Moreover, the ram's skulls recall those shown at the bottom corners of the frontispiece to *Hymn* (fig. 24), where the smoke exhaled by the ram at the lower left, reminiscent of altar smoke, twists up to a laurel wreath that is as far removed from the infant at the center of this drawing as the correspondent wreath is far removed from the poet in *Spring*. The huge boulder behind Melancholy in the tailpiece for *Hymn* (fig. 29) is to be found behind the altar in *Spring*; Melancholy's posture is mirrored by the bard's, and the rocks, roots, and dark foliage around her surround him too.

In "Bentley Bid the Pencil" Tayler shows that Pine's tailpiece for Ode

XXV, "Ad Lydiam," of Horace's first book (fig. 114) is the apposite analogue for the tailpiece to *Hymn*. Horace's old woman is neglected by young men, a theme echoed in *Spring* when the insects remind the poet-speaker that "Thy Joys no glittering female meets." The sterility and isolation of age, emphasized in the background of Pine's drawing by a priapic satyr, is the old woman's torment. It is interesting to note that the verse that explains the priapus, *Aridas frondes hiemis sodali dedicet*, was elucidated by Dr. Bentley, a fact his son must have known:

> The sense and interpretation of these words depend on the two former lines. Young men, says the poet, are more pleased, *magis gaudent*, with trees which are always green, such as are myrtle and ivy; but despise dry and withered leaves.[8]

Bentley reproduces the posture of unhappy Lydia not merely for the figure of Melancholy at the end of *Hymn*, but for the poet in the frontispiece who looks down and away from the withered tree before him. In Pine the satyr-like faces leering at Lydia from either side of her reappear in Bentley on the tombstone above the skull as "busts," the Latin root for which is *bustum*, place of pyre and burial.[9] Like the poet in the original drawing, both heads bear Gray's profile, in this case not expunged by Müller when he made the engraving. Gray is mocked by multiple reflections of himself.

In Pine's tailpiece a winged fury modeled on Caravaggio's *Medusa* rises over the neglected woman (cp. the bat above Dürer's Melancholy, fig. 83). Bentley drew a gorgon's head four times: as Madness for the frontispiece of *Eton*, on Athena's shield for the frontispiece of *Hymn*, in the inital letter of *Hymn* where she is significantly framed by her manacles, whip, and flail, and in the headpiece of *Hymn* where she descends on the disporting boys. In fact, the protagonists in all the poems are subjected to violence and destruction: the first is taunted by the (f)lies in *Spring*; Selima drowns; the old Etonian is attacked by vultures of the mind before the tranquil prospect of his school; the poet is pursued in *A Long Story* by two harpies; the infant is given to nurse Adversity with her flails and fetters; and the moralist, crazed with care, crossed in love, and marked by Melancholy for her own, is buried in the churchyard. In the frontispiece for *Spring*, roots rise round the seated figure like serpents, and branches fork down; the redoubling reflections of the frame swirl menacingly about him. These ominous signs of raving madness, the gorgon with her thundering voice and threatening mien, are part of his heavy burden.

On the right side of the frame, music makers are linked: below the lyre-playing cat and musician-ape, the skull of the lyricist next to the stream appears to sing even in death (as figuratively it does in the "Epitaph" of *Elegy*) like the decapitated head of Orpheus floating down the Hebrus. On the left side, below the book-reading boy and the artist-ape, a sepulchral altar supports the lyre.

Skull and lyre together, moved by intimations of mortality, appear to have generated the odes and the pictures suggested by them. Deep in shadow among the roots, cut off from the audience by the elaborate framework, the poet himself like Melancholy appears to be seated on the other side of a stream that divides life from death. Horror lurks in the dark shadows around him. The tableau of Gray's predicament conveys its "expressive horror and dignity," the key phrase Walpole coined to describe the essence of *The Bard* that only Bentley, he said, an artist comparable to Rosa and Poussin, could paint (*Corr.* 35.252).

The large downward pointing wedge in the fleuron made by the ape at his easel and the poet with his lyre receives answer in the frontispiece in the even larger triangle made by the juxtaposed lyre and spade. Although they are connected by the strapwork under the earth, the apex of their vectors lies precisely at the heart of the transcendent laurel wreath in both the original drawing and in Müller's engraving. By forsaking the world for art, the poet becomes a prisoner of his own nightmare; at the same time Bentley suggests through the structure of his designs that the poems may lead to their author's redemption. The brilliance of the star illuminating the wreath shows that, despite the weight of sorrow or even horror, Gray's melancholic songs paradoxically affirm life.

* * *

The headpiece for *Ode on the Spring* (fig. 3) lightly satirizes Gray's celibacy, particularly the kind of relationship Pine depicts for "Ad Thaliarchum" in the design that shows the lover's game of "course-a-park." Horace's earthy carpe diem solution would seem a proper response to the poet-speaker's depression at the end of *Spring*.

The headpiece illustrates the first ten lines of the poem. Under an ancient oak or beech, instead of the melancholic poet three Graces dance: "Lo! where the rosy-bosom'd Hours, / Fair Venus' train appear." Not precisely in their traditional guise, they all face forward. Their prominent breasts are emphasized in contrast to the bovine hindquarters of the tailpiece. "Rosy bosoms are conspicuously absent" in Gray's life, P. F. Vernon has written, thinking also of the line "Thy Joys no glittering female meets"; he maintains that "rosy-bosom'd Hours" is the poet's intentional joke against himself ("The Structure of Gray's Early Poems" 384). Clearly Bentley thought so too. In traditional depictions of the three Graces after Marsilio Fincino and other Neo-Platonists, Amor, who stands between Pulchritudo and Voluptas, is shown back-to-front because she represents the celestial power necessary to reconcile the other two.[10] Bentley irreverently makes her face forward to suggest Gray's frustrated desires, a subject that he later pursues in the illustrations for *A Long Story*.

These women, "the comely Graces" who "shake the ground with alternate feet" of Horace's "Ad Sestium" (*Odes* I.iv) (tr. Christopher Smart),[11] appear to dance *L'Allegro* to the melancholic bard's *Il Penseroso*. They objectify the frustration revealed in *Spring* more particularly than did the portrayal of his melancholy in the frontispiece. The notion that the headpiece, however innocent it may look, conveys deliberate sexual meaning is supported not merely by the context, or by Bentley's adjustment of a canonical emblem, but also by the obscene drawings he later produced, including those for Walpole's own pornographic writings.

The *Prospect of Vapourland* (fig. 62), for example, is again concerned with melancholy. Personified as a woman (as she is in the tailpiece for *Hymn*), she sits in the middle foreground in front of an explicitly drawn phallic tree trunk that defines the source of her misery. Her lover is dead. The stone she leans against is a man-shaped boulder, which either represents him or in this anthropomorphic landscape is himself turned to stone, possibly by the gorgons of madness like those described in *Eton*. Together they contrast sharply with the couple on the right who stroll arm-in-arm along the Physic Road, identified as such by Bentley on the back of the allegory.

In November 1753 Walpole completed an indelicate parody of Solomon's proposed division of a baby to satisfy the claims of two women (1 *Kings* iii, 16–28) (*Corr.* 13.25); Bentley provided equally indelicate illustrations (figs. 54 and 55) for this *Judgment of Solomon*. After reporting that the patriarch had to decide which of the two women, bride or whore, is rightful owner of a young man's phallus, Walpole wrote that it

> was what Virgin Eve beheld,
> The fairest plant of all the field,
> The tempting stem from whence she drew
> The fruit of joy and knowledge too.[12]

Walpole and Bentley imply that without sexual intercourse woman turns into Melancholy; the idea extends to both sexes, as is clear from *Vapourland* and *Spring*. In the pornographic work, the tree becomes an overt sexual symbol. Whether flourishing or withered, it also carries sexual implications in *Spring*.

The "rosy-bosom'd Hours" dancing before the tree tease Gray with a projection of one sexual fantasy; at the center of the drawing, two cherubs with dragonfly wings flutter between the trees tossing flowers. They illustrate the lines:

> While whisp'ring pleasure as they fly,
> Cool Zephyrs thro' the clear blue sky
> Their gather'd fragrance fling.

Probably modeled on the comparable figures drawn by Kent for the frontispiece of Thomson's *Spring* (fig. 101), they also anticipate the frontispiece to the Eton ode and of the headpiece to *Hymn* in which latent homosexuality is meant to be conveyed. They even recall, however faintly, the boy in the *Death of Orpheus*. Given the reflection of images from drawing to drawing, each enriching the other in meaning, one must question their purpose, for Bentley appears to taunt Gray with more than a hint of pederasty. In the context of the ode, zephyrs and Graces come to represent the temptations of sex.

The play on fronts and backs, beginnings and ends, from the frontispiece to the tailpiece, is repeated in the embellishment for the initial letter *L* of "Lo" (fig. 4). A bee rests near the top of the vertical shaft entwined with roses and lilies, or perhaps morning (mourning) glories, Dürer-like in treatment. Recalling seventeenth-century Dutch and English still lifes of flowers in which an insect usually signifies death, the composition makes a pun on "Lo" by becoming an emblem for low. At the same time this insect, clinging to the vertical shaft, another phallic emblem, is one of the many "Eager to taste the honied spring" as an agent of pollination. In two ways it reminds the poet of his mortality by placing the sterility of his solitary life against its power to fructify. The complex purpose of the initial letter forms an integral part of Bentley's thoroughly developed approach to illustration and is much more than fanciful decoration.

The last picture for *Spring* (fig. 5) is alive with humor. The image puns on the idea of a tailpiece; the rump of a cow with a long tail is an impertinent emblem for the end of the poem and for mortality. It gives ironic finality to the rebuke of the "sportive kind." The tension in the poem results from the self-deception and pretension of the speaker who elevates himself to the company of Horace, Virgil, and Milton when he echoes their high art, a plagiarism and affectation that deserves rebuke. To produce a corresponding effect in his drawing, Bentley turns the cow's rear toward us in a background of high-art elegance derived from the idealized pastorals of Claude and Watteau. Instead of visually representing the final event of the poem, Bentley matches his wit to Gray's with an effective strategy, even if one less sophisticated.

The landscape view introduces the succeeding odes; with the gazing cow whose back is turned to us, we look over the course of the stream towards its distant source beyond a chapel on the horizon suggestive of those in the illustrations for *Eton* and *Elegy*. The spring flows into the foreground like the progression of the poetry;[13] as one poem ends, another begins. Ultimately, we pass from this vernal scene to the frozen grave of the tailpiece for *Elegy*.

Notes

1. P. M. Spacks, *The Poetry of Vision*, 91. See also A. R. Humphries, "A Classical Education and Eighteenth-Century Poetry," *Scrutiny*, viii (1939); Geoffrey Tillotson, *Augustan Studies* (London: Athlone Press, 1961); F. Doherty, "The Two Voices of

Gray," *Essays in Criticism*, xii (1963), 222–230; P. F. Vernon, "The Structure of Gray's Early Poems," *Essays In Criticism*, xv (1965), 381–393.

2. The recollection of *Spring* in lines 101–104 of *Elegy* is fairly specific. We are told that under the beech the listless figure stretches his length at "noontide"; Mason records that the original title of *Spring* was *Noontide* (*The Poems of Mr. Gray* ii.73).

3. In "Short Notes" of his life Walpole said he was taught to draw by "Bernard Lens, master to the Duke [of Cumberland] and Princesses [Mary and Louisa]," with whom he played as a child (*Corr.* 13.7). A number of Bentley's figures recall Lens's—e.g., the Graces, Father Thames, and Henrietta Jane Speed and Lady Schaub; perhaps Walpole encouraged Bentley to copy the *Drawing Book*, namely to use standard, recognizable images, necessary to set off his satire.

4. *On Modern Gardening*, *Wks.* ii.539.

5. Walpole wrote in his edition (Hazen *Catalogue* #2044) below a footnote on Hatton: "In Ant. Bacon's papers published by Birch is an extract of a letter on the news of the court, in which one Capt. Allen tells Mr Bacon, that at the marriage of the chancellor's nephew Sr William Hatton, his Lordship danced the measures, and left his gown on the chair, saying, 'lie there, Chancellor.' vol. 1, p. 56."

6. John Sitter, *Literary Loneliness in Mid-Eighteenth-Century England* (Ithaca: Cornell University Press, 1982), 9.

7. Maynard Mack, *Alexander Pope, A Life* (New Haven, New York, and London: W. W. Norton & Co., in association with Yale University Press, 1985), 481.

8. *The Works of Horace*, tr. C. Smart (New York: Harper & Brothers, 1855), 26n.

9. By the joke Bentley has in effect "burned" Gray as a poet, just as the poet feared his aunts would burn him were they to discover that the "burial ticket" was the tailpiece to *Elegy*. This episode was described in the letter quoted earlier (*Corr.* 14.59). In all likelihood Walpole showed the letter to Bentley, who might in turn have made an allusion to it by this little scene.

10. Edgar Wind, *Pagan Mysteries in the Renaissance*, rev. ed. (New York: W. W. Norton and Co., 1968), ch. iii, esp. pp. 43–47.

11. In *Polymetis: or, an Enquiry concerning the Agreement Between the Works of the Roman Poets, and the Remains of the Ancient Artists* (London: R. Dodsley, 1747), the author Joseph Spence speaks of depictions of dancing Graces, thinly clad (72–73), and shows engravings of them, both in their usual pose and in dance (plate VII). According to the subscription list, Walpole bought five copies of this folio; it appears from his correspondence he gave one to Gray (*Corr.* 14.18), and it is probable that he and Bentley used it as a source for the illustrations.

12. Walpole included this poem among his *Fugitive Pieces*, although it was never published. The manuscript is presently at the Lewis Walpole Library.

13. The image could have been suggested by *The Progress of Poesy*, which Gray was working on throughout 1752 and hoped to finish for inclusion in *Designs*.

V
Designs for *Ode on the Death of a Favourite Cat*

BENTLEY may have wanted us to think that the spring from the preceding designs pours into the full-page frontispiece for *Ode on the Death of a Favourite Cat, Drowned in a Tub of Gold Fishes* (fig. 6), filling its tub and jars, for this picture and poem brim with a play of similar ideas. Like the poet-speaker of *Spring*, Selima is perched on a "rushy brink"—the edge of the chinoiserie tub decorated with flowers—and like him imagines herself on a level with classical heroes. *Spring* begins with echoes of Virgil that reveal the speaker's affectation; Selima's ode begins with an imitation of Dryden's *Alexander's Feast* that exposes her perception of herself as a goddess above the fish. Staged by a Timotheus-like Gray, both poems are about such delusions of grandeur. Each poem begins with dramatic irony and ends in an irony of situation. Bentley draws Selima, a dupe of vanity, admiring her reflection in the bowl, and for added emphasis of her self-glorification he shows her at the top of the frontispiece to *Spring* peering down at the poet-speaker whose lyre has been removed from his hands and placed in her paws.

In spite of her cat-like reflection, Selima sees herself as a nymph. She is unable to resist gold, a matter Gray cleverly realized not only by imitations of Dryden but by puns like that on goldfish—"midst the tide" they betray "a golden gleam" irresistible, Gray implies, to females and cats. Similarly, in *Spring* the speaker's perception of himself as a bard of the golden age includes a clever play on flies that like the symbolic fish are "afloat" in the "liquid noon . . . quick-glancing to the sun." Both cat and speaker are betrayed into platitudes before being brought to judgment. Caught up in their delusions, they fail to distinguish the true from the false. They attempt artificially to rise above their natural selves and must suffer for their presumption.

Censuring the link of cat and nymph in Selima's ode, Dr. Johnson said that Gray confused animal and human attributes, or animal instinct and human temptation, and was particularly critical of the last line. "If 'what glistered' had been 'gold'," he wrote in his *Gray*, "the cat would not have gone into the water; and, if she had, would not less have been drowned." Animal or human temptation, true or false gold, fish in a lofty vase or angel forms in a stream are among the many ambiguities Gray intentionally uses.[1] It is the distorted sensibilities of a human mind that interests him. The animal appetite, the irresistible hunt and taste of fish that draw Selima into the water, does not so much concern him as human vanity, greed, and arrogance. These Eve-like temptations make Selima aspire to be something she cannot be—a nymph or maid—and yearn for things she cannot have by right. Her passions are out of place for a cat, just as Eve's temptations were wrongful for a woman.

The word play in the ode is governed by the development of analogies. Gray's "violence both to language and sense" (Johnson's phrase) nevertheless remains within the bounds of the beast-fable genre, where such confusion is necessary to expose the dichotomy in human nature, in which arrogant aspirations are inevitably undermined by animal weakness. Selima's fate is the result of her inability to recognize her limitations as a cat; yet indeed she "would not less have been drowned" whatever the cause of her fall into the lofty vase.

Possibly Johnson was concerned that Gray had linked Selima to too many analogies, including Dryden's Alexander, Shakespeare's Portia, the mythical Narcissus and Persephone, and Aesop's dog in the fable of the dog and the shadow.[2] But that fault is perhaps part of Gray's strategy of exaggeration to expose Selima's arrogance and the all too cat-like foible that causes her to drown.[3] In his frontispiece Bentley contributes yet another analogue to the list: Gay's Fable XX, "The Old Hen and the Cock," a story about a young rooster who drowns when he attacks his reflection in a well. In Wootton's illustration (fig. 106) the rooster stretches over "the depth profound" to combat the advancing foe. Bentley's design captures a similar moment; a tabby becomes typical of a foolhardy, conceited hero as in mock-heroic comedy.

In *Spring* the speaker discovers that like the rooster he has thrown himself against his own reflection only to prove himself a son of Eve, the point of Gay's fable. Perhaps Gay and Gray remembered the ominous pleasure Eve took in her own reflection in a pool just after her creation, as described in *Paradise Lost* (IV.453–491).[4] These analogues, visible in the depths of the Selima poem, also lurk in the waters of *Spring*, and give the beast fable more than a simple moral, more than a clever revision of Shakespeare's "All that glisters is not gold." Mortification of vanity is required for salvation in both odes. With the poet's lyre in hand, we see in the frontispiece for *Spring* that she, Bentley's cat-Arion, is eventually transported to heaven on Apollo's dolphin, an emblem for the combined action of the sister arts. Bentley's frontispiece matches the light yet serious tone of Gray's mock-elegy; the wish to make poem and picture look like a mutual effort is shown by the initials on lyre and palette. Just as Gray has imbued Selima with a human psyche, so Bentley has placed her in a human environment.

Bentley conveys this theme dramatically by showing only a cat at the heart of each of the four drawings. Nothing about the plain unadorned tabby balanced on the rim of the bowl, or drowning in it, or sitting in a chair, or being ferried across the Styx at the end suggests a nymph or presumptuous maid.

This animal is untouched by personification, a matter stressed not only by its contrast to the mandarin cats on the borders of the frontispiece and the mourning cats at the edges of the headpiece, but also by the extraordinary elegance of the room in which we see her, where one might expect a nymph or presumptuous creature to be placed. The lavish room of the frontispiece rises above an enormous scallop shell; the scene does not show the birth of Venus, but rather the death of an ordinary cat with pretensions. Blake, on the other hand, in his illustrations for the ode changes his cats into nymphs and thus shifts his purpose away from the irony Bentley emphasizes.

Walpole's description for the frontispiece explains very little:

> The cat standing on the brim of the tub, and endeavouring to catch a gold fish. Two cariatides of a river god stopping his ears to her cries, and Destiny cutting the nine threads of life, are on each side. Above, is a cat's head between two expiring lamps, and over that, two mouse-traps, between a mandarin-cat sitting before a Chinese pagoda, and angling for gold fish into a china jar; and another cat drawing up a net. At the bottom are mice enjoying themselves on the prospect of the cat's death; a lyre and pallet.

On the left side of the frontispiece, Bentley's portrait of the river god with a wreath of sedge upon his brow and holding a triton-like paddle is mounted on a term. Like Terminus in Roman Mythology, and answering Atropos also on a term on the opposite side, he marks Selima's end by looking away from the scene and blocking his ears to her cries. He will give her no aid; the episode vaguely recalls Ovid's *Metamorphoses,* the story of Apollo and Daphne who cries out to her father, the river god Peneus, or the story of Pan and Syrinx, or that of Arethusa and Alpheus. More particularly, Bentley's river god recalls Pope's Father Thames who will not hear the screams of his daughter Lodona as she is about to be raped by Pan in Windsor Forest: "In vain on Father *Thames* she calls for Aid" (*Windsor Forest* 197). Like Lodona, Selima in her vanity has strayed beyond the limits of propriety and virtue, and thus must forfeit her life. Albeit in a mock-mythological context meant to amuse, the story has its serious side. Bentley's god, who hears no evil, is derived from the generality of river gods portrayed since classical times.

Bentley repeats geometric designs found in the fleuron and frontispiece to *Spring*. The drawing for the frontispiece to the cat ode is formed out of wedges and circles: we are prompted to see the whole scheme as a large wedge or funnel from the pagodas at the top, to the shell at the base; the lines draw together at the banner on which is written the ironic theme, "A Fav'rite has no Friend." By being favored Selima loses friends and becomes the object of universal jealousy; she must meet her fate alone. The graceful banner of the legend links the lyre and the palette which together as sister arts inside a shell tell the sad story in verse and picture.

A smaller funnel is formed by the tub with Selima balancing precariously on its lip. As she looks down into the water, she sees the image of heaven aglint with goldfish; her "fair round face" is wreathed by light, perhaps reminiscent of the incandescent star at the top of the frontispiece for *Spring*. Bentley and Gray borrow the traditional icon for *multum in parvo*, as used, for example, by Pope in *Windsor Forest* where the shepherd observes in the crystal Loddon "the headlong mountains and downward skies." But unlike the shepherd, the cat sees herself at the center of heaven; vanity turns her head and the world upside down. Instead of remaining a motionless Narcissus or Eve, instinct causes her to move for the fish and her "one false step is ne'er retriev'd." The allusion of this line to a woman's sexual temptation leads to the conclusion of the ode. Selima cannot see in the rounded shape of the tub a mirror image of the dome-like trap drawn for us by Bentley at the apex of the frontispiece; hence, unwarned, blinded by vanity, yet drawn forward by temptation, she loses her footing to fall, not to the downward skies of the reflected heaven, but to the hell below her, the hell that Bentley depicts below the poem in the tailpiece.

Funnels surround Selima in the frontispiece: to either side of her the bases of the caryatids; above her the brackets supporting the pagodas, the mousetraps, and vases; and below her the china jars. The tub, the source of the motif, is redrawn above the head of Destiny who cuts the threads of Selima's nine lives. Everything falls or spills and looks as if it were drawn down by gravity; the rococo strapwork itself appears ready to bend or twist down. The entire frame, making a gigantic pagoda, is reflected and defined for us by the two pagodas at the upper corners in which the mandarin cats, precariously perched, fish as Selima does inside the room. Their Chinese affectation tells us by inference something of Selima's vanity; with line and net they will hardly pull from their well-like jars the truth that is conveyed by the iconography of the drawing and that recalls the famous passage in Sir Thomas Brown's *Pseudodoxia Epidemica*, I.v.: "For questionless, in Knowledge there is no slender difficulty; and Truth, which wise men say doth lye in a Well, is not recoverable by exantlation."[5] The frame encloses Selima like a mouse trap and separates her from the reader. Her predicament is encapsulated, just as the detailed and layered frame removes the poet from the reader in the frontispiece to *Spring* and emphasizes his solitude. The details of these reflections are not derived from the ode; Bentley invented them to illustrate his interpretation of it.

Shadows, volutes, curves, terms, lamps, vases, flowers, cats, mice, traps, and fish fill the drawing with mirror images as the poem is filled with echoes.

At the bottom of the drawing the palette with its quiver of brushes is mirrored by the strings of the lyre. The reflection on the side of the bowl (window panes, a pun for pain) and the revealed chamber behind it extend Bentley's theme.

In certain important respects the satire of the second plate of Hogarth's *Marriage à la Mode* (fig. 117) is parallel to Bentley's. Ronald Paulson tells us that the "fireplace and mantel, the center of the picture, is a horrible example of William Kent interior decoration"; Bentley's recognition of this fact, as well as his knowing that the room "was copied from the drawing-room of No. 24 Arlington Street," Horace Walpole's London house,[6] would have attracted his eye to the print. Over young Squanderfield's head there is a large ugly clock, "part of an elaborate girandole full of rococo or 'rock-work' " with a life-sized cat above the dial, two fish to either side, and a Buddha below in shadow. The whole thing, a memento mori, might have suggested to Bentley his rococo plan. The empty, despoiled lives depicted in Hogarth's print reveal the consequences of human vanity. So too, in Bentley's drawing the furniture, Chinese porcelain, pagodas, and heavy oriental frame—even goldfish which are not indigenous to England but imported—point up the affectation and uselessness of possessions in a crisis. They ridicule collectors, especially those intrigued by the fashionable taste for chinoiserie and European finery. Tayler has pointed out that Gray and Bentley skirted unacceptable satire on their patron, yet despite this satire it is also significant that reflected on the tub is a sash window, an innovation associated with the rage for Palladian architecture,[7] instead of the native gothic casement that Walpole and Bentley had chosen for Strawberry Hill.

The elegance of the room behind the curtain becomes a foil for Selima's vanity. The contrast between the chinoiserie bowl and the humble English well in the ramshackle barnyard of Wootton's design for Gay's Fable XX (fig. 106) dramatizes Selima's difference from unpretentious cats, the robust world of Toms and Susans. In the affectation of the creature, Bentley has caught the disparity in her character: "Demurest of the tabby kind . . . she saw; and purred applause." The cat, of course, makes a comment on polite society, its sheen and brittle manners. It is no accident that her left front leg is reflected by the shadow of the highboy leg, and again by the serpentine tail of the fish. The exposure of artificiality is stressed not merely by the presence of mice in the pretty interior, but by the clyster pipe with which one mouse (at the bottom of the picture) grapples in order to aim at Selima's already well-exposed rear.

The mandarin cats fishing from the pagodas in the upper corners of the frontispiece probably reminded Walpole of his own desire for a Chinese summer house next to Po Yang, his goldfish pond at Strawberry Hill. In 1751 or 1752[8] Bentley made sketches for him of two pagodas that, mounted high on rocks and cascading down the page, are remarkably like those in the design for Gray (fig. 7). The several references in the correspondence to goldfish (e.g., *Corr.* 9.134, 155) and the variety of architectural elevations that Bentley made for Chinese garden houses prove the interest Walpole took in them, and hint that he fancied himself inside sipping tea or fishing like the elegant cats we see in Bentley's drawing. The placement of such angler daydreams within rococo and Chinese contexts was already commonplace. As early as 1740 George Bickham designed a frontispiece showing a gentleman, a lady, and four boys fishing on the banks of a stream within a rococo-chinoiserie frame for *The British Angler: or, a Pocket-Companion for Gentlemen-Fishers*, by John Williamson (London: J. Hodges, 1740). Bentley's tabbies have cast themselves into unnatural roles, and indicative of Selima's fate they have blinded themselves to reality by their playacting. Even as mourners in the headpiece, where they stand in black hats with downcast eyes, they continue their drama, and like Orpheus in Dürer's woodcut, they pose. The horror of Selima's doom seems to glance off them without meaning, their thoughts preoccupied by their attitudinizing.

Set into the treacherous elegance of the frame at the top of the frontispiece and between the "expiring lamps," symbolic of foolish virgins falling for temptation, Selima's smug little face with closed eyes cannot see the mouse under its nose, let alone the significant traps above it. For the idea of the cage, Bentley might have glanced at Wither's emblem ("When *Magistrates* confined are, They revell, who were kept in feare"). It shows mice dancing around an imprisoned cat (fig. 91). The fishing line and nets, the strings on the curvilinear lyre, the brushes stuck into the round palette, the window mullions reflected in the tub, the strapwork on the highboy and the scrolls on the lintel, and even every tiny line of the composition drawn by Bentley to look like an engraving (suggestive of the pun on grave and Gray), all these details reflect the fountain-like wires of the cage above Selima and the nine threads that Atropos is about to cut.

* * *

In Walpole's words the headpiece (fig. 8) shows "the cat almost drowned in the tub. A standish on a table to write her elegy. Two cats as mourners with hat bands and staves. Dead birds, mice and fish hung up on each side." The mourning cats, staving off sorrow, are as ostentatious in their apparel as are their counterparts in the pagodas of the frontispiece. Hardly chastened, they have learned little even from their own dead victims, the hanging birds, fish, and single mouse whose fellows in the frontispiece have made such a mockery of Selima. Selima drowns inelegantly; her once shining coat is matted with wet and one sopping paw is ineffectually raised as she cries to deaf ears. The room, mockingly elegant, crowded with furniture and empty of friends, emphasizes the indifference of the world to her fate, as does the china bowl itself on which in gayest art the azure flowers are "dy'd," a word on which Bentley puns when he changes them to dead twigs above Selima in the tailpiece. As po(e)sies they immortalize the cat, signified by the pyramidical frame whose apex rises above the standish. Under the standish and held down by it is the elegiac ode. The shape of the ink-well mirrors the basin beneath, and the feather, perhaps from one of Selima's victims, dipped into soot water, will now lift her on poetical wings from oblivion as Apollo's fish carries her to heaven in the frontispiece to *Spring*.

Together the headpiece and the title printed below it have a sculptural effect that suggests a cenotaph on which the image itself, like an inscription, tells us a great deal about the life and death of Selima. Moreover, the lines of the title increasing in size upward are like steps leading to the entrance of a tomb guarded by sentry cats; we see beneath the roof the bowl-shaped coffin inside. Headpiece and title unite into a single composition. The size, spacing, and blackness of the letters give them an aesthetic role, for they, aside from their textual signification, help to illustrate the meaning graphically. In a corresponding way, the scene is like picture writing and functions as a hieroglyph.

As the title diminishes in size line by line, we step down, as it were, into a verbal redaction of the scene. The text begins with the decorated initial letter (fig. 9), in which demurest Selima, as Walpole explains, snoozes in an elbow chair. She has wrapped herself about the *T* in "Twas," no doubt a memento mori too. Her expression is like that of the tabby seated between "expiring lamps" in the frontispiece: Selima is smug to a T. The curve of the chair arm recalls the highboy leg, the fish, and the leg of the cat that will be beguiled by the slippery verge, all shown in the frontispiece.

As with the initial letter, the scared animal Bentley depicts for the tailpiece (fig. 10) is entirely of his own invention. Dated "1751" opposite his signature in the original drawing,[9] the tailpiece illustrates no detail in the poem, but it extends Gray's humor and clarifies his ironic theme. The cat, who had perched on the bowl in the frontispiece, drowned in the headpiece, and taken a nap in the initial letter, is now conducted to hell in the tailpiece. Again she remains an emphatically plain tabby, sharply distinguished from the four tabbies personified on the frames of the first two designs. Yet the mythography, expressive of the horror of classical Hades, makes a dramatic frame for the figure of Charon who ferries "the ghost of the deceased cat" across the Styx, where she "sets up her back on seeing Cerberus on the shore," a setting amusingly appropriate for a cat on her way to a cat hell. Selima's tail and back reflect the mouth of the cave, and it reflects the shape of the tubs in the earlier scenes. Our response to the mirroring images and to Bentley's invention binds the sequence together and illustrates the ode with vitality and insight.

Gray echoes elements of pastoral elegy in his mock-heroic poem; Bentley uses details of high Italian art to achieve satiric effect. Frederick Antal writes that the composition of the tailpiece "recalls Tibaldi's mannerist frescoes in Bologna, engravings after which were perhaps to be found in Strawberry Hill" (*Hogarth* 156). However when he calls the tailpiece "ferocious," he overlooks the subtle way both poet and artist have separated us from the event. They hoped that Walpole would smile away his sorrow and be consoled to see Selima given commemorative immortality; a mere cat, she nonetheless is dignified by the notice of Atropos and by her entrance into the Elysium of classical heroes. Even when Bentley reminds us of Virgil's description of the gateway to Hades in Book VI of the *Aeneid* (where at the opening cave protected by the gloomy lake Avernus we are prompted to hear the baying hounds as we look into the depths), we laugh at the joke and do not recoil in terror, revulsion, or sadness. In retrospect the caryatids of the frontispiece now seem to be guarding a variation of the portal into hell with its shroud-like curtain blown aside. The Selima of the endpiece may very well be looking up from the bottom of the tub to see its lip transformed into the mouth of the cave. The blossoming branches have died, and the river god, having laid down his oar, has picked up a pole and become Charon.

Notes

1. For two modern discussions of the word play in the poem, see William Empson, *Seven Types of Ambiguity* (New York: New Directions, 1947), 139–140, and Tayler, *Blake's Illustrations to the Poems of Gray*, 68–69.
2. The dog drops his bone and loses it in a stream because he has attempted to seize its reflection.
3. Gray's "Presumptuous Maid!" echoes Addison's "Presumptuous Man!" in *Cato*, Act II.ii.61, where Cato declaims against Caesar to his agent, Decius, and Pope's "Presumptuous Man!" in *Essay on Man*, I.35.
4. Milton echoes Ovid's account of Narcissus in *Metamorphoses*, III.402–510.
5. *The Works of the Learned Sir Thomas Brown, Kt.* (London, 1686), 14.
6. Paulson quotes Arthur Dobson. *Hogarth's Graphic Works*, i.270–271.
7. B. Sprague Allen, *Tides in English Taste (1619–1800): A Background for the Study of Literature*, 2 vols. (New York: Rowman and Littlefield, 1969), i.41–47.
8. Prompted by its similarity to the frontispiece for *Favourite Cat* the editors of Walpole's *Correspondence* date this sketch 1752 (*Corr.* 35.131). Yet because Bentley dates the tailpiece (fig. 10) 1751, the frontispiece may have been completed in 1751 also.
9. This is the only drawing on which Bentley writes a date.

VI
Designs for *Ode on a Distant Prospect of Eton College*

AT Eton, Gray led an insulated life. R. W. Ketton-Cremer has written that his happiness at school "was absolute"[1] and that there was "a singular placidity, an almost pastoral air, about the life which Horace Walpole and his circle of intimate friends appear to have led at Eton."[2] The correspondence of Walpole and Gray seems to bear this out, although Walpole admitted in a letter to Montagu that he "was sometimes troubled with a rough creature or two from the plow; one that one should have thought had worked with his head, as well as his hands, they were both so callous" (*Corr.* 9.3–4). Ketton-Cremer concedes in his biography of Walpole that Walpole, Gray, West, and Thomas Ashton came together to form the Quadruple Alliance amid scenes "of tremendous fights and savage floggings, of occasional riots and rebellions, of permanent and bloody warfare against townsmen and bargees" (33); and in his biography of Gray he calls the Alliance "a singularly fastidious group" (6), in which these boys of similar temperament and delicate health gave each other poetic pseudonyms and read and wrote literature together.

Eton may have been one of the few schools where a boy who was not tough had a chance of happiness; at eighteenth-century public schools tyranny and cruelty prevailed. Locke urged parents to keep their sons at home; Steele, Smollett, Thomas Day, Chesterfield, and Gibbon wrote to the same effect.[3] In *Joseph Andrews* Parson Adams declares that "public schools are the nurseries of all vice and immorality" (III.v); he may have echoed the sentiments of Fielding his author, who himself was a student at Eton.

Bentley's illustrations for Gray's nostalgic *Ode on a Distant Prospect of Eton College* project this darker vision. Replacing the wreath of *Spring* and the head of Selima, the head of Folly is lifted to the apex of the frontispiece for the ode (fig. 11). Folly's face is placed between a brightly burning light of knowledge and open book (compare Selima's head between two "expiring lamps"), details that suggest that during the "thoughtless day" of youth, learning would be folly for students: "thought would destroy their paradise." Supporting Folly's head, the scrolls of the broken pediment are blacker and thicker than their counterparts in the first two frontispieces and, because they look ready to uncoil, seem menacing. Folly's sneer establishes the theme.

Bentley mocks Gray's speaker, an old Etonian, for his blindness to bullying, boasting, indolence, tyranny, sadism, and pederasty, sins that are barely disguised in this drawing of seeming innocence. Grotesque and ill-proportioned, the boys appear as vicious as the horrors about to drop on them; they make the picture, despite its comic burlesque, the most savage of the book's designs. They expose the folly of this poem's narrator and challenge his idyllic dream of Etonian youth. By parodying the activities described rather than illustrating them, the drawing sharpens the ironic perspective into which the narrator should be placed. It makes emphatic that his nostalgia in the first half of the poem is as crazed as his nightmare in the second; each represents an extreme, one is balanced by the other. When Müller cut his engraving, he softened the figures and gave the design an unwarranted charm that almost neutralizes the satire.

Walpole's explanation is as follows:

> Boys at their sports, near the chapel of Eton, the god of the Thames sitting by: the passions, misfortunes, and diseases, coming down upon them. On either side, terms representing Jealousy and Madness. Above is a head of Folly: beneath, are play-things intermixed with thorns, a sword, a serpent and a scorpion.

In "Two Eighteenth-Century Illustrators of Gray," Tayler argues that unlike Bentley Blake wanted "to correct by pictorial emphasis what he felt to be a rather morbid turn in the poet—his pallid caution, his melancholy, his retreat from life": he showed that "the vultures of the mind" were only "the ugly embodiment of Gray's own mental imagery" (123). Tayler assumes that the twofold nature of Gray's ode, by which highly artificial verse distances and controls powerful emotions,[4] makes it brittle and stilted. In Blake's *Illustrations to the Poems of Gray*, she asserts further that the Romantic artist, frustrated yet excited by this polarity of artifice and feeling, effected a reconciliation: his art purges Gray's craft through an exposure of its subliminal causes. On the other hand, Tayler continues, Bentley "frames the action (and so distances it) in a pictorial tradition whose verbal analogue is Gray's decorous poetic tradition" (43). He adopts the poet's strategy but with a difference; even though the elaborate borders, personifications, and ornate embellishment distance action, the drawings lack, in Tayler's words, the poem's "passionate concern." Rather, she writes, they are merely clever, witty, and empirical.

This assessment needs qualification. Tayler has unduly connected the narrator of the ode with Gray; they are not the same. Bentley's picture does not stress a biographical connection, especially when compared with his frontispiece for *Spring* where the details are only loosely associated with the ode it ostensibly represents. In the frontispiece for *Spring*, the crowded reflections and intricacies of the frame swirling round Gray's seated figure (in the original drawing there is no question about his identity) demonstrate that, when

Bentley made a biographical allusion, he understood as did Blake the "vultures of the mind" to be the poet's own mental imagery; the biographical emphasis here in part resulted from the dual purpose of introducing both *Spring* and the other five poems.

In the frontispiece to the Eton ode the scene of boys and descending "passions, misfortunes, and diseases" is generated by the imagery of the poem with few biographical implications. The crowded figures appear to violate the tradition Tayler refers to, a tradition established on one hand by pictures like Salvator Rosa's *Saul and the Witch of Endor* (its demons are a forerunner of Bentley's) and on the other hand by baroque assumptions like Anton Domenico Gabbiani's "Francesco Redi Crowned by the Muses" (fig. 99).[5] The pose of melancholic Redi, which is like Bellori's *Muta Poesis* (fig. 79) and the figure of Gray in the frontispiece to *Spring*, is an example of the convention that Bentley exploits. Moreover, he parodies Kent's pastoral vision in the frontispiece for Thomson's *Spring* with its angels descending in a cloud (fig. 101) and in the low alternative for Gay's Fable XXXIX, "The Father and Jupiter" (fig. 107). The effect of the Eton ode illustration is certainly not pastoral. If the cathartic action of Blake's visionary designs purges Gray's "rather morbid turn," Bentley's satiric use of a pictorial tradition more properly undermines the "decorous poetic tradition" that Gray puts into his narrator's mouth. Bentley's ugly frame and scene attack the indecorous sentimentality of pastoral visions, a strategy that recurs throughout *Designs* but with greatest force in the burlesque of Poussin's *Arcadian Shepherds* for the frontispiece of *Elegy*, as I will show.

In his frontispiece for the Eton ode, Bentley unites the pretty rococo of Kent and the robust saturnalia of Renaissance woodcuts, as seen in the title page for volume ii of Holinshed's *Chronicles* (fig. 66), but with a very different effect from either. Squeezed between Jealousy and Madness, the convulsion of figures becomes a convulsion. The torturers descending from heaven crowd together into a rococo heap; the boys in unpleasant proximity mirror them. Sadism and insanity with a hint of orgy reflect from group to group. The bulk and density of their bodies appear to tip over the towered chapel and push it out of the picture (a subtlety lost in Müller's engraving), with the result that in this top-heavy construction everything looks oversized and twisted. The theme recalls the satire of the *Centaur* where oversized Manpferdt represents sterility and perversity in seminaries.

Jealousy and Madness show the contrasting states of the narrator's mind: the pallid caution and retreat from life in the first part of the poem, and the half-hysterical enumeration of evils in the second. It is a mistake to see this narrator as a stoic with a tragic vision of life, or as a poet in collision with history who "poses childhood scenes against the fallen world of adulthood," as John Sitter has recently asserted in *Literary Loneliness in Mid-Eighteenth-Century England* (87ff.). Rather the dream-like quality of the speaker's evocation of youth followed by the vividly personified malefactors of adulthood is Gray's calculated contrast. Above the lyre, Jealousy recalls the young and handsome bard of the title page fleuron; the snake gripping his heart represents the constricting pain of jealousy that afflicts all mankind, young and old. From the serpent comes the self-told lie about something that never was, the "innocence" of school boys:

> Say, Father THAMES, for thou hast seen
> Full many a sprightly race
> Disporting on thy margent green
> The paths of pleasure trace,
> Who foremost now delight to cleave
> With pliant arm thy glassy wave?
> The captive linnet which enthrall?
> What idle progeny succeed
> To chase the rolling circle's speed,
> Or urge the flying ball?

Bentley understood that the periphrasis—the almost literal transcription of the motion of swimming and the hoop—has displaced the adult from his childhood. Its airless images, shattering the world into sharply delineated bits, paradoxically become the vehicle of nostalgic removal and unreality, and create the morbid sentimentality Gray successfully dramatizes.

Gray knew that the vision of boyhood in the first half of the poem was false; his invented narrator does not remember anything like the Quadruple Alliance, rather he idealizes the rowdy, athletic boys against which the Alliance was formed. The bullies are transformed in an idyll of schoolboy life as it could never be experienced. Whereas innocence in youth, Gray's narrator suggests, intensifies the pain and treachery of adulthood (an idea intimated by the snake, scorpion, sword, and thorns intermixed with the playthings beneath the picture), Bentley demolishes the thought that youth ever was golden in the first place and by the central scene exposes such delusion as madness. The parodied innocence of the boys exaggerates their ugliness; similarly, the pastoral appearance of the picture exaggerates the self-deception of the narrator in powerful dramatic irony. If Bentley's tactic can be likened to Gray's lapidary style, whose polish makes the figures of memory glisten, then his is to reveal that the speaker suffers from amnesia.

Bentley depicts the fall of the sentimentalist. The pun on Eton/Eden implies that original sin was committed in both, and that schoolboys are far from innocent. In Bentley's burlesqued pastoral, nearly every character looks downward; the furies descending in the black cloud push everything before them and are about to choke from view the upward pointing windows and pinnacles of the chapel; the motion and shapes of all in the composition lead the eye to the bottom of the frame where the serpent falls out from leaves and flowers. Generated by the poetry, the illustration appears to have dropped like a foldout from the open book placed beside Folly above; if, figuratively speaking, the snake lay hidden in its leaves and flowers, so too do the boys of the Eton ode become serpent's teeth to its nostalgic dreamer. So too, it could be said, the sharp ironies hiding inside Gray's and Bentley's anthology dart forth like serpents.

Bentley hints that one consequence of sentimentality is "moody Madness laughing wild," as is suggested by his allegorical representation of the verbal and graphic arts. The figures on the frame distinguish them from one another. The lyre on the plinth supporting Jealousy and the palette below Madness, as well as the work between them that has produced the scene on the playing fields, intimates that Jealousy has drawn the fury passions down upon his own head, a fate against which the narrator in *Hymn to Adversity* pleads:

> Oh, gently on thy Suppliant's head,
> Dread Goddess, lay thy chast'ning hand!
> Not in thy Gorgon terrors clad.

His sentimental song (the lie strummed on his lyre) has not only led to his description of "moody Madness laughing wild," but has also generated the further response of the artist, who discovers behind the nostalgic veil the deranged pathology of the boys. Bentley's portrait of madness, more horrific in the original drawing than in Müller's engraving, recalls the couplet from which the phrase "fury passions" originally came in Pope's *Essay on Man:* "The Fury-Passions from that Blood began / And turn'd on Man a fiercer Savage, Man" (iii.167–168). Pope argues that this madness is self-inflicted, resulting from man's violation of social love. Bentley turns the fury passions not into Gray's vultures, but into vipers of the mind: clad in gorgon terrors, Madness reveals an imagination that is as much a prisoner of snakes as the heart of Jealousy; in fact, the serpent, reappearing again in the left hand of the fury just above the hoop and wriggling out from under the leaves below, is the representative image for this drawing. The gorgon is an incarnation of the knowledge that Thought, subtlest beast in the field, must destroy a sentimental paradise. The boys, not told they are men, are flattered in their favorite foibles by the narrator who, as Goldsmith would say, applauds their faults and commends their folly. This Bentley ridicules.

Moreover, it follows from his bowed head that Jealousy is a manifestation of Melancholy. As the bard sits opposite the ape in the title page fleuron, so Jealousy is placed opposite Madness; one kind of insanity receives answer from the other. The nostalgic narrator begets in the ape a picture of what the marriage of the arts produces in the purlieus of this Eton, and we see their strange progeny between them. From his Melancholy has sprung Madness: the two, male and female, even make manifest types of Satan and Sin; at the Gate of the garden of Eton, they are Adam and Eve, one flesh, one made from the other, who beget under the grinning head of Folly the subjects of death's "painful family."

Pallid caution and melancholy are qualities attributed to Gray by Tayler. By placing Gray's initials as well as his own, so conspicuously like labels, on the plinths supporting Jealousy and Madness in the original drawing, Bentley makes an oblique biographical reference and hints at something deeper than is expressed in the ode; when Müller omitted the initials for the engraving, as no doubt he was told to do, he muted the direct association between the allegorical figures and the poet and artist. But nevertheless, possibly encouraged by Walpole, Bentley has subtly documented his difference in temperament from Gray's. The poet's orderly mind and methodical scholarship contrasted with the artist's irregular habits and erratic insights; the meticulous style of the verse vies with the spiraling involutions of the drawings. Even the handwriting of the two men shows something of this difference: Bentley's script is loose and large with long loping letters; Gray's is tight, compact, extraordinarily neat, and it never wanders off the line. Bentley crosses out; Gray rarely. Gray withdrew from the world in fastidious isolation; Bentley was a family man who pursued wild schemes and was fiscally irresponsible. The intricacies of the frontispiece for Eton seem an extension of Bentley's psychology, just as the tidy ode is an extension of Gray's.

Yet it must be said that Bentley's exotic genius was stimulated by this polarity, probably because he saw in the other his antithesis. He must have suspected that Gray saw in him a mirror image and knew the interchange of their media would be fruitful. Bentley took unexpected care over his draughtsmanship, even to the engraving-like lines. The melancholy, anxiety, and latent fury that underlie the poetry, those subliminal emotions that required the curb of a highly polished surface, are reflected in Bentley's portraits: if the saucy monkey and Madness with her twisting serpents and taut muscles share qualities, then opposite and unlike them the mournful bard in the fleuron and Jealousy with folded hands, knotted snake, and bowed head under the weight of a square box convey tense restraint. The sister arts pull each other inside out. The contrasted figures in the drawings reverse in one another latent and overt qualities.

It was the projection of their idiosyncracies into their works that helped artist and poet to safeguard their sanity and confront their demons at the sage remove of irony. Gray deals with his morbid or even violent turn by dramatizing it in his poetry; Bentley "frames the action (and so distances it)," as Tayler writes, but with much more "passionate concern" than she implies.

Gray produces dramatic irony when he sets the speaker's vision of boyhood in the first half of the poem against his hallucination of devils in the second; Bentley places Jealousy against Madness on opposite sides of the frame as a representation of the speaker's two contrary states of mind, and something of the contrasted complexities of poet and artist. The boys centrally placed are a product of this double counterpoint.

In design and poem we also remain aloof, no matter how tempted to indulge in our own nostalgia. Bentley separates us from the allegorical landscape behind the terms just as he divides us from the poet-speaker of *Spring* and Selima by elaborate frames. The curtain held back by Madness operates exactly as the one by the river god revealing the cat at her perilous moment. Through their works artist and writer purge themselves of their demons; by their satire they vex us into thought.

The borders through which we peer are like gates. The door to Eton is a revision of the portal invented for Selima: Destiny becomes Madness, and the river god, who stops his ears to the cries of the cat ("A Fav'rite has no Friend"), is now portrayed as Jealousy. Moreover, both frames seem variations on the doorways to Hell described in Virgil, Dante, Spenser, and Milton. Bentley's contemporaries would have been familiar with these descriptions and would have seen the newly built and celebrated entrance to Bethlehem (or Bedlam) Hospital for the insane. Although unlike in detail to Bentley's design, Bedlam's gateway was adorned with two statues, one of "Melancholy Madness" and the other of "Raving Madness," carved by Caius-Gabriel Cibber, the father of Colley Cibber, a fact to which Pope refers at the beginning of the *Dunciad* in the version published in 1743:

> Close to those walls where Folly holds her throne,
> And laughs to think Monroe would take her down,
> Where o'er the gates, by his fam'd father's hand
> Great Cibber's brazen, brainless brothers stand.
>
> (i.29–32)

In *Anecdotes of Painting* Walpole finds that Caius-Gabriel's "two figures of Melancholy and raving Madness" are "the most capital" of his admirable works (*Wks.* iii.340), but he condemns Pope for "the injustice" of calling them Colley's brothers. Bentley reinterpreted the idea for the Eton ode (excluding Colley and Dr. Monroe, of course) with Pope's lines in view.

From the downward pointing torch of Madness, smoke drifts round her lower torso to make the demon-stuffed cloud behind her; it shows the consequent "murth'rous band" of tyranny—Envy with her snake, blind disdainful Anger, comfortless Despair, sculking Shame, pining Love, and behind them Queen Death. The monsters that Aeneas sees just inside the gate to Hell

(*Aeneid* vi.273ff.) and the satanic figures and pageants of Spenser and Milton are evoked. Pictorially, the descending furies recall Dürer's *Four Horsemen of the Apocalypse* (fig. 88) and Callot's *Temptation of St. Anthony* (1635) (fig. 76), a picture that Bentley may have used as a source for his own *Temptation of St. Antony* (ca. 1755), although the subject was popular among seventeenth-century painters, including Rosa. For comparison with his frontispiece for the Eton ode, Bentley's dusky watercolor (fig. 60) is a telling design.

Its theme is perverse sexual temptation. A sergeant major, copied from the drummer in Hogarth's *March to Finchley*, marks time to the marauders and gives the depicted orgy the feeling of a ritual; as in Hogarth he is a foil to the threatening debauchery and chaos that is signaled by the allegorical animals: hounds, hare, cock, and toad. The swirling devils and grotesques of Callot are neatly humanized here and of a more readily identifiable type; they are also more realistic than the allegorical furies in the Eton ode which correspond with them. Just as the "passions, misfortunes, and diseases" descend on the boys, the huntsmen descend on St. Antony. He is surrounded by tormentors: a student who has kicked off his shoes at the entrance of the cave and plies a bellows, possibly one of Swift's Aeolists (*A Tale of a Tub* viii) or a matriculant at Lagado (*Gulliver's Travels* III.v); a fishwife who might drive even a saint to pederasty; and a sailor with exposed buttocks. St. Antony kneels before the cross exactly as the boy before the cage in the scene of Eton College; Bentley shows the consequences of unnatural celibacy and isolation. If the cross itself is a symbol for removal from life and, as such, suggests monastic retreat from evil, so the boy sees in the birdcage an image of his own predicament. Arriving staff in hand like the "kindred Spirit" in the frontispiece to *Elegy*, the surprised pilgrim, like Diogenes, holds aloft a lantern to peer into this dark, unfathomed cave; his counterparts are Father Thames, who surveys the scene before him, and finally we ourselves, who look through the portal guarded by Jealousy and Madness.

Both the huntsmen and torturers surrounding St. Antony as well as the furies and youths in the frontispiece for the Eton ode seem visitants from Bedlam. The environment of the boys is as unnatural as St. Antony's. The illustration suggests that the voices they hear in every wind are those of the devils behind them:

> Still as they run they look behind,
> They hear a voice in every wind,
> And snatch a fearful joy.

The "fearful joys" they snatch are shown: the design unfolds an alternative to Acrasia's Bower of Bliss; Jealousy and Madness guarding the entrance take the places of Genius and Excess. The "bold Adventurers," like Lodona in Pope's *Windsor Forest*,

disdain
The Limits of their little Reign,
And unknown Regions dare descry . . . ,

and the consequent impropriety of their violation is shown; Bentley drew a general satire on public school life in which is exposed the improper sentimentality of the narrator.

On either side of Folly's head, the oil lamp and open book (emblems suggesting education and study) are taken from the beginning lines of the fourth stanza:

While some on earnest business bent
Their murm'ring labours ply
'Gainst graver hours, that bring constraint
To sweeten liberty.

Bentley has carefully removed them from the scene below; one wonders whether the boys represent the sweeter liberty remembered by the old Etonian-narrator during the "constraint" of his "graver hours." It is possible to think of the book as one of "two basic school texts in eighteenth-century England for verbalizing the visual and visualizing the verbal . . . Prodicus's *Choice of Hercules* and the *Tabula Cebetis*,"[6] the first, Shaftesbury's description of the hero confronted by pleasure and virtue, and the second Cebes's account of the treacherous ascent to virtue and wisdom. Both evoke Spenserian pageants.[7] Despite their Arcadian ambiance, these boys are hardly like Hercules whose choice was heroic virtue. In the *Tabula Cebetis* Cebes speaks of a wall painting that shows a press of people at the Gate of Life. After being greeted by Divine Genius, they are met by Deceit, who gives a draught of ignorance and error, and by blind Fortune standing on a round stone, half-crazed, who indiscriminately distributes and collects favors. Each soul must then confront personifications of evil and temptation in its passage up the hill toward the temple of Wisdom and Happiness. Eighteenth-century readers reared on Cebes and accustomed to looking at derivative prints like Gabbiani's *Redi Crowned by the Muses* would recognize Bentley's allegory in the frontispiece.

But the *Eton College* version appears more ominous and darkly comic, seen through a gate to Hell guarded by Jealousy and Madness. By playing upon a memory of Cebes, Virgil, Spenser, Milton, and their flattering derivatives like Addison's *Vision of Mirzah*, Bentley ridicules the tendency to make pastoral adaptations sentimental, especially when the action of sentimentality is followed by an equal and opposite reaction in cynicism, as in Gray's ode. There is no personified Divine Genius, Deceit, or Fortune. At the capstone under Folly's chin, a pile of birch faggots, alluding perhaps to the famous "birchen altar" upon which boys were made to kneel for thrashing,[8] symbolizes tyranny and sexual perversity.[9] All the figures are unclad (even Death's shroud is blown away) and the disproportionate size of the naked boys emphasizes their grossness; all are stripped of pretense. At the base of the distant hill, nearly obliterated by the cloud of terrors, two of the youths "urge the flying ball," or so it appears in Müller's print; in the original drawing they seem to be cutting down a tree (compare the woodsman of the headpiece to *Elegy*, fig. 32). If they are destroying Arcadia, then the pastoral is not simply burlesqued as in Gay's *Shepherd's Week*, but despoiled as in Pope's *Windsor Forest*.

The group on the lower left examine a cage;[10] as I have suggested before in connection with St. Antony, it is similar in purpose to the trap at the top of Selima's frontispiece in its ironic implication that the boys are caught too. With the descent of the cloud, the lid will close on them like that of a coffin, a hint of which is given in stanza four (the "constraint" of "graver hours"). The bars of a cage carried on the top of a boy's head parallel the buttresses, pinnacles, and window mullions of the chapel—perhaps the onetime residence of Divine Genius, or alternatively, the temple of Wisdom and Happiness toward which the boys should move—and imply that here it represents to them another prison; with all else in the drawing, it is placed inside the imprisoning frame. Our attempt to evade one kind of entrapment merely produces another, Bentley seems to say. If law, whether clerical, academic, or social, constrains yet sweetens liberty, we nonetheless find the insidious fact forced upon us that under the eye of Folly we sink into the ever more subtle manacles forged by desire, envy, anger, fear, and shame or, in the case of the narrator, by sentimentality and cynicism.

However much at play, these boys are not carefree. The one leaning over with arms folded is already about to be touched by Envy; envy underlies his contemptuous look. Another, his hair like gorgon snakes blown by the wind, frantically rolls the hoop right to the center of the design; hardly an image of eternity in a traditional sense, it seems the axle round which the vortex of figures turn. It is the midpoint of a chiasmus of reflecting images along crossed vectors, the first of the lyre to Death's rib cage and the second of the palette and brushes to the birdcage. The mouth of the urn, a reflection of the hoop along the second vector, recalls Selima's basin. The boys in the river hint at homosexual temptation; they make a mockery of Kent's Damon and Musidora in the illustration for Thomson's *Summer* (fig. 102) and popular bathing Venuses such as those painted by Boucher. They also recall the illustration for "Salmacis et Hermaphrodite" in Michel de Marolles's *Tableaux du Temple des Muses* (IV.xxxi, p. 243), a story from Ovid's *Metamorphoses* (iv.285–388) that has a bearing on Bentley's homosexual theme.

Father Thames seated in the bullrushes (another pun?) looks with detachment at the folly about him. He could have been copied from any number of elegant depictions of river gods; for example, from portraits of Father Tiber or other classical depictions of river gods as shown in Spence's *Polymetis*, plate XXXI, where Father Tiber reclines against a horn of plenty and two boys, Romulus and Remus, look up at him from the teat of a wolf, and where Father Nile above a crocodile leans against a sphinx as a crowd of tiny children scamper over him. Raphael, Rosa, Cheron (in the frontispiece to Prior's *Poems on Several Occasions*), Gabbiani, or Gribelin (in the headpiece to *Windsor Forest* in Pope's *Works* of 1717) drew similar river gods. As perhaps Gray thought of Pope when he wrote the ode, so Bentley might have remembered Father Thames of *Windsor Forest* when he made his drawing:

> High in the midst, upon his Urn reclin'd,
> (His Sea-green Mantle waving with the Wind)
> The God appear'd: he turn'd his azure Eyes
> Where *Windsor*-Domes and pompous Turrets rise,
> Then bow'd and spoke; the Winds forget to roar,
> And the hush'd Waves glide softly to the Shore.
>
> (349–354)

Yet the Father Thames of the illustration also represents another image of Melancholy and by association becomes a further depiction of Gray as he is shown in the frontispiece to *Spring*. Unlike Pope's god, Bentley's is the image of disenchantment. Because withdrawn and contemplative, he suggests the aesthetic removal of poet and artist and, in fact, all observers of the scene. Bentley might have had in mind Pine's river god in the headpiece to Ode XIV, "Ad Postumum," of Horace's second book (fig. 115): the surrounding emblems show that from this god's urn pours the Stygian stream or the black waters of the Cocytus. Pine's headpeice and tailpiece significantly darken the implications of the ode: Horace says we must give up worldly pleasures and visit the mountain of Sisyphus whether we like it or not; Pine adds the bane of madness by placing Sisyphus in a frame of writhing snakes surmounted by a gorgon not mentioned in the poem. The detachment of Bentley's river god reclining on his urn in the midst of the mad vortex of figures, and beneath Madness, conveys an effect similar to that of Pine's god at the head of Horace's ode. Indeed, Father Thames may look over a further bend of the river upon which Selima is ferried in the preceding illustration. Behind the hoop-rolling boy, the hill more appropriately belongs to Sisyphus than to Cebes.

* * *

By contrast to the frontispiece, the headpiece and the initial letter (figs. 12 and 14) are unadorned; they project the visual content in the first seven lines:

> Ye distant spires, ye antique towers,
> That crown the wat'ry glade,
> Where grateful Science still adores
> Her HENRY'S holy Shade;
> And ye, that from the stately brow
> Of WINDSOR'S heights th' expanse below
> Of grove, of lawn, of mead survey.

For the headpiece Walpole explains:

> Science adoring the shade of Henry VIth. Two angels bearing shields inscribed with that king's name support a Gothic building, in allusion to his foundations at Eton and Cambridge.

The mention of both Eton and Cambridge expands the boyhood experience and touches upon Bentley's own past at Cambridge. Bentley's rough drawing (fig. 13) clearly shows the spires of Eton at the bottom left and King Henry at the upper right; the composition resembles the frontispiece more closely than the final version. Possibly to avoid an association of the king with the descending horrors that are approximately in the same place emerging from a cloud, he moved King Henry to the upper left, put him within a vault, and expunged the pinnacles of Eton College Chapel entirely. If his first thought was to draw satire, it appears he changed his mind; rather respect for the founder of the school is his theme, which was in keeping with Gray's own veneration of him. According to Ketton-Cremer, Gray was "haunted" by the memory of King Henry, whose "fine bronze statute" at Eton

> had been placed in the centre of School Yard; and every day, as he passed to Chapel and to the long hours of work in Lower and then in Upper School, the story of the Founder was brought home to him in all its sadness. 'The murther'd Saint', 'the meek Usurper', 'her Henry's holy Shade'—time and again that devout and gentle presence was to figure in his poems. [*Thomas Gray* 5]

The scholarly, quiet, self-effacing, and melancholic Gray is associated by Bentley with the king, not with the narrator of the poem, and not with the boys of the frontispiece.

The format of the headpiece even suggests that between the first and second drafts Walpole may have shown Bentley his own elegy "In Memory of King Henry the Sixth" (1738), the first of the *Fugitive Pieces*. Wishing to pay his tribute to the charitable monarch, Walpole cannot find his tomb:

> my eyes in vain require
> Th' engraven brass and monumental spire.
> HENRY knows none of these—above! around!
> Behold where e'er this pensile quarry's found,
> Or swelling into vaulted roofs its weight,
> Or shooting columns into gothic state,
> Where e'er this fane extends its lofty frame,
> Behold the monument to Henry's name![11]

The fane is King's College Chapel, Cambridge; Bentley has drawn the peak of its nave and, with his placement of the king, perhaps remembered the apostrophe to Henry at the end of Walpole's poem to regard "from thy lucid orb" those who sing his praises, especially as founder of King's College and Eton.

In the final draft adoring Science appears less slavish and more respectful. From the books surrounding her come true knowledge and perhaps the disenchantment and resignation of wisdom that leads to Gray's forlorn solitude and, at the same time, forestalls the sentimental nostalgia or precludes the bitterness of the poem's narrator. The glib cynicism "'Tis Folly to be wise" does not come from Science, but the stoical acceptance of life and philosophy that has permitted Gray to stage the dramatic irony of the ode. Upon the altar burns the sacrifice—is it of worldly vanities?—the high worship (at the apex of the pyramidical vault high on the page) that is dedicated to all that the king represents, evidenced by the smoke that rises toward him; the smoke in fact makes a large Lancastrian rose and betokens, in a typical Bentleian gesture, that Henry "rose" from the dead by his endowments.

The initial letter shows "Part of Windsor-castle." In front of the flag flying above the round tower, the *Y* stands gigantic and stark. It is the standard emblem for the crossroads of Hercules and may allude to the choice presented to the students by "ye" distant spires and antique towers, between the mad corruption of the frontispiece and the solemnity of "grateful Science" of the headpiece. The low point of the frontispiece, at the bottom of which is shown the bottom of the swimmer, contrasts with the high tone of the headpiece; the low and the high are illustrated graphically by their placement on opposite pages.

Human activity is conspicuously absent in the headpiece and initial letter. Not even the lawn, garden, or water mentioned in the last lines of the first stanza printed on the same page is shown:

> Whose turf, whose shade, whose flowers among
> Wanders the hoary Thames along
> His silver-winding way.

The vacuity of the initial letter corresponds to the emptiness of the narrator's classical or stoical pretense. For him Madness and Science (the "Thought" that "would destroy" the paradise of the boys) are variant states of one another; the ironic counterpoint of the frontispiece, where the boys, turf, flowers, and river are carefully drawn in satire, reveal this truth.

The tailpiece provides in vignette the theme of the frontispiece.[12] Walpole explains that it consists of "two boys drest in watermen's cloaths, rowing another. A view of Eton college at a distance." The splendid view of the school is the predominant feature, a sailboat on the river provides a tranquil touch, and a sunset recalls the final emblem in Whitney's *Choice of Emblems*, "Tempus omnia terminat," a poem that in turn recalls Horace's *Ad Sestium* (I.iv): "Pale Death knocks at the cottages of the poor, and the palaces of kings, with impartial foot."[13] From the pretty rush base of the picture a waterfowl is frighted and a tufted reed is bent.

Close inspection of the "two boys" in a boat "wearing watermen's cloaths, rowing another," reveal that all three are louts, one in a heavy coat taunting a hatted oarsman, while a naked passenger looks on. Bentley makes no attempt to portray sensitive youths such as Walpole, Gray, Ashton, or West who roamed the river banks together reciting classical poetry and making their own compositions. On the contrary, the students he depicts in the illustrations for the Eton ode destroy mawkish nostalgia. The tailpiece of boys on the Thames corresponds to the tailpiece of Selima on the Styx; in each, innocence comes to an end with the inexorable approach of doom. Bentley suggests by the parallel that on the muddy verge of this pastoral scene, with the spires of Eton Chapel glinting in the sunlight across the water, the feet of the old Etonian were beguiled, just as were the paws of Selima on the chinoiserie bowl.

Notes

1. Ketton-Cremer, *Thomas Gray*, 8.
2. Ketton-Cremer, *Horace Walpole*, 32.
3. Vivien Ogilvie, *The English Public School* (London: Batsford, 1957), 112; Derek Jarrett, *England in the Age of Hogarth* (London: Hart-Davis, MacGibbon, 1974), 76ff.
4. Tayler follows Chester F. Chapin, *Personification in Eighteenth-Century English Poetry* (New York: King's Crown Press, Columbia University, 1955), 70, and P. M. Spacks, *The Poetry of Vision*, 100–101.
5. Bound in Redi, *Sonnetti* (Florence, 1702). "A melancholic Redi is depicted being crowned by Poetry at the foot of Mount Parnassus, where the temple of Virtue stands. The other Muses attend nearby. Apollo traverses the sky in his chariot, accompanied by Mercury and personifications of timeless Fame. In the distance, Dante and Petrarch ascend another slope of Parnassus. The city of Florence is evoked by the River God Arno in the foreground." John T. Spike, *Baroque Portraiture in Italy:*

Works from North American Collections (Sarasota: The John and Mable Ringling Museum of Art, 1984–1985), 90.

6. Paulson, *Emblem and Expression*, 30. See also Paulson, *Hogarth*, i.265–266. Stephen Orgel, ed., *Cebes in England: English Translations of the Tablet of Cebes from Three Centuries with Related Materials* (New York and London: Garland Publishing, Inc., 1980). An example of a contemporary derivative of the *Tabula Cebetis* is Samuel Johnson's "Vision of Theodore, the Hermit of Teneriffe" (1748).

7. That these pageants or dreams were generally placed in sentimental contexts is significant here, e.g., Addison's *Vision of Mirzah* (*Spectator* #159) and young Bevil's reference to it in Steele's *Conscious Lovers* (I.ii). Bentley ridicules this propensity.

8. Wilbur L. Cross, *The History of Henry Fielding*, 3 vols. (New York: Russell & Russell, 1963), i.48.

9. Compare the birch in plate 3 of Hogarth's *Harlot's Progress*.

10. For these boys Bentley may have remembered an etching for *Aesop's Fables* by Claude Gillot. Walpole owned an oblong octavo containing seventy-five engravings later used for Antoine H. de la Motte's edition of the fables (ca. 1720) (Hazen, *Catalogue* #2325). Number seven shows three boys huddled beneath a tree examining a cage.

11. Walpole notes that the last line "is copied from the inscription over sir Christopher Wren, who is buried under the dome of St. Paul, of which he was the architect" (*Wks.* i.2). King's College and Wren's appreciation of it was of key importance to Walpole's and Bentley's gothic architecture.

12. Elements of the tailpiece and frontispiece contrast with the romantic and pastoral vision shown in a line engraving of the playing fields of Eton, by R. Silvester, published in 1803 and reproduced in Tuberville's *Johnson's England* (Oxford, 1933), ii.216. This print was identified for me by Paul R. Quarrie, College Librarian, Eton College. Bentley's anti-pastoral purpose becomes clearer when his illustrations are compared with, say, Alexander Cozens's drawing of Eton College, engraved by Pine and published by W. Collier in 1742.

13. Christopher Smart, tr., 6–7.

VII
Designs for *A Long Story*

THE beauty of the frontispiece for *A Long Story* (fig. 16) strikes one immediately as a marvel of rococo invention that derives from Watteau, Berain, and Picart. The way the figures sweep round the frame suggests that the inner scene is merely a moment in a larger drama; bursting out of the picture almost like Tiepolo angels, their defiance of gravity is the secret of visual energy and feeling of depth. Bentley's images are not boxed in by arbitrary borders, but leap through broken boundaries like syncopation in music that releases the imagination yet incorporates the action of the whole.

The portraits of the "Warriors" or "Heroines" with their billowing, winglike sleeves and flowing gowns are particularly happy. Compared with the other designs, this one seems the most polite and especially suited to the elegant audience addressed by Gray. Walpole, however, begins his "explanation" with, of all things, an outhouse:

> The Muses conveying the Poet under their hoops to a small closet in the garden. Fame in the shape of Mr. P[urt] is flying before; and after him the two female warriors, as described in the verses. On one side is my lord keeper Hatton dancing; and among the ornaments are the heads of the Pope and queen Elizabeth nodding at one another; behind him is a papal bull, a phial of sublimate, a dagger and a crucifix; behind her the cannon called queen Elizabeth's pocket-pistol.

The polite ambiance of Bentley's picture conforms to the imagery of Gray's poem. Yet while unmasking pretense and folly, it also answers another lie of the lyre and ridicules Gray's infatuation for one of the high-born ladies.

Acting as a blind for the indelicacy of the allusions, the prettiness of the drawing in an inverse proportion actually exaggerates the effect of the scatological reversals and timorous sexuality of the poet. In order to trace "the paths of pleasure" for Gray and Walpole, Bentley evokes romance of the past by several means: gothic architecture, the magic of Spenser's world, and portraits of the Pope, the Queen, and Sir Christopher Hatton, Elizabethan owner of the manor house. These details of fashionable taste, with their eclectic mix of classical and gothic ideas in a rococo context, recall the spirit of the verse and cast a glamorous, nostalgic spell that Bentley turns to the purpose of his satire.

The high French polish of a Watteau-like scene strengthens the contrast and impudence of the outhouse within it, surely a unique combination in the history of graphic art. Bentley uses a Hogarthian strategy; like the clyster pipe at the base of the frontispiece for Selima, or the boys' behinds at the bottom of the design for the Eton ode, the outhouse undercuts pretty affectation. The bard led to it beneath the skirt of a buxom Muse produces an effect that might be compared to the surprise found in the Merchant's Garden in Chaucer or Celia's dressing room in Swift, although Bentley's elegant drawing is filled with more light-hearted humor. His satire is less dark than in his *Centaur,* where social refinement contrasts with the base desires of polite ladies for a private meeting with Manpferdt, thus increasing titillation.

The theme for the frontispiece is taken from stanzas 18 and 20.

> On the first marching of the troops
> The Muses, hopeless of his pardon,
> Convey'd him underneath their hoops
> To a small closet in the garden.
>
> * * *
>
> Short was his joy. He little knew,
> The power of Magick was no fable.
> Out of the window, whisk, they flew,
> But left a spell upon the table.

Bentley particularizes and sharpens Gray's wit by making us see a connection between the Muses and the ladies soaring above them, even though they appear as discrete pairs in both poem and design. For each group one figure is drawn with a full face and the other in profile. In both groups the women have flowing skirts or garments. The shell-shaped cuffs of the "Heroines" are reflected in the shell-topped lyre held by the center Muse. In the drawing the two pairs chase the poet. Each wishes to capture and enclose him; the ladies flying above will draw him into the great house shown in the right background, while the Muses lead him to the outhouse in the left foreground. These juxtapositions prompt us to conclude that the ladies and Muses are double portraits of the same women, Lady Schaub and Henrietta Jane Speed. The "Heroines" have given the occasion for the verse and inspired it; hence, they simultaneously assume muse-like roles. Bentley's naughty coincidence makes their flight not only a defiance of gravity, but also a defiance of Gray, as is suggested by the hidden pun; they mount a challenge to the grave poet. We also see, by virtue of the interplay of figures, that the contest between the "Heroines" and Muses is contrived, because, without seeming to do so, the poet lets himself be captured by both.

In "Bentley Bid the Pencil," Tayler suggests that by means of this association the artist has actually drawn the poet beneath the hoops of Henrietta

Jane Speed, the girl he was rumored to love, a recognition which may be one reason for Gray's repeated insistence that poem and illustration be dropped in later editions. The poet hides but wishes to be found. As in the game "course-a-park" depicted by Pine for "Ad Thaliarchum" (fig. 113) or like Sylvia who runs from Daphnis in Pope's "Spring" ("How much at variance are her Feet and Eyes"), Bentley too shows the variance between the poet's feet and eyes. He makes clear that the poem itself was the vehicle for flirtation which ensured Gray's capture; he knew that *A Long Story* was a "spell" left by Gray upon the table at the manor house for the "Heroines" to see. But if Gray's verse sweetens his motive and pays deference to the ladies, Bentley's illustration does not.

"Short is his Joy!" is the exclamation used by Pope to describe the exultation of the pheasant in flight just before it was shot down in *Windsor Forest*, one of the more famous passages in that poem (I.113). The same exclamation likens the poet to the bird. By drawing the poet underneath the Muse's hoops, a scene reminiscent of the bird within the cage held by the boys in the frontispiece to the Eton ode, Bentley teases Gray for flattering himself that he, Gray, is the much desired object of the chase, a revelation to the public that would have dismayed him as much as did his portrait in the original drawing for the frontispiece to *Spring*. Moreover, placing the frontispiece for *A Long Story* after the designs for the Eton ode with their theme of boyhood infatuations, Bentley may have had in mind the final irony in Horace's *Ad Sestium* (I. iv): after your death, Sestius, the speaker admonishes, "you shall neither decide the dominion of the bottle by dice, nor shall you admire the tender Lycidas, with whom now all the youth is inflamed, and for whom ere long the maidens will grow warm" (Smart 7). Possibly this passage helped to bind the theme of the Eton ode illustrations to the frontispiece for *A Long Story*, where the young poet becomes the love-object of the maidens.

In the design the eye drops from the ethereal angels above the clouds to the sturdy Muses next to the privy and then to the bard cringing under their skirts; despite the apparent beauty of the figures, rococo elegance high on the page is undercut by low humor at the bottom. All the details are an extension of the poet's vanity, which like the pheasant, will be shot down. The graphic juxtaposition of high against low, of polite embellishment against coarse allusions, turns the pictorial scheme into mock-heroic satire with a significance that goes beyond the bounds of the verse.

To strengthen his ridicule Bentley uses a recognizable format for his design, exemplified by Picart's satire on the John Law scandal of 1720 (fig. 97) and by the prefatory illustration from the studio of Bernard Lens and John Sturt for Swift's *Battle of the Books* (1710 edition) (fig. 96). Behind Picart's angel looms the dark image of Satan relishing the mayhem caused by Law's worthless bank bills; behind the angel for Swift is the spider, Keeper of the King's Library (i.e., Dr. Bentley), who spins a web from its entrails while below him is depicted the battle of the books. In the frontispiece to *A Long Story*, the warriors are positioned behind Fame which, according to the set pattern, signifies their troublemaking or diabolical role; the battle is the battle of the sexes which the poet is letting himself lose. Bentley suggests that the irony comes of Gray's coyness and willingness to capitulate, which has encouraged the ladies to set their trap. The consequence of his capture will hardly be the blissful imprisonment he anticipates, for in the tailpiece (fig. 20), Gray's head with its distinctive nose, mounted like a trophy in a broken pediment, hangs above gorgons. The coalescent roles of "Heroines" and Muses in the frontispiece extends to their respective houses. Just as the door to the outhouse is open, so too is the door to the manor house, one in perfect reflection of the other. Bentley further downplays the allegory by transforming the typical annunciatory angel who blows on the double trumpet of noble and ignoble reputation; he now becomes a portrait of the Reverend Robert Purt, a rumormonger and gossip, rector of Settrington and onetime tutor of the Duke of Bridgwater at Eton. It was Purt who told the ladies where the author of *Elegy* could be found.

When Queen Elizabeth and Pope Pius V nod prettily to one another at the top of the frontispiece, they mask a tumultuous period in English history. Despite the pope's holy title, Bentley reminds us of his impiety, bigotry, and unbounded treachery by placing together the dagger, sublimate, crucifix, and bull of excommunication against Elizabeth. Despite her femininity, the Queen's "pocket pistol" hidden behind her was sufficient to defeat the Armada and secure a Protestant England. The arrogant pope was defeated by a woman. The implication for Gray is unambiguous and amusing; he hoped by using his black arts, his spell, to entice the ladies, but they, as Gloriana's knights, get the better of him.

The graceful ceiling drop above the action is emblematic of his fall. It is reflected and enlarged by the triangular form made by the men on the left and woman on the right who meet at the figure of the crouching poet. The pope, Purt, and poet are linked to symbols of eloquence, the papal bull, trumpet, and lyre, but in Bentley's mock-heroic environment these items signify hypocrisy, trumpery, and lies. These men are hurt by the unintended consequences of their communications: the pope's bull and black deeds paradoxically redounded to Elizabeth's fame and confirmed her power; the poet's black arts glorified Lady Schaub, Lady Cobham, and Henrietta Jane Speed and gave them power over him; Purt's tattle ironically increased Gray's credit at the expense of his own. The reversals of the illustrations, which complement the strategy Gray used to court the ladies in the poem, a strategy of fiction, exaggeration, and misplaced emphasis, put the whole event of the flirtation into an ironic perspective.

Apparently, Sir Christopher Hatton (with his hat on) dances to the music of the trumpet and lyre as though he were a participant in an Elizabethan revel. Walpole annotates his edition of *Designs* (Hazen, *Catalogue* #2044) by a footnote on Sir Christopher who, in order to dance at his nephew's wedding, placed his gown on a chair with the words, "Lie there Chancellor."[1] His dance now ridicules the poet (drawn by Bentley beside him) much as it had earlier mocked the pope and Philip II:

> His bushy beard, and shoe-strings green,
> His high-crown'd hat, and sattin-doublet,
> Mov'd the stout heart of England's Queen,
> Tho' Pope and Spaniard could not trouble it.

Hatton now stirs the hearts of Gloriana's new warriors.

The hidden power of these Amazon knights, linked to the queen along the right side of the triangle that identifies them as her liegewomen, is mock-heroic, not unlike that of Belinda at Hampton Court in *The Rape of the Lock*. Their weaponry, mentioned in stanza 10, is not derived from Homer, but is unsheathed by Bentley in the middle of the picture with the reappearance of the women as Muses.

> With bonnet blue and capucine,
> And aprons long they hid their armour,
> And veil'd their weapons bright and keen
> In pity to the country-farmer.

Their plump nudity, their breasts and sturdy legs, utterly dwarf the poet under their skirts. Possibly Bentley continues the joke in the headpiece to *Spring* where the "rosy-bosom'd Hours" might also be portraits of Schaub, Speed, and Cobham.

When Gray wrote that from the manor house came "A brace of Warriors, not in buff, / But rustling in their silks and tissues . . . ," he might have intended a pun on *buff*, a colloquial word for the buff coat of military attire, or for bare skin. Bentley also appears to pun on armor/amor or, closer to the point, shows that under "their aprons long" the Muses hid their amour. They taunt the poet by imprisoning him under their hoops, which are the implements of their "tyranny" amusingly displayed. Broken boundaries suggested by the warrior angels above echo perhaps the sexual boundaries that Gray secretly wished to break; they make his confinement below the Muses emphatic. These women are "hopeless of his pardon," not because of the unbending will of the inhabitants of the manor house, but because they, Schaub and Speed, are the objects of his infatuation.

Bentley's picture stresses Gray's intention that the verse be a medium for flirtation and an articulation of desire. The poet ostensibly peers up at the angels, but inspection shows that in reality, in this country scene (Bentley plays on the word country), he looks at something else. Placed in his line of sight, the lyre reflects the pudendum. Little is veiled "in pity" to the country-poet.

He recoils in astonishment, or so it seems. "Meaner Beauties... vainly ape" the "art of killing" practiced by these women, a line that seems particularly apt when sexual intercourse was often described as death or an execution. In effect, prisoner Gray is led to an execution; indeed, he compares himself to Maclean, the gentleman-highwayman and hero of the ladies, who was tried and put to death in the autumn of 1750. The reversal of male and female roles is part of Bentley's joke. Possibly he is reminding us of the usual consequence in mythology that the love of a god or goddess meant death.[2] When the divinities swoop down on the poet, he crouches in a gesture emblematic of death; the outhouse door to which he is led opens a way to the underworld.

The developing imagery in the preceding illustrations makes the Muses correspond to the earlier gatekeepers, to Jealousy and Madness in the Eton ode frontispiece, and to the river god and Atropos in Selima's frontispiece. It reinforces the sexual implications of the other illustrations; when they in turn remind us of the link between sex and death, the frontispiece for *A Long Story* seems more sinister. Because the Muses represent the same women as the "Heroines" or angels and look as though they themselves had leapt off the cloud above, they seem by association to be renewed manifestations of Madness and Atropos. Sir Christopher standing on the left side of the frame turns his back to the drama below him, just as the river god ignores Selima, and as Jealousy is oblivious to the Etonians.

The design for *A Long Story* recalls the frontispiece for the cat and also for the Eton ode. When one frontispiece is laid over the other, the women precisely correspond to the baleful horrors also borne up by dark clouds, and the poet falls among the boys with their cages. At first he believes he has eluded his pursuers; like the boys he will discover that he is entrapped. Those heavily ribbed skirts are his prison bars; the door opened by the Muses deepens the confinement. As one of the Etonians, he has been caught by bedlamite "horrors" whose guise is allegorical in a new way and whose house, appropriately, is not Parnassus but the outhouse; robust like the large women in Dürer's *Death of Orpheus*, these "Heroines" will "rid the manour of such vermin." The metamorphosis of the angels and the death of the poet seem announced by the dual trumpets blown by a Gabriel-like Purt.

In the verse the poet in the outhouse laughs in his sleeve; Bentley shows how misplaced such laughter is, for as I have already suggested, the doors to the outhouse and mansion are one and the same. The verse tells us of the poet's enthrallment by beauty, wit, and titles, by fretted ceilings, splendid portraits, windows that exclude the light, and passages that lead to nothing. It ends with an invitation to dine at the mansion, as the poet had secretly hoped it would. Bentley's drawing taunts Gray with the ironic consequence of enslavement to "high borne" harpies who show him where the passages lead, namely to the bottom of the garden.

Bentley's own *Temptation of St. Antony* (fig. 60) is governed by a similar vortical pattern, and so helps confirm that these reversals were supposed to be understood in this way. Huntsmen, hounds, and hare careen through the smoke above the poor benighted saint just as the Amazons soar above Gray, and the Furies above the boys in the design for the Eton ode. Instead of a crucifix, the poet crouches before the privy, and the swirling skirt under which he hides is his darkened cave. The frontispiece to *A Long Story* illustrates temptation again.

Because of their parallel with the Furies in the Eton ode, we know what the women in *A Long Story* represent, yet their difference heightens the effect of Bentley's sexual teasing. When Bentley leads the eye down the vortex of the angels and whirling skirts to the hole inside the privy, he communicates an unmistakable idea. He is more direct when he takes the eye to the same place down the *V* of the tree trunks that mirror and turn upside down the limbs of the muse (Henrietta Jane Speed) holding a pudendum-shaped lyre. Furthermore, the hole inside the privy, another reflection of the ceiling drop, is a version of Selima's tub inside its chamber. The parallel connects the poet with the cat-nymph, a creature of vanity and desire, and the bowl with sexual temptation. By transference, the decorative room in which the tub is placed becomes the pretty interior of the manor house and warns of danger there. In effect, the poet is told that at the slippery verge the image of the outhouse should warn him away; even as it invites, it should forestall the false step he is about to take, especially as, like Selima, he has failed in his plea to Apollo. Bentley reminds this poet whose sensibilities have been beguiled that not all that tempts his heart is lawful prize. His inspiration, under the guidance of these muses, Swiftian in nature, is more like an afflatus, but one that should produce catharsis.

The twofold portraits of the women and their contest for the poet anticipate Bentley's illustrations for Walpole's *Judgment of Solomon*, an unpublished *Fugitive Piece* completed in November 1753. These designs (figs. 54 and 55) that explicitly connect sex and death help to confirm the hidden theme in the frontispiece to *A Long Story*, including its twisted view of sex, its confusion of procreative and defecative functions, and its latent misogyny. In the drawings for *Solomon*, which show the bride and whore arguing over their right to a lout's gigantic organ before the king, classical and rococo ideas are mingled in such a way that the rococo by contrast appears sensual and dangerous; its complication conveys an animistic or even anthropomorphic effect in the headpiece with the throne, the curtain above and to the right of Solomon, the lions around him, and the muscular figures before him. Part of the humor is the contrast between the lout's false modesty—his embarrassment over his missing shirt—and his Herculean virtue so prominently displayed. The mock solemnity of the headpiece corresponds to the ironic elegance of the frontispiece for Gray.

Evidently, the tapestry scene of Solomon's Judgment in the fifth plate of *Marriage à la Mode* (fig. 118) was one model for the Solomon;[3] the more telling analogue is a figural duplicate to the headpiece, Kent's design for "The Court of Death" (fig. 108),[4] Gay's Fable XLVII of 1727. The fable concerns the election at the Court of Death of a minister of state; the "eban wand" is not granted to Fever, Gout, Syphilis, or any of the other claimants who shout their merits, but to Intemperance "who finds employment" for all the others. In Kent's picture, Time holding his scythe stands behind a Solomon-like Death; he becomes the executioner in Bentley's tailpiece. Kent's disease-ridden hag, Intemperance, is ushered forth to receive her wand; the wand becomes the lout's organ in Bentley's picture. Because Intemperance is an analogue for Bentley's bride and whore, we know that the judgment of Walpole's Solomon will be death to the man whatever the decision; not Time, but Woman, no matter whether bride or whore, will destroy him.

Moreover, the reversal of the figures in Bentley's tailpiece for *Solomon* complements the ironic reversals in the tale. Justice without her scales—they are shown in the initial letter—rests the blade of her sword against her shoulder as she pulls back the curtain at the very moment when Solomon's decision is challenged by the wife who stays the hand of the satyr-like executioner, but who, nevertheless, will herself, as the possessor, become Solomon's executioner. The treatment of the wife and satyr seems taken from Hogarth. Placed next to the whore, Justice herself with her raised sword is sexually provocative, an appropriate suggestion, given the pun on execution. The sword, columns, other upright projections, and the bearded, grinning lions of the tailpiece, stress the husband's fate and the perverse humor in Walpole's final quip: "Those accents Truth must prompt, which tell / None but a Wife could love so well." The effect of Bentley's use of Hogarth's plate and Kent's illustrations for Gay as analogues corresponds to the counterpoint in Gay's use of tunes from D'Urfey's ballads in *The Beggar's Opera*, or more generally his exploitation of the fable form in his *Fables*.

Irene Tayler writes of the frontispiece to *A Long Story* that Bentley wittily amplified Gray's deference to Schaub and Speed "by extending the compliment implicit in the poem's conception yet one step further" ("Bentley Bid the Pencil" 210). Tayler insufficiently stresses, however, the mock-heroic context that is established by the many parallels and reflections in Bentley's work which make us question this "compliment." Most things in Bentley's drawings turn into something unsavory. He is not interested in the women as individuals and may not have met them; his receipt of a sketch of the manor house to redraw for the headpiece might imply that he had not visited it. The Muses and the "Heroines" probably differ from Schaub and Speed as much as the handsome figure under the skirts differs from Gray, but since there are no known portraits of the two ladies at that early date, it is impossible to tell. Undoubtedly, Bentley's humor is at their expense. According to the strategy we have come to recognize, he disguises by their beauty a malevolence that the poet "literally" brings down upon his own head. The bard in the picture is pursued by one pair, hidden by another, yet both pairs are one and the same, creatures of his imagination, "vultures" (here with angelic masks) of his own mind. When Tayler writes that the Muses Lady Schaub and Henrietta Jane Speed are "etheralized by harps and laurels," she does not mention the effect of Bentley's satiric strategy.

Gray's words are the inspiration for Bentley's picture, but the picture does not translate into a comparable language. The fable and bard are visualized, assessed, and challenged. Picture and poem are not entirely synonymous; rather they encroach upon and change one another.

* * *

The headpiece, initial letter, and tailpiece (figs. 18 to 20) emphasize the elegance that awaits Gray at the mansion. Walpole merely says of the headpiece: "A view of the house which formerly belonged to the earls of Huntingdon and lord keeper Hatton." Not only has Bentley given dimension and detail to the rough sketch for the building that Gray sent him (fig. 17) but on the right he has added the steeple of the famous church at Stoke Poges. This addition reminds us that the poet came to the attention of the ladies in the first place because they had discovered that the author of *Elegy* lived nearby. In the frontispiece below the dancing figure of Sir Christopher, Gray is conducted toward the dead tree and coffin-like closet; in the foreground of the headpiece, the sporting figure dancing on the keystone of the bridge, whose shape ultimately recalls Selima's cave in her tailpiece, is surely meant to tease Gray with an ironic intimation of his fate, an invitation to dine and consequent entrapment.

The design for the initial letter *I* of "In," described simply as "A coronet, fan, muff and tippet, in the manner of Hollar," evokes the seductive splendor inside the mansion into which the poet has won entrance. The fan lies inside the muff; muff and tippet, furry objects of enclosure, are sexually provocative, as are a multitude of other details connected to the play on "in," including the name of Hollar ("hole her").[5]

Though the tailpiece shows "Ghosts of ancient ladies and old maids, peeping over the gallery" at the poet's trial, it is a picture of hoydenish hags whose appearance and gaping mouths recall Madness, not to mention all those gorgons in Pine after Caravaggio or the Medusa in the first plate of Hogarth's *Marriage à la Mode*. Bentley's preliminary sketch of these "ghosts" is to be found on the back of his drawing of Stoke House (fig. 21). Their repugnant company is the poet's destiny at the great house, a fate as fearful as Selima's.

Having let himself be captured, he will be doomed by the vixens to an eternity of "Rubbers."

Raised to the broken pediment and like a commemorative bust or death's head on a tombstone signifying his sexual execution, the poet looks down frozen to stone by the horror of his fate before the bar, where he stands "as mute as poor Maclean," the highwayman.[6] The expressive horror and indignity of the moment is shown by Bentley. He has drawn Gray's unmistakable profile, exactly as he had for the busts on the tomb representing *Elegy* in the frontispiece for *Spring*. This sly link of the poet to the action in *A Long Story* completes the allegory, although admittedly, a specific portrait under the skirt of the Muse would have been more daring. Bentley is to Gray what Gray is to Selima in the *Ode on the Death of a Favourite Cat*: he is like the Timotheus of that ode, the "Malignant Fate" complacently smiling after he had staged the cat-nymph's fall. Possibly the skull that tops Cheron's tailpiece for *Alma, or the Progress of the Mind* (fig. 95) suggested the idea of the tailpiece for *A Long Story*: the bust also replaces and thereby recalls the heads of Selima and Folly in earlier frontispieces.

Walpole liked the tailpiece drawing well enough to preserve four rough drafts, two of which Kirgate later pasted into his extra-illustrated copy (figs. 22 and 23). Examination shows that Bentley had the essential idea in mind from the start, but enriched it at each stage with significant detail. In the final drawing he softened the portraits and gesticulations of the women and thereby removed some of the satire designed for Walpole's personal amusement. Grignion took the softening process a step further to produce the less dramatic scene that we see in the engraving.

Notes

1. See chapter IV, note 5.

2. Wind, *Pagan Mysteries of the Renaissance*, chapter X, "Amor as a God of Death."

3. Bentley may also have remembered Cheron's headpiece for the first book "Knowledge" in Prior's *Solomon on the Vanity of the World* in *Poems on Several Occasions* (1718). Sitting on his throne, Solomon receives knowledge from the learned men about him or dispenses it to them.

4. Kent used a similar design for his illustration of Lucifera's Palace in Birch's edition of *The Faerie Queene* (illustration #7, i.52). For these illustrations of Solomon and Lucifera at court, Kent's source was Verrio's *Study for Charles II Giving Audience at Christ's Hospital*, which was also the model Hayman used for his *Artists Presenting a Plan for an Academy to Frederick*. See Brian Allen, *Francis Hayman* (New Haven and London: Yale University Press, 1987), figures 36 to 38.

5. William Shenstone wrote, "I am thankful that my name is obnoxious to no pun." *The Works in Verse and Prose*, 3 vols. (London: J. Dodsley, 1765, 1769), ii.137.

6. Bentley wrote a satire to coincide with the trial, condemnation, and execution of James Maclean (or Maclaine), "*A Petition to the Right Hon. Mr. [Pelham], in Favour of Mr. MACLEAN*. By a Lady" (London, 1750). It was intended to recall Gay's *Beggar's Opera*.

VIII
Designs for *Hymn to Adversity*

THE frontispiece for *Hymn to Adversity* (fig. 24) imitates many pictures similar in historical and religious vein, such as those painted by Guido Reni, one of Gray's favorite artists. In fact, the composition recalls fairly closely Reni's *Madonna con il Bambino, San Domenico e i Misteri del Rosario* (*Madonna del Rosario*) at the Basilica of Saint Luke, Bologna, yet whether Bentley ever saw the painting or a copy is unknown. He certainly would have seen prints of Raphael's *Judgment of Paris* and *Vision of Ezekiel* (this last influenced Gray's description of the poet in *The Bard*), which would have provided models for his own Jove. As a counterpoint to the high art of Reni and Raphael, he probably looked at Gravelot's illustration for Fable VII, "The Countryman and Jupiter," of Gay's 1738 collection (fig. 111). This poem, like *Hymn*, is a derivative of Horace's *Ad Fortunam* (*Odes* I.xxxv), but because a fable, the speaker is admonished in gentler terms than the speaker in Gray's poem (if "truth, honour, virtue and peace of mind" are your "scruples," give over Fortune, and instead "write, practice morals, and be poor").

Bentley's illustration reflects the details of many other contemporary works, from ephemeral satires like the frontispiece for Bolingbroke's *A Dissertation upon Parties* (fig. 100) first published in *The Craftsman* and in subsequent editions,[1] to large canvases portraying infants. Some of the latter were exhibited at the Foundling Hospital in 1746 under the sponsorship of Hogarth, including his own *Moses brought to Pharoah's Daughter*, Hayman's *Finding of Moses*, and Highmore's *Hagar and Ishmael*. It also seems clear that the general framing of Bentley's composition was influenced by the dimensional architecture in the paintings of Tiepolo, Reni, Raphael, and Thornhill. With plinths and terms around the floating figures, the design recalls the grandiosity of ceiling and wall paintings; apparently, it was thought so elegant by the editors of *The London Magazine* that they had it re-engraved for the July 1753 issue (xxii.333) (fig. 25). The impression of a mural is reinforced by the half visible escutcheon with Walpole's arms at the bottom of the original drawing, a detail Grignion expunged in the print.

In many poems by Gray, Jean Hagstrum has observed that the "lines constitute a painting" and that often the poet "presents a natural scene in which pictorial and visual details are subordinated to a quasi-mythological persona whose function is to organize the details and interpret them as manifestations of some kind of animistic order and meaning." Of *Hymn* in particular, Hagstrum maintains that Gray's imagistic effect "is created by personified abstraction: a pictorially conceived moral quality is presented as in an allegorical painting, attended by a train of minor but related personae" (*The Sister Arts* 290–291). It is this personified abstraction that Bentley revises and interprets. His design reflects the grandeur and solemnity of the poem whose stately measure is confirmed by a Spenserian hexameter at the end of each stanza. In answer to Gray's neoclassical imitation, Bentley's imitation of a High Renaissance mural seems appropriate; but his "mural" avoids the sentimentality of other contemporary imitators of Italian art in England, such as Kent who had done work for the Walpole family at Houghton.

Bentley counters the sentimentality of such pictures by using an "annunciation" scene to show the origin of affliction and sorrow. His purpose is not to depict a putto-like child, but to present the paradox of salvation that requires hardship and mortification for its fulfillment. The frontispiece, like Reni's *Madonna del Rosario,* shows god-the-father Jove handing down an infant to a pretty, madonna-like Adversity with curls and feminine figure. But when we see what she holds under her arm, we realize that she will flail and manacle the baby. The prospect is so frightful that the Medusa on Athena's shield, who represents Madness, turns toward Adversity (in spite of the direction of the shield) with wide eyes and a shriek of terror. For emphasis, the staring and screaming head of Madness appears a second time: in the initial letter she is framed by Adversity's instruments of torture (fig. 27).

Adversity is addressed as

> Daughter of Jove, relentless Power,
> Thou Tamer of the human breast,
> Whose iron scourge and tort'ring hour,
> The Bad affright, afflict the Best!

She is painted for the frontispiece as the "stern rugged nurse" of the first half of the second stanza:

> When first thy Sire to send on earth
> Virtue, his darling Child, design'd,
> To thee he gave the heav'nly Birth,
> And bad to form her infant mind.

Whether Adversity should be identified as Ate, or Blind Folly, as Mitford maintained, or as Athena, as has been more generally assumed, or simply as personified Affliction without association with a traditional goddess is a question that has been a matter of some debate.[2] Bentley's picture decides the issue: she is placed next to Athena, obviously with Gray's concurrence. In his explanation Walpole identifies the individuals in the print: "Jupiter delivering infant Virtue to Adversity to be educated. Minerva and Hercules on each side."

Bentley wishes us to see that Adversity and Jupiter are types of Minerva and Hercules by the juxtaposition of the pairs and their figural similarity. His contemporary audience was conditioned to accept this linkage, for it would have been familiar with an English mythology made popular by Sir James Thornhill in his murals for the Upper and Lower Halls at the Royal Naval Hospital, Greenwich, and in the dome at St. Paul's Cathedral. In Thornhill's allegory of the Protestant Succession, Hercules is the embodiment of Heroic Virtue, and Athena, of Wisdom; together they expel from England Calumny, Detraction, Envy, and other evils. It is these elements that are burlesqued in the frontispiece for Bolingbroke's *Dissertation upon Parties*. Under the influence of Thornhill, Hogarth adopted the same symbolism for the engraving of George Augustus, Prince of Wales, and the design for the Great Seal of England on the silver salver made for Sir Robert Walpole.[3]

In Bentley's design, Minerva and Hercules having pushed back a curtain display Gray's scene in Heaven; they hold a wreath that recalls the laurel crown of the frontispiece to the book, or perhaps they are passing it from one to the other as the child is passed by Jove to Adversity below. The frontispieces for *Spring*, the Eton ode, and *Hymn* suggest the difficult ascent up the hill of clouds to Olympus and to virtue (or bardic apotheosis) after the model of the *Tabula Cebetis*. Virtue, now changed by Bentley into a boy, holds a sprig of laurel signifying his ambition to succeed; he is handed down to Adversity who will raise him, in both senses of the word.

Each figure in the frontispiece is given representative emblems: Hercules, his helmet, club, and lion skin (on the model of the Farnese Hercules); Minerva, her armor and gorgon shield; Adversity, her whips and fetters; and Jupiter, his staff of office and his eagle grasping thunderbolts.[4] These are emblems of struggle, courage, steadfastness, discipline, responsibility, and authority. The design for the eagle was taken from Mario di Fiori's *A Concert of Birds*, a picture that hung in the Breakfast Room at Houghton. Bentley, who would have copied the the engraving of it at Strawberry Hill, may also have had in mind Walpole's eagle "found in the gardens of Boccapadugli within the precinct of Caracalla's baths" (later kept in the Gallery at Strawberry Hill) because, according to Walpole (*Wks*. ii.463), Gray "drew" its flagging wing in his *Progress of Poesy*:

the feather'd king
With ruffled plumes, and flagging wing:
Quench'd in dark clouds of slumber lie
The terror of his beak, and light'nings of his eye.

Borne up by the smoke from the sacrificial ram, Bentley's more active bird seems volcanic, a creation of the black smoke that opposes the friendlier cumulus of Heaven. Its dire effect matches Medusa's head on Athena's shield, also darkened by shadow. In its claw it holds Jupiter's thunderbolts, which in turn find ominous reflection in the whip, flail, and manacles under Adversity's arm. These links reveal not simply a hidden malevolence of Jove, despite his serenity of the moment, but also the recalcitrance of man that requires the violent discipline of Adversity.

Heroic Virtue (Jove) and Wisdom (Adversity) represent the torment necessary for the inculcation of virtue as well as man's necessary acceptance of suffering. That human beings must undergo pain to acquire humility, to become compassionate and philosophic, and to learn the value of detachment and wise melancholy was, of course, a commonplace, classical rationalization for adverse fate, a rationalization Gray directly derived in this instance from Horace's *Ad Fortunam* and Aeschylus's *Agamemnon*. He took the motto for the poem, "wisdom comes through suffering," from Aeschylus.

Tayler shows that Blake found this passive resignation repugnant. The acceptance of infant Virtue by Adversity clutching her whips and manacles represented in his mind a macabre casuistry. He modeled one of his illustrations for the ode on Bentley's beautiful tailpiece; thoroughly upset by Gray's submission to misery, he made the milk of the nurse lethal to the infant who lies dead in her arms ("Bentley Bid the Pencil" 212). But what appeared to Blake to be latent masochism or sadism is not so. Gray's poem and Bentley's designs generate no sympathy for the child out of a misplaced concern for its innocence or goodness. By changing the sex of Gray's Virtue to male, Bentley establishes a link with the boys shown in the frontispiece for the Eton ode (as well as in the headpiece for *Hymn*) who lack innate goodness and for whom sentimental indulgence should be censured. Moreover, the vigilant eagle, kept aloft by smoke from the torch of Madness, echoes the purpose of the demons in the Eton ode frontispiece, but unlike the demons it reminds us that stiff, rigorous discipline is necessary for charity, justice, and pity, objectives of the child's moral instruction. Without it virtue will be supplanted by the "Orgies of Folly, Noise and Laughter" (as Walpole describes the scene of the headpiece) and ultimately, one supposes, by the evils in the illustration for Bolingbroke.

Yet the pathos of *Hymn* occurs with the supplication to Adversity that she be gentle with her pupil, the speaker himself, and appear in her benign form rather than clad in gorgon terrors; passive acceptance and noble fortitude are not the sole subject of either the poem or the frontispiece. Fear is the moving force of the ode as much as compliance. It leads to a veiled threat in the last stanza, where an overzealous goddess is warned that severity might turn her pupil to despair and make him impervious to the knowledge and compassion requisite for virtue. In the frontispiece, Bentley faithfully interprets Gray by not showing a simple submission to fate. The crowded figures mirror one another, Minerva and Adversity, Hercules and Jove, the eagle and the gorgon on the shield; they intensify the reality of punishing discipline, retribution, and madness, and thus act as an antidote to the faintly ridiculous and lugubrious, even pompous, elegance of the Renaissance imitation and to the sentimentality often inherent in the rococo style.

The encapsulated mythography of the drawing gives no hint of an alternative to Adversity and therefore excludes choices other than cruel discipline for the development of virtue. Because Gray's personification of Virtue amounts to a non sequitur (one cannot educate Virtue to be virtuous), it follows that in the design Bentley purposely connects his personification with the all-too-human delinquent boys at Eton. If Adversity were to abandon her responsibility, Virtue would become no better. It is against this chance that Gray pleads in the third stanza, the details of which Bentley illustrates for the headpiece (fig. 26).

In the headpiece Adversity, agent of parents, schoolmasters, and the fierce divinity of heaven, swoops down upon the boys, "Self-pleasing Folly's idle brood, / Wild Laughter, Noise, and thoughtless Joy," to disturb their "Orgies," as Walpole says in his explanation. Like the Etonian miscreants, and even, perhaps, the less offensive zephyrs of the headpiece to *Spring* who flutter through the air and drop posies like the little spring poems that beguile the poet-speaker but in the end chasten him, these boys vex us into correction. They may have been modeled on Cheron's youths representative of the childish preoccupations that ruin adult minds in Prior's satire *Alma, or the Progress of the Mind* (figs. 94 and 95). With open mouth and flying hair ("thund'ring voice and threat'ning mien"), Adversity is no longer the pretty nurse of the frontispiece but instead she is like a gorgon, akin to Dürer's women in the *Death of Orpheus* or Virtue in *Der Hercules*. She is wrapped in a black cloud, as black as the eagle's of the frontispiece, and also as black as the cloud on which "Misfortune's baleful train" arrives in the Eton ode. She carries in her left hand the birch from under Folly's head. She represents, in fact, a further transformation of Minerva, even to suggesting perhaps the identification of the goddess with the gorgon on her own shield. If Minerva-like Adversity descending in a cloud is a reminder of Raving Madness in the frontispiece for the Eton ode, then beside her, behind the altar, the boulder and dark cave may belong not merely to the Melancholy of the tailpiece for *Hymn*, but to Melancholy Madness. This sequence of provocative transformations also parallels the change of the pretty "warriors" in the frontispiece for *A Long Story* into the gorgons found in the tailpiece for the same poem.

When the boys flee they drop their pastoral instruments, their tambor, pipes, and playthings, in order to "leave us leisure to be good," the speaker of *Hymn* says, and also, we presume, to leave him leisure to write admonitory hymns. Placed between Folly's idle brood and Adversity, the sacrificial altar in the foreground may be Bentley's representation of the bard's attempt by his supplication to interpose between the fierce goddess and the boys, which is to say, ourselves; in the background behind the altar, the cave of Melancholy presages the tailpiece portrait of the goddess in her benign form. Bentley deepens and universalizes the meaning of the headpiece by a visual analogue, the woodcut of Adam and Eve's expulsion from Paradise designed by Hans Holbein the Younger for his series *The Dance of Death* (fig. 89). The analogue hints that since the fall all men must be curbed by adversity in order to achieve redemption. The dead tree on the left of Holbein's print, balanced by Death holding a lute on the right, also repeats the pattern of the title page fleuron and recalls the Orphean theme threaded throughout the illustrations, especially as it has been placed in the context of the Choice of Hercules.

In the initial letter (fig. 27) showing, as Walpole explains, "A Gorgon's head, and instruments of punishment," Medusa is framed by the *D* of *Daughter* and fetters; she is hardly what one would expect for a portrait of Jove's daughter and completes the metamorphosis suggested in the headpiece where the pretty madonna of the frontispiece is turned to a fury. By framing Adversity in the giant *D*, Bentley reflects and redacts the heavily framed scene of the frontispiece but, in this compression, emphasizes only the essential terror of Jove's command.

Tayler speaks of Blake's and Pine's recognition of the "close association between depression and rage" ("Bentley Bid the Pencil" 212) and refers to the tailpiece made by Pine for Horace's Ode XXV of Book I, *Ad Lydiam*. It shows a gorgon hovering above the melancholic Lydia (fig. 114), a design that Bentley used as a model for his own tailpiece for *Hymn* (fig. 29). Blake "was to complain that the *rage* was missing in the 'Hymn to Adversity'." Bentley, Tayler continues, separated rage from lamentation by portraying the latter ("grieving yet dignified submission to Adversity") only in the tailpiece to *Hymn*, whereas rage, driven to Madness by the fury passions, was portrayed only in the frontispiece to the Eton ode. To emphasize this separation, Tayler asserts that the Fury of Pine's tailpiece does not appear "in any illustration" to *Hymn* (213–214), yet we have seen that she is present in the frontispiece and is suggested by the headpiece. Moreover, because she dominates the initial letter launching the poem, she helps to establish a highly specific association between rage and depression and is thus crucially important to Gray and Bentley.

The dominant emotion in the ode, I suggest again, is neither rage nor depression in isolation, but the terror induced by fear of a blacker affliction not yet received, a fear brutal enough to become a fury passion or vulture of the mind, namely madness. Adversity is asked:

> Oh, gently on thy Suppliant's head,
> Dread Goddess, lay thy chast'ning hand!

Not in thy Gorgon terrors clad,
Nor circled with the vengeful Band.

Hymn concerns the two kinds of melancholy that Gray distinguished in his letter to West of 27 May 1742 (Toynbee and Whibley #110), "white Melancholy, or rather Leucocholy" and black melancholy. The first he describes as something short of Joy or Pleasure, yet "a good easy sort of a state" whose only fault is "insipidity... apt now and then to give a sort of Ennui, which makes one form certain little wishes that signify nothing." The second "is sure of every thing that is unlikely, so it be but frightful; and, on the other hand, excludes and shuts its eyes to the most possible hopes, and every thing that is pleasurable; from this the Lord deliver us!" In the ode, written three months later but just after West had died, the two forms are deepened, the first with a "philosophic train" that can still soften the heart, and the second with gorgon terrors that can wound the heart and harden into despair, the psychic or spiritual paralysis of acedia.

Instead of separating the two states of lamentation and madness, Bentley appears to balance one against the other, the gorgon's head in the initial letter against Melancholy in the tailpiece. The moving significance of the tailpiece is contained in the figure of lamentation who becomes philosophic Melancholy; in other words, when Bentley suggests the opposition of rage and depression, he simultaneously transcends and combines them. With the wisdom and courage of Minerva, to whom Gray adds piety, the figure of the tailpiece turns her back to the demon and keeps her eye to the ground in order not to be turned to stone. She does not represent misery, for she combines the attributes of

Wisdom in sable garb array'd
Immers'd in rapt'rous thought profound,
And Melancholy, silent maid
With leaden eye, that loves the ground.

Unlike Gray and Bentley, Blake overcomes (or precludes) madness by a cathartic rage, whether violent or passive, an emotion that leads to the anger of rebellion. Tayler argues in "Two Eighteenth-Century Illustrators" that the Romantic poet offers a "corrective" to Gray in his illustration of the line "Hyperion's march and glittering shafts of war" from *The Progress of Poesy.* In the middle of a rising sun, Blake places a divine archer with his bow drawn to symbolize "the enlightening power of poetic genius," as though the archer were a visualization of his own lines from the "Preface" to *Milton:*

Bring me my bow of burning gold!
Bring me my arrows of desire!

Bring me my spear! O clouds unfold!
Bring me my chariot of fire!

"Had Gray been willing to shoot his arrows of desire more freely," Tayler writes, "he might, with all that power of 'sensibility', have driven out his own night creatures and mounted a glorious chariot of fire" (123).

Without Blake's confidence, Gray could not find rebellion credible; Bentley's illustrations emphasize Gray's view. The gentle and terrible goddesses in *Hymn* and in the drawings hardly suggest any possibility of raging rebellion that might overthrow or purge their melancholy but suggest instead the inevitability of adversity and the fortitude necessary to deal with it. For Gray it seems rage is indistinguishable from raving madness, a self-defeating response akin to hysteria. Bentley and Gray understood that melancholia without escape would become, not rage, but madness, as is proved by their collaboration both in the frontispiece to the Eton ode and these drawings for *Hymn*.[5]

Pine's recognition of the "close association between depression and rage" is actually closer in spirit to Gray and Bentley than to Blake. When Tayler remarks that the Latin diction in *Ad Lydiam* "evokes images appropriate to the furies, and connects them with the Thracian Maenads who, when repudiated by Orpheus, ran mad and tore him apart" ("Bentley Bid the Pencil" 213), she touches upon Horace's emphasis on the victim Lydia. Lydia had inadvertantly become the fool of her own coyness, a form of hubris, which brought the gorgon circled with the vengeful band down upon her own head. The horror that Pine shows is the frightening relationship of Lydia's melancholy to madness.

The same Orphean theme is latent in Gray's six odes, particularly in *Spring* and *Eton*. The menace that hovers above Lydia in Pine's engraving has a palpable presence in Bentley's frontispiece to *Spring* and the tailpieces to *Favourite Cat* and *Long Story*; it is explicitly shown in the drawings for *Eton* and *Hymn*. In *Spring* and *Eton* Gray's speakers, like Lydia, are cowed by malevolent fate; in the first the speaker finds he has been in "perpetual possession of being well deceived," as Swift would say; in the second he avers that the baleful horrors will descend on adults regardless of what they do. *Hymn* develops the Lydian idea in a different way: philosophic Melancholy, by virtue of her contrast to her black sister, acquires an unexpected loveliness. This is the theme of Bentley's tailpiece.

If Melancholy in the tailpiece suggests that the poet has had a glimpse of the gorgon and is very nearly turned to stone, she is also reminiscent of *Muta Poesis* (fig. 79). Her portrait recalls Shakespeare's "Patience on a monument Smiling at grief" who suffers "with a green and yellow melancholy" (*Twelfth Night*, II.iv.113–115); she represents Gray's attempt to reconcile himself to adversity and to avoid madness. By means of Melancholy, Bentley suggests that the poet has distanced desolate emotions and has made of them an art object. The controlled tensions and lapidary beauty of the metrical structure in his poem discovers a Roman grace; similarly, Bentley's illustrations for *Hymn* reflect Gray's restraint and unexpected reaffirmation in a balance of images, and in his control of emblems and analogues. Salvation is marked by the transformation of Adversity, finally, into philosophic Melancholy. Statuesque but beautiful in her sorrow, she becomes the image of wisdom—marmoreal, yet meditative and dignified. Her effect at the end of the sequence of the drawings is similar to the hexameter line at the end of each stanza. She embodies the wish of *Hymn*.

Preoccupied with melancholy like many of their contemporaries, Walpole, Bentley, and Gray seemed especially affected by Pope's *Eloisa to Abelard*. From this poem Walpole took the name *Paraclete* for the hall that Bentley designed for Strawberry Hill. Gray's "Epitaph" in *Elegy* contains an echo of Eloisa's soliloquy of love to Abelard after the burial of her "cold dust": "Here all its frailties, all its flames resign, / And wait, till 'tis no sin to mix with thine" (175–176). According to Walpole's *Description* of Strawberry Hill there hung in the Tribune on the side opposite to the door "A drawing by Mr. Bentley, representing two lovers in a church looking at the tombs of Abelard and Eloisa, from these lines of Pope, 'If ever chance two wand'ring lovers brings / To Paraclete's white walls and silver springs, &c.'" (*Wks.* ii.488). Bentley's tailpiece for *Hymn* is in part derived from Pope, as well as from Gray:

> But o'er the twilight groves, and dusky caves,
> Long-sounding isles, and intermingled graves,
> Black Melancholy sits, and round her throws
> A death-like silence, and a dread repose:
> Her gloomy presence saddens all the scene,
> Shades ev'ry flow'r, and darkens ev'ry green,
> Deepens the murmur of the falling floods,
> And breathes a browner horror on the woods.
>
> (163–170)

"Dreariness" or "gloom" are the words Dr. Johnson uses to define horror in the last quoted line, a line of particular attraction to the Strawberry Hill circle. In Gray's *Hymn* the "expressive horror and dignity" of Melancholy reflects her immersion "in rapt'rous thought profound," a state at once beautiful and terrible. She revises the figure in the frontispiece for *Spring* who, sitting under his gloomy canopy, has thrown about himself a death-like silence and dread repose.

Bentley's exclusion of Pine's gorgon seems to violate the pattern established by one of its sources, the bat above Melancholy in Dürer's *Melencolia I* (fig. 83). The removal conveys transcendence of the gorgon through a discovery of Christian-like humility. The poem and drawing are closer in spirit to Johnson's "celestial Wisdom," a wisdom that comes with Christian acceptance of the inevitable afflictions catalogued in *The Vanity of Human Wishes*. Of course, it is a strategy to keep raving madness at bay. In the parenthesis of stanza 5, Gray implies, as does Johnson in *Vanity*, that only "the impious" will be visited by the gorgon, namely by Horror's funeral cry, Despair, Disease, and Poverty. But this is clearly no more than a suppression of the fury; Bentley in his tailpiece makes the suppression implicit in the dark rocks and gloomy woods, a latent presence intensifying the seductive quality of the foreground figure. By contrast, the speaker in the Eton ode succumbs to the gorgon.

An important clue to Bentley's meaning is a rough draft for Melancholy, a brown and gray wash drawing preserved in Kirgate's extra-illustrated edition of *Designs* (fig. 30). This nude with a sad and beautiful head modifies its particular sources, Ripa's *Malinconia* (fig. 78) and Pine's headpiece to *Ad Fortunam* (fig. 116). Bentley has already discarded the idea that Dürer conveys in *Melencolia I* as part of the tri-partite *Meisterstück* (including also *Knight, Death and Devil* and *St. Jerome in his Study*), where Melancholy asserts her power against the world; Panofsky has said that she is a representation of intellectual life in competition with God, as opposed to the *vita contemplativa* of St. Jerome. Pine's scene for *Ad Lydiam* shows life in competition with age and the malignant isolation that results. But Bentley visualizes harmony between a madonna of the rocks and her surroundings, a sympathy or *concordia discors* deepened by his suggestion of the further analogue of Bellori's *Muta Poesis*.

Perhaps Bentley looked at Dürer's *Penance of St. John Chrysostom* (fig. 84) and its source Jocopo de' Barbari's *Cleopatra*, as identified by Panofsky (77). In the left background of Dürer's engraving, the saint, naked with unkempt hair, crawls away ignominiously after his alledged seduction of an emperor's daughter. Having succumbed to sexual appetite, he is made to live like a beast until forgiven. Natural and inescapable depravity brings affliction; violence, rage, and self-assertion are not remedies. His salvation is suggested paradoxically by the beauty of the predominant figures in the portrait, his victim and their child. Panofsky explains that Dürer "in suppressing almost entirely the dismal saint in favor of this touching group . . . transformed a spurious story of 'sin and punishment' into an idyll of tender humanity and primeval innocence" (77). Fierce Adversity gives way to a human Melancholy in Gray's final verse; her tender humanity is accentuated in Bentley's picture. The change from the watercolor to the more graceful figure of the engraving might also have been helped by reference to an untitled etching by Rosa (fig. 81).

Bentley took pains to refine his comely portrait even in the engraving. Opposite to the tailpiece in Kirgate's extra-illustrated volume is pasted a proof copy on which he has written to Grignion at the bottom: "This proof is a great deal too black. I should be glad to have 3 proofs more but I wou'd have them wip'd a great deal more & the press not set so tight" (fig. 28). It is the only design preserved with such instructions. Among the dark boulders beneath distant cypresses, emblems of death, Melancholy's restraint is both Christian and classical. Despite her bowed head and placement within the inverted triangle of the dead tree and tombstone-like rock, she, genius loci, makes a pyramid pointing to heaven and to the lines:

> Teach me to love and to forgive,
> Exact my own defects to scan,
> What others are, to feel, and know myself a Man.

By art Gray and Bentley have displaced bitterness and madness. If Melancholy is Eloisa to Gray's Abelard, in the sequence of Bentley's drawings, she seems also to be a transformation of Henrietta Jane Speed. She represents ultimately the transfigured spirit of the poet depicted in the frontispiece of the book. The pride Bentley took in his achievement is proved by Eccardt's portrait of him, completed in late 1753, where he holds this drawing of Melancholy (frontispiece).

On 8 October 1751 (*Corr.* 14.53), Gray remarked to Walpole that he did not think *Hymn* would furnish "out a head- or tail-piece." On 28 August 1752 (9.143–144), Walpole told Montagu that the poet was so impressed with the tailpiece that he wanted Bentley to draw him something out of Dryden's *Theodore and Honoria*; in Walpole's mind the wish was shocking and resulted from Gray's "loving melancholy, till it is not strong enough." He even hinted that this love was like drink to a drunkard. The desire for a picture from Dryden's fable based on Boccaccio's tale of Nastagio degli Onesti (eighth story, fifth day of the *Decameron*) would have seemed less astonishing to Walpole had he known of Botticelli's picture of the story's climax, with which Gray was undoubtedly familiar.[6] Gray may have wished to pay Bentley a compliment by suggesting indirectly that he should imitate this Italian master; he did not expect to be laughed at.

Several years later, in 1759, Bentley made one last nightmarish portrait of Melancholy, in which her link with the gorgons of madness and with sexual frustration and death is explicit. It is like Pine's illustration of Lydia with its priapus in the background. Entitled *Prospect of Vapourland* (fig. 62),[7] Bentley's picture is not derived from Dryden's fable; whether this largest of all Bentley's preserved designs was begun in compliance with Gray's request cannot now be known, yet it develops the preoccupation of poet and artist for Melancholy.

Gray's selection of Dryden's fable as a subject for a complementary picture suggests that the melancholy within him demanded another, more violent version. Possibly the beautiful figure (who "immers'd in rapt'rous thought profound" had quelled for the poet the raving madness he feared) seemed actually to foster another lie in her formal similarity to the figure of *Muta Poesis*. Bentley caught in the tailpiece something of the way the poet on his lyre had not merely placed an aesthetic distance between himself and the gorgon in order to still her thundering voice, but was hiding her very existence from himself. Bentley's instruction to Grignion to make the engraving less black was part of the conspiracy. Yet Gray's unwholesome addiction to the tailpiece coupled with his desire to have another more sinister portrait, also revealed his profoundly paradoxical need to arouse the fury and then to quell her again. On his Pegasus he, like Perseus, wanted to decapitate her.

In the ninth section of Swift's *Tale of a Tub*, madness, we are told, "proceeds from a Redundancy of *Vapour*," and in Johnson's *Dictionary* "vapour" is defined as "fancies unreal," or in the plural, illness caused "by diseased nerves; hypochrondriacal maladies; melancholy; spleen"; these definitions clarify Bentley's intent in *Prospect of Vapourland*. His picture also brings to mind Pope's "Cave of Spleen" described in canto iv of *The Rape of the Lock*:

> A constant *Vapour* o'er the Palace flies;
> Strange Phantoms rising as the Mists arise;
> Dreadful, as Hermit's Dreams in haunted Shades,
> Or bright as Visions of expiring Maids.

The explanation in Bentley's hand on the back of the drawing defines the *modus operandi* of the scene, the verbal-visual pun:

> A Prospect of Vapourland. The Batavia Plane Tree. The Dragon Tree. The *Ficus Peoeides maximus, caule Hibernica foliis hirsutis*. The Rattan Palm Tree. *Lapis andromorphites*. The Gibbet Tree. Mount Lion. Phisic road. Calves-head Hillock. The Sky after Polonius.

The Batavia (Bat aviary) Plane tree foliates with bats; the Dragon Tree consists of a trunk of human heads (rising like Hogarth's *Laughing Audience* or *Characters and Caricaturas*) that leaf out in a cone of serpents like those of Medusa in the frontispiece to the Eton ode or the initial letter to *Hymn;* the *Ficus Peoeides maximus* (suggested by Adam's fig leaf, by the fig as a fertility symbol, and by the colloquial, obscene pun) is the trunk of a man whose phallus props up one corner of the tent (*hibernica*) also held by the Rattan Palm and Gibbet Tree; and the Rattan Palm (rat and palm) shows rats rushing up and encasing the tree trunk to cascade in leaves. In front of this phantasmagoria the *Lapis andromorphites* is a man-shaped boulder (perhaps Pope's hermit) against which reclines a woman (possibly Pope's expiring maid) leaning on her elbow and with one breast exposed. She, Melancholy, in the extreme suffers from the "green and yellow melancholy" of Shakespeare's "Patience," yet also recalls a typical figure of mourning as shown in Louis Cheron's frontispiece for *The Works of Tibullus, Containing his four Books of Love-Elegies* (tr. John Dart, London, 1720) (fig. 80).[8]

Melancholy pulls Bentley's prospect into focus. Her back to the *Ficus* and the Gibbet Tree implies a sexual frustration like that of Horace's Lydia; Pine's priapus depicted behind Lydia has been changed into both the *Ficus* and the Gibbet Tree, just as the winged fury has turned into the Dragon Tree.[9] Within this allegorical landscape Melancholy becomes an emblem for the adverse fate of the lovelorn; in a scene filled with phallic objects she represents, with the death of her lover, sexual isolation and failure. Adversity has come to her clad in Gorgon terrors and surrounded with the vengeful band. Alluding to the vapors of madness "The sky after Polonius" perhaps refers not merely to work of the Bolognese painter Tommaso di Andrea Vincidor (who was referred to by Dürer as Thomas Polonius), but also to *Hamlet* (III.ii), where the character Polonius agrees with the mad-seeming hero that the clouds are shaped like camels, weasels, whales, or whatever monsters one chooses to see. Melancholy makes a sharp contrast to the couple walking together on the Physic road, whose backs are turned to the nightmare, an image of healthful, social love. In the tailpiece to *Hymn* Melancholy's benign manifestation results perhaps from her placement below *Man*, the final word in the verse above her, yet even so, one senses the frenzy beneath her skin.

The *Lapis andromorphites*, which Melancholy leans upon and which corresponds to the urn in Cheron's drawing, has possibly been frozen to stone by the gorgons of black melancholy that the woman represents. Legs crossed, arms folded, and head bowed, the man is the personification of misery. Her head like a death mask is emblematic of his isolation, petrification, impotence, and death.

The underlying menace in so many of the illustrations (the title page fleuron, the frontispieces to *Spring* and to the Eton ode, and the tailpiece to *Hymn*) seems realized by this scene. It suggests that Bentley also remembered Kent's portrait of Despair in Book I of *The Faerie Queene* who, before his cave, unites the effect of Melancholy and the *Lapis andromorphites* (fig. 82). At the end of *Hymn*, Melancholy leans against a *lapis andromorphites* too, but in the shape of a gravestone, a subtle memento mori.

Notes

1. With its ironic use of Olympian imagery, this picture might also have influenced the frontispiece to the Eton ode. It shows Sir Robert Walpole on a cloud pyramid between Fortune, Mercury, and Plutus; Corruption hands money to suppliants below; and the weeping figure of Liberty sits before the hydra of Faction and Corruption. For further explanation, see Carretta, *The Snarling Muse*, 56–57.

2. *The Complete Poems of Thomas Gray*, 204, note 1.

3. Paulson, *Hogarth's Graphic Works*, i.93–94; *Hogarth*, i.124ff., 175.

4. In Spence's *Polymetis*, plates I and II show Zeus with a scepter in his left hand, lightning (fulmen) in his right, and his eagle beside and below him. Plate IV shows depictions of Minerva with her emblems; and plates XVII to XIX are of Hercules with his.

5. Madness and melancholy were commonly linked in eighteenth-century literature; see Jarrett, *England in the Age of Hogarth* (London: Hart-Davis MacGibbon, 1974), ch. 8.

6. There is no mention of Botticelli in Gray's journal kept during his "Tour in Italy" ("Criticisms on Architecture and Painting during a Tour in Italy," in *The Works of Gray*, ed. J. Mitford, vol. iv, 1836, 225–305), yet that does not necessarily preclude his remembering the picture at Florence. Apparently, he kept no journal when there. Hagstrum in *The Sister Arts* admits to the temptation of seeing "a reflection of the 'Primavera' or the 'Birth of Venus' " in "Gray's richly sensuous mythological allegory" of the first epode in the *Progress of Poesy* (304).

7. Brown and gray wash with ink over pencil, 18½ by 25⅛ inches; verso inscription in Walpole's hand "By Mr Bentley, 1759." Now at the Yale Center for British Art.

8. In the English translation of Ripa's *Iconologia* of 1709 (London: Benj. Motte), the stone and leafless tree are said to signify that "Malinconia . . . is *barren*, in Words and Deeds" (55), an idea both Pine and Bentley have played upon in their different ways.

9. Bentley pursued the connection between Melancholy and the serpents of Madness in his play *The Wishes, or Harlequin's Mouth Open'd* (1761). The heroine Isabelle, depressed because her father has cruelly prohibited her from seeing her lover, goes to the garden to weep, where by chance she prevents the gardner from killing a snake. The creature changes into the fairy Manto (i.e., "to Man") who grants her the power of wishes. Manto first appears as a viper because, as she says, few women "are not snakes sometime in their lives." With "a little snug venomous bite to some particular friend," the urbane Manto continues, the transformation begins, and "nothing else but a continual exertion of this faculty of snapping improves one into a Dragon" (Act I, sc. i). By this analogue to Eden, Bentley suggests that the consequences of unnatural isolation is malice, impotence, and madness.

IX
Designs for *Elegy Written in a Country Church-Yard*

BENTLEY'S frontispiece for *Elegy* (fig. 31) is not the comparatively straightforward expression of Melancholy found in the tailpiece for *Hymn* where the figural coincidence with Bellori's *Muta Poesis* points to the feeling in all the designs drawn for a poet "marked by Melancholy for her own," but it has a more subtle purpose. A key element is the distance created by the poet between the reader and humble rustics; the massive gate also separates the viewer from the "cool sequestered vale" and the silent tenor of the countryman's life glimpsed in the distance. Walpole footnotes Gray's passage on the "sequestered vale" in his edition of *Designs* (Hazen #2044) with a reference to *Spectator* #610, where we are told that human values are different from those of "spirits or angels" who look down upon mankind. Whereas we "are dazzled with the splendor of titles, the ostentation of learning, the noise of victories," they look for the "philosopher in the cottage, who possesses his soul in patience and thankfulness"; they find "great men . . . in shades and solitudes, in the private walks and by-paths of life," not at the head of armies or governments.

Bentley's heavy portico and shadows in black ink convey "the expressive horror and dignity" of the final hour, and separate us from humble countrymen who possess their souls in patience and thankfulness. Closer inspection shows that the scene has a second purpose, one which for all its difference and complexity complements the first. Bentley's genius lay in dark comedy. Analogues, punning images, and lugubrious details produce in this last frontispiece a surprising theater of elegiac ironies. One cannot help concluding that the artist wanted to capture something of the poet's annoyance over the popular and sentimental reaction to the high art of his *Elegy*, first published in 1751, a poem with ideas that "find a mirror in every mind" and "an echo in every bosom," as Dr. Johnson said.

John Sitter maintains that the speaker in *Elegy* is in "collision" with history because of his sense that he has been betrayed by society (*Literary Loneliness in Mid-Eighteenth-Century England* 96ff.), and that likewise Gray himself implicitly yearns for the simple life and the "sequestered vale." Yet if Bentley conveys this yearning, he also burlesques the popular, sentimental reaction to the poem. His strategy recalls the one he used in illustrating the Eton ode and *A Long Story*, and for many of the earlier drawings as well where visual puns are a vehicle for satire. In *Elegy* Bentley seems to play on the idea of *grave* in a picture that is drawn to look like an *engraving* for the ultimate, *Gravian* poem in the volume. The Swain announces the *grave* subject as he points to the *engraved* text on the stone above the *grave*; this gesture and the Stranger's shadow reveal to us what is written on the monument; one engraving answers the other, just as other details answer other details, and the whole scene answers the poem. The Stranger's *foot* rests on the *footstone*; the shadow of his *head* at the base of the *headstone* is balanced by the *death's head* grinning in mockery at the top, and the skull and stone parody the human body. Stranger, grave, and Swain together reflect the shape of the vault in the foreground and become a second articulation of its "storied" theme. In the frontispieces for the odes on the cat and Eton College, the initials of the poet and artist are placed together, Gray's on the left, Bentley's on the right. Only Bentley's initials appear now as a monogram at the lower left; it would seem as though Gray's are meant to be signified by the *grave* itself, the focal point of the drawing.

For the frontispiece of *Elegy*, Jean Hagstrum identified an important analogue from high art, one that Gray no doubt also had in mind when he wrote the poem, namely Nicholas Poussin's second version of *The Arcadian Shepherds* (fig. 77). Engraved many times by different men (Picart was one[1]) it was, Hagstrum writes, the "classical expression of the elegiac mood" in the early eighteenth century.[2] Echoing the action of Poussin's kneeling shepherd, Bentley's rustic traces with a finger the letters on the monument; he does not beckon to the Stranger (Gray's "kindred spirit") or point to the stone "beneath yon aged thorn" as in the verse. The Stranger leans on his staff like Poussin's shepherd, and like Poussin's kneeling man casts a shadow over the grave to suggest his own mortality, an idea Bentley has made particularly emphatic by the exact placement of the Stranger's shadow.

But Bentley and Poussin work on a different scale with different objectives. Whereas Poussin's theme of *Et in Arcadia ego* is simply and beautifully visualized, Bentley's theme grows complex in its obvious and self-conscious parody of the painting. It is not just a restatement of its idea or meant only to recall it. Rather the drawing burlesques Poussin's icon for death, which had become a stereotyped vehicle for sentimentality, not unlike the swelling emotional reaction to *Elegy* itself. Bentley uncovers and counteracts such sentimentality by the impertinence of his visual puns. He exploited Poussin in a different spirit from that suggested by Hagstrum.

A double analogue from low art helps to clarify Bentley's objective. He was inspired by Kent's illustration for the first of Gay's 1727 *Fables* and by Gravelot's for the last of the 1738 series. Kent's design for "The Shepherd and the Philosopher" (fig. 105), mentioned before in connection with the title page fleuron, shows the shepherd leaning on a staff as he teaches the philosopher about enduring values, a parallel to Bentley's Swain. In Gravelot's picture for "The Ravens, the Sexton, and the Earthworm" (fig. 112), the sexton leaning on his spade, the church behind him, the gravestones, and even the skull below the crypt on the lower right (it might have suggested the skull under the monument in the frontispiece to *Spring*) prompt the viewer to recognize parallels in *Elegy*. In the latter fable the sexton's chief concern is the fee that death will bring him; he is nevertheless shocked to learn that the distinction between the carcasses of the squire and his steed is only a matter of taste to the ravens and earthworm. Consolation is offered by the worm who tells him that the true "dignity of man" was "never vermin's food" or for that matter a larger fee, but virtue "seated in th' immortal mind."

Much in Fable XVI finds eloquent echo in *Elegy*, perhaps most strikingly when Gay, speaking of the vanities and riches of the world, asks, "Can those prolong one gasp of breath, / Or calm the troubled hour of death?" (53–54).[3] Gravelot's sexton in turn recalls the farmer in his own earlier illustration for Fable VII, "The Countryman and Jupiter" (fig. 111) (mentioned in the chapter on *Hymn*) where the language, especially with its corresponding rural evocation, is also echoed by Gray. Gay's lines about ambition became a central theme in *Elegy*:

> Or were you dignified with pow'r,
> Would that avert one pensive hour?
> You might give avarice its swing,
> Defraud a nation, blind a king:
> Then, from the hirelings in your cause
> Though daily fed with false applause,
> Could it a real joy impart?
> Great guilt knew never joy at heart.
>
> (45–52)[4]

Bentley, I believe, recognized these connections and wanted us to do so. Such parallels do not merely point to pictorial or poetical analogues, but call up a memory of childhood fables and their humbler morality.[5] They exaggerate in order to repudiate the sentimentality in the multitude of prints and poems which, although inspired by Poussin's great art, lack any true worth and show how far vanity and ambition can remove the sophisticated from the more clear-sighted country folk. When Bentley illustrated Gray's own version of Poussin, he used satire to correct a wallow in self-indulgent sorrow.

The high vault in Bentley's design takes up at least half the drawing; it stiffens the rococo into the perpendicular style and makes a more elaborate architectural frame than in any of his other illustrations. It recalls the heavy, dark bower of branches enclosing Gray in the frontispiece to *Spring* whose circumscribed images have now turned into a harvest of funereal emblems. The monumental arch seems to absorb all the other frontispiece borders that precede it, a passageway built on a foundation of parallels that reach back to the initial frontispiece, to Charon and Atropos, Jealousy and Madness, Sir Christopher and the winged ladies, Athena and Hercules, and also to thc gate of Hell in Virgil, to life in Cebes, and to Bedlam Hospital in London. They all recall and memorialize the passage from womb to coffin. Subordinate to the enormous frame, Poussin's and Gravelot's images are reduced in size to mere cameos.

Walpole's explanation emphasizes architecture:

> A Gothic gateway in ruins with the emblems of nobility on one side; on the other, the implements and employments of the Poor. Thro' the arch appears a church-yard, and village-church built out of the remains of an abbey. A countryman showing an epitaph to a passenger.

The arch organizes the scene beyond it as does the diaphragm of a camera, a simile Panofsky used to describe an identical technique in Dürer. Bentley may have studied the woodcut *Meeting of Joachim and Ann at the Golden Gate* (fig. 85), where the gateway is reflected by doors and windows in the distance to make the theme emphatic. The Dürer is explained in part by architectural embellishment: "Decorated with a border of interlaced branches, in which are set small statutes of Moses, three Prophets, David and Gideon, this Gate fulfills the double purpose of frame and 'repousoir'," Panofsky explains (100). Similarly, the shape of Bentley's portal is repeated by the window in the niche on the left side of the gateway, the door and window in the ruined church behind the Swain, the half vault behind the Stranger, and even by the Swain and Stranger themselves. Vaults and doorways proliferate to stress the theme of passages, all of which "lead but to the grave," or to the vault of the tailpiece toward which the Stranger's staff in the frontispiece seems to point.

The Stranger, or "kindred spirit," as he is called in the poem, has walked with staff in hand through the turnstile, yet another gate on the left; he recalls Dürer's figure, staff in hand, hurrying into the vista from the same direction. The posture of the Swain recalls St. Ann. One wants to see Joachim between them: perhaps implicitly the grave is his, for it teaches its disturbing lesson yet gives ironic solace. The subtler analogue of the Dürer enriches the counterpoised allusions to Poussin and Gravelot; this additional play and the diaphragmatic gate, if nothing else, help to reveal the scorn Bentley clearly felt for sentimentalized versions of Poussin in elegant prints, as well as for the popular reaction to *Elegy*, many lines of which were already becoming clichés.

The embarrassment of Gray over the popularity of his poem caused him to take a different approach toward his pindarics; the motto chosen from Pindar for the *Progress of Poesy* says, "not for the general public." It was now preferable after all to be a "Youth . . . to Fame unknown." Poussin's emblem is used to the same effect as the pastoral ambiance in the frontispiece for the Eton ode; it becomes an elegant foil to the melodramatic poet of the "Epitaph." Kent, Gravelot, and Dürer, together with visual puns and the heavy gate, enable Bentley to reinvest Poussin with expressive if ironic force.

The tiny skull and bones atop the grave reflect the head, sword, and staff of the Stranger, as well as helmet and weapons on the left of the arch. Crossed bones and crossed weapons recall the bones, farm implements, spade, hourglasses, and skulls that decorate the title page of Dodsley's first edition of *Elegy* (1751) and point in this case to paradoxical vitality in decay. Life and death, death and life, echo and re-echo as the emptiness of the left side of the vault contrasts with the abundance on the right, while the helmet, sword, and lance are drawn opposite the spade, fork, rake, and ax. The grandeur of the vault in good repair on one side is contrasted to the crumbling of common brick on the other; past history symbolized by gothic architecture faces a present-day harvest that will ensure a future. Like the gateway in the frontispiece for the Eton ode, there is a contrast between neatness (Jealousy) and disorder (Madness), representing here the meanness and vacuity of the great in relation to the fecundity of the struggling serf. The accoutrements of a knight, his weapons and mail against deep shadow of night, contrast with the implements of the poor in shining sun; cenotaphic armorial quarterings face a cornucopia of fruits, flowers, and vegetables; bare blocks of stone at the base of the gothic structure are removed at the right to reveal a tuber buried in the darkness of the earth foundation from which new life begins to sprout.

The trees growing out of the vault accentuate decay, yet Dürer-like in treatment, they were possibly suggested by *The Nativity* whose composition mirrors *The Golden Gate*. The humble efforts of the rustics, having made a church out of the collapsing abbey, emphasize temporality, yet also renewal. The Stranger's staff parallels the arm of the Swain, each pointing to the grave; peering down, Stranger and Swain seem also reminiscent of shepherds in a nativity scene, the living tuber beneath them suggestive of regeneration. Contrasts between life and death, wealth and poverty, light and dark, high and low, reverberate everywhere; images reflect back and forth like the tolling of a bell.

The split in the monumental archway dividing rich from poor and past from present is reflected by the edge of the distant tower where the wheel for the rope of the curfew bell intersects the wheel of the rose window, cut in half in the rebuilt steeple. The church is not Stoke Poges, but an impossible structure; it even has the look of an Italian campanile, a hodgepodge of mixed architectural styles to satirize contemporary taste. The lightly sketched tower and gateway look like follies of the rich rather than sturdy country buildings.

Gothic architecture with its forest of pinnacles romanticizes the natural scene, yet often becomes an absurd imitation of it. Bentley illustrates the past by use of medieval England and the gothic style which Walpole wished to revive. The frontispiece in fact may be a subtle burlesque of Strawberry Hill with its armory of weapons and trophies, "the boast of heraldry, the pomp of power." Bentley made a drawing of the Armory at Strawberry Hill which Walpole dated 1753 (fig. 64). In 1747 Walpole bought the small plain house on the banks of the Thames at Twickenham and soon began super imposing a fictitious gothic front over the original brick. So too, in the frontispiece, Bentley carefully drew artificial gothic pinnacles against a background of brick. His attractive design may have contributed to the picturesque vogue for medieval glamour, yet he ridiculed the rage for sham ruins and, like Gay in *Shepherd's Week*, satirized the tendency of the upper classes (those who will look at these illustrations) to indulge in ludicrous and romantic fantasies on pastoral life.

The speaker of *Elegy* could never have voiced his pastoral lament had he not himself left the sequestered vale. The artist knew that pastoral yearnings are in direct proportion to distance from Eden. Because we are not the jocund swain, we become susceptible to cynicism on one hand and to the pomposity of sentimental visions of rustic life on the other. The absurd details mock popularizations of Poussin's peasants who are set in a false arcadian scene where even death is artificial and made glamorous. Grignion engraved the frontispiece with the unreal wax-like pinnacles above the niche exactly as drawn; having lost rigidity, they appear to change shape before our eyes. The closer one looks at this and other details of the illustration, the more forcibly one is struck by a stage-set quality. The plastic forms refuse to be confined by architectonics; everything seems fluid. Yet the farming implements, fruits, grains, sack, cider barrel, and basket show the growing, dying, transcient things of real laborers. If Bentley scorned the sentimentalist's reduction of death to tidy emblems and reviled the sterility of an artificial life that was commemorated with follies, storied urns, and animated busts, he also depicted the real beauty of a country harvest. The play of reflections and analogues and the tension of ambiguities make the pictorial elegy paradoxically vital.

* * *

The headpiece (fig. 32) of "Country-labours" shows men in action: two sturdy farmers reap grain that moves in the wind, another swings an ax, and a third drives his cart through a stream as one of the horses bends over to drink.

Oft did the harvest to their sickle yield,
Their furrow oft the stubborn glebe has broke;
How jocund did they drive their team afield!
How bow'd the Woods beneath their sturdy stroke!

(25–28)

The illustration looks like an early Stubbs; it may be intended to recall, if only in a vague way, Kent's design for Thomson's "Autumn" (fig. 103), or even Poussin's "Summer" in his series *The Four Seasons*. Life and its fruits, the neatly kept farmhouse in the distance, and great-bottomed men who get to the bottom of things as they fell or reap, all make a serpentine movement downward to the water which if allowed to fall would flow into the opening lines of *Elegy*. The sinking motion anticipates Gainsborough's downward curves.[6]

The toil of rude forefathers of the hamlet is answered by a passive meditation indicated by the church in ruins and owl of the initial letter (fig. 33): "from yonder ivy-mantled tow'r, The mopeing owl does to the moon complain." The tiny figure strolling in deep shadow is clearly the poet of the fourth line, "And leaves the world to darkness and to me." His microscopic figure, especially in relation to the high tower, the enormous letters of the print, and the huge designs, suggests that he has been dwarfed by his gigantic, evolving meditation on death and that the poet is eclipsed by the fame of his poem. In contrast to the muscular laborers of the headpiece stressing the universality of the lush harvest scene, the benighted poet hobbles on a cane, about to pass through the crumbling abbey (as through his meditation) to the churchyard gates just discernible to the right. The stark miniature so obviously an icon produces a satiric effect like that of *The Arcadian Shepherds* in the frontispiece. When the moping owl with outspread wings flies from the *T* (for tower) over the molester of its solitary reign, it answers the imagery of Gray's tolling lines; the owlish "o's" evoke in a similarly witty manner the poet's large melancholy.[7]

It is of interest to note that in the context of the most gothic of these illustrations, Walpole and Bentley did not choose black letter, which they apparently eschewed as they did monkish emblems. Their decision to use Roman type everywhere, in all their publications even at the height of their gothic revival, is further evidence of their neoclassic orientation and a measure of the depth of their gothic fantasies.

Walpole explains that the tailpiece (fig. 34) shows "a country burial" with a "torch fallen into an ancient vault." Kirgate's three proof-engravings (figs. 35a to 36a) give evidence of the evolution of Bentley's drawing. The first within double ink margins looks like the burial ticket described by Gray in his letter to Walpole of 8 July 1752. Apparently Bentley sent a copy of it to William Sleater, the Dublin publisher, who had it re-engraved for his edition of the poems printed in 1768 (fig. 38).[8] Bentley's second version of the tailpiece reverses the procession, adds the vault, and enlarges the scene, but it is still bounded by a line. The third and final draft, with marching mourners returned to their original right-to-left direction, has grown even bigger; the ink margins that provide a frame have been removed.

When told in the "Epitaph" that the "Youth to Fortune and to Fame unknown" had given "to Mis'ry all he had, a tear," and "gain'd from Heav'n ('twas all he wish'd) a friend," Bentley might have been reminded of "The Hare and Many Friends," the last fable in Gay's 1727 work. In this fable, the rabbit, pursued by the huntsmen and hounds, is not saved by his "friends," for he who wants many friends will "rarely find" a true one. It is interesting to note that Gay explicitly identifies himself with the victim: "A Hare, who, in a civil way, / Comply'd with ev'ry thing, like *Gay*." Gray's solitary youth, on the other hand, wished for no more than one true friend. Two details suggest that, when Bentley enlarged this final drawing for *Designs*, he looked at Wootton's illustration for the hare (fig. 110). First, behind the sad victim in Wootton's foreground, a horse, bull, goat, and sheep file like a cortege into the distance. Second, their visible tails mark the end of the hare's story and suggest the pictorial strategy that Bentley used for the tailpiece to *Spring*. It will be remembered that in this first tailpiece, showing a distant steeple, he seemed in effect to look ahead over the sequence of drawings to the illustrations for *Elegy*; now by calling up a memory of Gay's fable a second time, Bentley looks back to the beginning of the book.

Throughout the volume he repeatedly points to the affinity between the fables and Gray's odes. Significant details from numbers I and L, the first and last of Gay's 1727 collection, and XVI, the last of his 1738 collection, seem to coalesce in *Elegy*, to remind us of a single method that helps to give pictorial coherence to the sequence. By the complex and dramatic play of his sister art, Bentley reveals a humble source for the poems he illustrates, yet also shows their transcendence of it.

It would be surprisingly inconsistent if, by the designs for the *Elegy*, Bentley had not wanted to bring together details from the sequence of designs. In the frontispiece for *Spring*, the altar and chaplet of flowers at the lower left, representative of the ode, are balanced by a Roman sepulchral altar on the right, representative of *Elegy*. Their placement foreshadows the beginning and end of the book; their reflection of one another recalls the line about the race of men who "shall end where they began." At the center the "listless" figure of the poet actually reclines "at the foot of yonder beech" of both *Spring* and *Elegy* and pores upon the same "brook that babbles by" through both. The illustrations that follow show indirectly the speaker either "craz'd with care, or cross'd in hopeless love," and finally in the grave marked by Melancholy for her own. Dominating the scene, the tree over the crypt is not merely the final transformation of the tree over the melancholic bard of the frontispiece for *Spring*, or for that matter the tree over the grave in the frontispiece for *Elegy*. It recalls, repeats, and replaces the flourishing laurel of art in the fleuron and, as the last tree depicted, it also answers the very first, the stark tree above the artist ape, whose final act was to make it the prominent image above the crypt of the bard. Moreover, the tailpiece about death culminates the succession of tailpieces, all appropriately about the end of things. The final design, like *Elegy* itself, incorporates the funerary formula *Siste, viator*; it begs the wayfarer-reader to stop and reflect upon the picture before him and the procession of illustrations that like mourners have led him to it.

The water spilling through the illustrations from the Spring seems to settle and turn to ice above the crypt; if Selima fell to a watery grave, the poet of the "Epitaph" appears buried in an icy one. The wilted, frost-bound sedge is symptomatic of the thematic fall. Bentley's scene betokens the end of the seasonal movement in his illustrations which roughly parallel those of Kent's for Thomson's *Seasons*, or Poussin's *Seasons*, or a multitude of other contemporary progressions. According to Mason, Gray himself considered a similar flow, for he originally entitled *Spring* "Noontide" and "meant to write two more, descriptive of Morning and Evening," which Mason went on to speculate were the ode on *Vicissitude* and *Elegy* (*The Poems of Mr. Gray* ii.73). Although the drawings suggest a seasonal development, Bentley reworks the pretentious and sentimentalized ideography of the received pattern in order to show that accrued presumption and self-deception are involved, just as Gray's poetry repeatedly becomes an exposure of complacency and vanity.

The massive portal of the frontispiece to *Elegy* turns into the vault of the grave, and together they suggest the inside of a church. In retrospect it seems that we have been conducted through a number of porches that have led to this final interior, each in its turn soaring over a particular ode. The design sequence acquires the temporal movement of the poems, yet articulates the same, timeless theme of the last ode. The poems under their portals have been enriched, sometimes invasively, but generally complementarily, by analogous, not duplicate, pictorial allegories. Evoking the idea of *multum in parvo*, each encapsulation reflects many ideas without confusion and shows us how small images can open into large. The vista we sense before us as we move into each picture takes us, as in a play replicated from print to print, to the same focal point. Like Selima we may be attracted by superficiality, but when we look deeply into the pictures, we discover that the alluring images are made of a truer gold than we had imagined.

Many images in the frontispiece are reversed in the tailpiece. The earth is beneath the apex of the arch in the former and above it in the latter. In the frontispiece the sun shines from the left, possibly the east, whereas in the tailpiece, from the right, or the west. The passenger in both faces right; in both he is accompanied by someone else, the countryman who points to an inscription on the grave and the clergyman who will read from the prayer-book in his hand; in both his shadow is cast upon a grave, although in the tailpiece it lies on a tomb behind him above which grows an evergreen topiary to signify life everlasting. Over three dark archways reminiscent perhaps of the Caves of Care, Melancholy, and Despair or Avernus, pall bearers and mourners march into the light. Light and life to the left contrast with darkness and death to the right; just right of center, the floor of the vault is broken, as is the step at the base of the portal in the frontispiece, which is forced apart by new life.

The crypt (the "bosom of his Father and his God") built for the poet marked by Melancholy for her own, mirrors the tailpiece of *Hymn to Adversity*, and particularly Melancholy herself. The vault and torch are a simpler realization of the idea she conveys, as though Bentley had stripped her of all ornament. Smoke from the torch underlies the image of the funeral as it did the baleful furies of the Eton ode; the two images combine into the essence of her vision. In the tailpiece for *Hymn* the large wedge made by the trunk and tombstone-like rock in which Melancholy sits is repeated in the *Elegy* tailpiece by the dead tree on the left and crag on the right. It encloses the upward pointing vault that in turn intimates the bard's "trembling hope." Even the poet in the frontispiece to *Spring* reflects the shape of the vault and prefigures the recurring motif; the smoke rising from the altar, against which the lyre bound by elegaic flowers leans, presages the smoke from the taper. The epitaphic script of the verse above the mourners looks like an outgrowth of the branches spreading to the margins like lines of print. As such, the italics extend pictographically the "bare ruined choirs where late the sweet birds sang." Indeed, the leaves of the text have fallen away from us like the secondary characteristics in Addison's summary of Locke in *Spectator* #413.

At the very base of the drawing, Bentley's faint monogram would have been the final image in the printed work to be noticed, had Grignion not omitted it from the engraving. By its placement centered beneath the title "Epitaph" printed in capitals with verses and illustration in between, Bentley may have wished the monogram to link him to the poet-speaker of *Elegy* and to signify his collaboration with Gray. Directly under the dropping point that supports not merely the vault but also the world and text above, it hangs in blank space, the void marking the final silence of the speaking picture and the beginning of wordless infinity, like the stilled pendulum of a clock or clapper of a bell.

Notes

1. Niquet, Mathieu, and Reindel were others (Hagstrum 297). Hagstrum discusses Bentley and Poussin on pages 296–297.

2. Kent may also have imitated Poussin's *Arcadian Shepherds* in his frontispiece for *Dione. A Pastoral Tragedy*, in volume 2 of Gay's *Poems on Several Occasions* (1720).

3. Compare lines 43–44 in *Elegy*. Gay's lines 61–69 enlarge upon the same theme in similar language.

4. Compare lines 62ff. in the *Elegy*.

5. In the early 1750s Bentley's growing family included three or four young daughters. His attention was undoubtedly drawn to the *Fables* because of them.

6. See Paulson, *Emblem and Expression*, 218ff.

7. The idea of the bird hovering above the initial letter might have been suggested to Bentley also by the design for the initial letter in John Sheffield's play *The Tragedy of Julius Caesar* in *The Works of John Sheffield, Earl of Mulgrave, Marquis of Normanby, and Duke of Buckingham*, 2 vols. (London: John Barber, 1723), i.213. The engraving shows the Roman eagle hovering just above and behind the horizontal bar of a huge H, and over the world.

8. This edition also includes a version of Bentley's frontispiece showing the Swain and Stranger at the grave. The gateway has been eliminated, the church in the background has been made regular (more like Stoke Poges), and a tower with a funeral cortege has been added in the left background; these changes remove the satire and restore the sentimental idea (fig. 37).

X
Conclusion

BENTLEY'S great achievement in *Designs by Mr. R. Bentley, for Six Poems by Mr. T. Gray* is twofold: first, Bentley made a coherent work with odes and illustrations on an equal footing, each answering the other synergetically; second, he united six poems by stressing a common theme. He helped to redeem the casual efforts of illustrators like Kent in his designs for Spenser's *Faerie Queene* in which the images reflect haphazardly from art to art. He improved upon the work of Hogarth and Pine, and as Tayler has affirmed, his illustrations for Gray fill a key place in the evolution that led to Blake.[1]

The essential strategy was to place each poem into an envelope of drawings, a quadripartite surrounding of frontispiece, headpiece, initial letter, and tailpiece. Each drawing, uniquely suited to the text, is joined to the other designs by a complicated development of analogical forms and recurring, significant details. Similarly, the play that develops within each group of four pictures is replicated from group to group, like six episodes in a single drama. Bentley thus intensified the meaning of each separate poem and disclosed the underlying theme of all six together, a feat which created a unified work with a larger dimension than the sum of its parts. It must be remembered that the poems were not written to be illustrated, yet the drawings based upon the verse result in a relationship that combines and heightens both media.

Gray provided Bentley with exactly the right kind of material for the interplay of text and picture. The vivid personifications and evocations of place transfer easily to the visual dimension; moreover, the subject matter of the six poems in *Designs* perfectly suited Bentley's temperament and background. Gray's verbal images portray a mortification that results from self-deception or malign fate, in such a way that the speaker or protagonist either discovers himself to be the victim of his own vanity or imagines himself to be crazed with life's cruel contradictions; Bentley's illustrations, even when irreverent or impertinent, augment the vexatious truth that is discovered in each poem. The ridicule, mockery, exposure, or scorn in his pictorial satire is of a kind that derives from Swift and Hogarth, in whose tradition he, Bentley, was nurtured and enriched. But this tradition proved unsatisfactory for *The Bard* (see Appendix I). When Gray abandoned introspective melancholy and instead represented the bard's effective challenge to adverse fate, resulting in rage, incantation, and suicide, he left Bentley no choice but to draw a conventional scene by way of illustration.

In *Designs* the images that reflect from text to picture and from picture to picture do not merely translate the verbal to the visual art, but also introduce disturbing associations and evaluative ideas. This marriage recalls Pope's characterization of wit and judgment, which "often are at strife, tho' meant each other's aid like man and wife"; the incongrous pictorial connections or allusions coerce each reader to reconcile what he sees with what he reads; it makes his engagement in the interplay of the sister arts dynamic. His pleasure in the book arises from his participation with the artist and poet in their creative process. This was especially true for Walpole, the reader Bentley had in mind, for Walpole kindled and through daunting wit sustained the ingenious innovation. Without his sponsorship and challenge, *Designs* would never have taken the shape or had the complexity it had. Yet unfortunately, the engagement of subsequent readers diminishes as they become ever farther removed from the eighteenth century and Strawberry Hill, with the details of the drawings becoming impersonal, obscure, and less pointedly pertinent or, depending on the context, impertinent.

The illustrations for Gray were not produced in a vacuum. Their format and integration reveal systematic study and thoughtful preparation. The absence of a single known drawing by Bentley done either before or after his tenure at Strawberry Hill (with the exception of one engraving for *The Bard*), as well as his correspondence with Walpole whose "Vasari-hood" is always plainly evident, confirms that the designs were a combined effort. As collector, critic, and amateur art historian, Walpole became an ideal patron, teacher, and observer of Bentley, although the extent of his coaching is difficult to gauge, because like his model Lord Burlington, whose quiet encouragement of Kent he admired, he was self-effacing. Yet however one assesses the collaboration at Strawberry Hill, the achievement in *Designs* directly depended on the far greater genius of Gray, whose stature increased as Bentley and Walpole bounded, teased, and snapped at his tender heels.

Renaissance woodcuts, emblem books, Italian, French, and Dutch illustrations, the work of Kent for Pope, Gay, Thomson, and Spenser, the illustrations of Pine for Horace, and particularly those of Gravelot and Hogarth for a large number of items, were the chief objects of the two men's scrutiny. Walpole was the first to catalogue Hogarth's satirical prints and paintings; he was primarily concerned, according to Paulson, "with Hogarth's subjects—murderesses, actors, and prison wardens—but he was undoubtedly not immune to the liveliness of expression" (*Hogarth: His Life, Art, and Times* i.194), and certainly not to satirical technique. With Walpole's help Bentley coupled Hogarth's strategy to the flowing line and airy shapes of European rococo ornament.

He not only studied Walpole's vast collections of illustrated books, elephant folios of polite art, and pictorial satires by Hogarth and his circle, but also examined hundreds of political prints, from which he discovered methods of visual caricature and strategies of ironic imitation; his four literary satires published from 1750–1751, including *The Centaur*, attest to his attraction to political ridicule from the start of his association with Walpole. If this contemporary work helped to stock his arsenal, he did not use it so much to subvert Gray's poetry, as Blake would do on occasion, but to meet it with a counterpoised, pictorial development that visualizes the thoughts and circumstances of Gray's protagonists, yet undercuts them by revealing either their vanity, complacency, arrogance, or sentimentality. The illustrations are meant to evoke the atmosphere of the odes and expose, as do the odes themselves, the painful humiliation of their protagonists.

In the preface to *Angel of Apocalpyse: Blake's Idea of Milton*, Joseph Wittreich forewarns his readers that the understanding of an artwork "depends upon the determination of its contexts," and he quotes Earl Wasserman's observation that interpretive disagreements result from differences over "what the relevant context is, over whether we have the right framework for putting the work together organically" (xiii). The necessary exegetical environment for the illustrations is to be found at Strawberry Hill, the nursery of Bentley's genius.

The engraved-like appearance of the drawings belies their ultimate effect. Compared with the smooth lines of Müller and Grignion, they are not rigidly precise but have an unfinished yet much more lively quality about them. Indeed, Bentley's purpose was to burlesque the pretty rococo engravings generally produced and to counter the public's sentimental reaction to them. Walpole expressed to Gray contempt for people who thought the drawings looked like engravings: they "have not eyes—such are almost all who have seen Mr Bentley's drawings, and think to compliment him by mistaking them for prints" (*Corr.* 14.65). To Bedingfield, Gray wrote that the engravings convey some idea of Bentley's "taste & invention" but nothing "of his spirit or execution" (Toynbee and Whibley #222). And Mason remarked, as noted in Chapter I, that "the original drawings . . . are so infinitely superior to the published engravings of them, that a person, who has only seen the latter, can by no means judge of the excellencies of the former." Yet he added, anticipating the criticism of people like art historian C. F. Bell, that the "grotesque fancy in the Designs," even when muted in the engravings, was the reason for their failure "to please universally" (*The Poems of Mr. Gray* i.226). The witty and complex interplay of text and design proved not to be for the general public.

When Bell dismissed the Bentley-Gray volume as "a barbaric, amateurish curiosity" in comparison with the elegant publications in contemporary France,[2] he failed to see that Bentley's objective was less to produce elegant decoration than to parody the polished surfaces of Watteau and Berain, whose work he was capable of imitating had he wished to do so, as is clear from the frontispiece to *A Long Story*. Just as Hogarth had complemented Gay's *Beggar's Opera* with a picture that by a parody of elegance ridiculed the hypocrisy of polite society (Walpole owned Hogarth's first sketch in oil and the large engraving), so Bentley pitched against Gray's artifice, which consisted of ironic echoes of Virgil and Milton, a complex pictorial analogue whose images, though suggested by the verse, also embodied ironic reflections of standard works of art. Bell misunderstood the distinctive craft in this interplay of picture and poem; he did not perceive that the unpleasant distortion in the "pastoral" frontispiece for the Eton ode is necessary for the exposure of the narrator's sentimentality and classical affectation, or that the effect of the frontispiece for *Elegy* relies in part on a parody of Poussin and Gravelot.

The distress one hears in Gray's voice in the six poems (or more properly in the voices he invented for them) becomes a harbinger of change that we see in *The Bard*, a change of direction that the artist could not follow. The vexation and mortification of each speaker, including the sprightly humorous, mock-serious tone and "tritical" moralism in *Favourite Cat* and *A Long Story*, scarcely hide a deeper terror or desperation that wants to cry and roar all night, to scream out against malignant fate, or even to shake a fist (or lyre) at the philosophical resignation and evaluative, stoic-like detachment to which Gray feels he must submit. But because in Gray this classical restraint is uneasy and artificial, it tends to blunt sensibilities, which is exactly what Blake wanted to correct. Bentley's snake-haired furies, on the other hand, do not record a longing for catharsis so much as show the self-defeating consequence of melancholic madness. The emphasis in the designs is not the malignancy of Fate, but rather the sentimental effusion, affectation, and self-deception, the lie on the lyre in point of fact, that makes a fate malignant. Bentley goes straight to the truth.

The poet took melancholy more to heart than the artist. For Bentley and Walpole at this time, melancholy was a fashionable posture with theatrical potential that could be beautifully exploited in poetry, in revived gothic architecture and sham ruins, and ultimately in the illustrations for Gray. Because Walpole and Bentley found this kind of self-conscious dramatization stimulating, they provided themselves with stage props and a language of wit to express it. Gray's melancholy by contrast had the immediacy of real mortification and a sense of loss, although it must be admitted, as Bentley hints in his illustrations, the poet indulged in these emotions with satisfaction.

Whether in a humorous or serious vein, the images of melancholy and death convey the mood of the anthology. They draw the illustrations together from the Orphean bard of the fleuron to the smoking taper of the last tailpiece. The definitive representation of Melancholy that transforms the Misery of the emblem books into a statuesque beauty at the end of *Hymn*, and whose benignant form seems to quell a gorgon heart, so transported Gray that Walpole and Bentley recoiled. The unwholesome pleasure they detected in Gray's obsession with melancholy had been suggested by Bentley in the thwarted love-theme threaded throughout the illustrations; Melancholy's implied sexuality becomes manifest with reference to the analogue of Pine's Lydia and then later to her visualization in the *Prospect of Vapourland*. The figure at the bottom of *Hymn* is invented by Bentley as a synthesis of Wisdom and Melancholy, but because she does not attend Adversity's "solemn steps" as in the ode, she also recalls Pope's Eloisa. She thereby joins love to death and embodies a morbid self-pity combined with hope of eventual fulfillment that follows thwarted love. Bentley's image interprets rather than represents the idea of *Hymn*; the portrait demands of the viewer the construction of an appropriate exegetical framework.

Bentley and Walpole prompt us to see that, in a properly illustrated book, Locke's secondary characteristics should undergo an expansion. If the title page fleuron with monkey, leafless tree, and barren Parnassian hills represents the landscape robbed of its secondary characteristics (to return to Addison's language in *Spectator* #413), then the bard under the flourishing laurel of art in the fleuron, and the imagery in all the subsequent drawings, not only restore to the world its sensuous beauty but also give it a super-added garment, the tertiary characteristics of verbal signs. We no longer rejoice like the "enchanted hero of romance" with the restoration of color, sound, and smell (as Addison describes), but feel like the melancholic poet himself whose visions, the creatures of his mind, have received in Bentley's hands allegorical embodiment. More than a woman, Melancholy becomes an image of latent madness; her appearance is benign, yet she conveys malignity. If she has the beauty of Wisdom, she also recalls Ripa's and Dürer's impotent angels, or Pine's Lydia who is tormented by the discovery of lost opportunities. She seems to gather round her the furies depicted in the foregoing illustrations. The tree stumps and stones that surround her subtly anticipate the explicit symbols of *Vapourland*.

In the frontispiece to *Spring*, the figures like the "constant *Vapour* o'er the Palace" of Spleen enclose the melancholic bard under the beech tree. Emanating from his mind, the cloud of images first captured by Bentley in the arched fretwork above the bard were then reticulated in each successive drawing. Each catches anew elements of the essential melancholy and reshapes them; each in effect demystifies the rising phantoms and finally lays them to rest in the crypt of the last page.

The repeated sequence of four drawings in all six poems is, as I have said, like episodes of a drama with novel settings and similar characters in different costumes. The sequence begins with dramatic irony, where the theme in one way or another is the protagonist's (or reader's) self-deception, and ends with irony of situation, where the discovery and consequence of self-deception is shown. Because he creates fictions, the poet is a liar by profession; Bentley fulfills the purpose of irony by making emphatic that Gray's protagonists who indulge in fictions must be rebuked by a harsher expression of truth. The poet musing on the spring turns out to be "the youth to fortune and to fame unknown" of the "Epitaph" in *Elegy*, whose death is repeatedly anticipated from drawing to drawing, particularly in the tailpieces: in *Spring* by his absence from the arcadian landscape and by the distant bell tower; in *Favourite Cat* by Selima who finds herself on the Styx having to deal with Cerberus; in *Eton* by the threat of doom in a paradise that has degenerated into a scene of bullying on another Stygian river; in *A Long Story* by the bust of the poet in the broken pediment above Tisiphones; in *Hymn* by the transformation of Adversity and Virtue into Melancholy and a *lapis andromorphites*; and in *Elegy* by the crypt over which the shadow of a "kindred Spirit" has lain.

Bentley and Walpole recognized that Gray was haunted by his own images. The elegance of an idea, such as Melancholy, could so take possession of the poet that reality became circumscribed by it. He became mesmerized by the coherence he created in a poem, whose symbol, such as Melancholy, explained the world with paradigmatic power. Bentley's perception of this entrapment is demonstrated in all the designs, most clearly in the frontispiece for *Elegy*. Leading us through the portal, Bentley reminds us of the symmetry of Poussin's theme. Then by the witty coincidence of Kent's and Gravelot's analogues, the impertinence of visual puns, and the absurd, jumbled architecture of the distant steeple, not to mention the gate itself, he deconstructs the scene and frees us from its fascinating power. Like Orpheus perhaps, we peer back through the gate to see the Poussin-inspired image dissolve. It seems as though Bentley has dismembered his own work in order to dispossess us of its sentimental suggestion, yet then he sends us, like Hercules, to redeem it—or better, prompts us, like Aesculapius, to rebuild the whole again. In this way Bentley provides us with a firmer grasp on the idea than we had before, as well as an understanding of its composition. The picture recovers new integrity in a different, richer, more painful theme of evaluation. The process may separate us from the image, but it informs, or rather reforms, us by its reconstruction. We are left with the conclusion reached by Gray's narrator in *Ode on the Spring* that he must confront the reality of his own self-deception where he saw himself a self-enamored fool, like a puppet in borrowed grandeur.

The architecture of the drawings is important. The necessity of structure, yet the necessity to escape it, is a key paradox in Bentley's conception. Frames or portals in frontispieces literally enclose scenes but simultaneously open unexpected vistas to the mind, especially as they lead in and out of the odes. The progression of ideas acquires a discursive feel. If each design brims with the peril of sentimentality like a chinoiserie bowl, it also offers the necessary revelation, involving a judgment of its own content, so that we can step back, the wiser, from a slippery verge. Each set of four illustrations reworks the preceding set like multiple doorways that produce for us an ever sharper irony to deepen our depth of field.

Bentley set out to please Walpole by building a complex structure of analogues for his illustrations. He suited his patron's wit with its mixture of humor, raillery, and even unkindness, often at the expense of Gray, their mutual friend. Disquieting details and superimposed viewpoints are joined together by the architecture of the book, as a gothic revival house unites its ornate chambers. This is the "design" of *Designs* and may explain the importance of Dodsley's change of the half-title from *Drawings, &c.* to *Designs, &c.* The size, shape, and arrangement of verse and drawing, with print on only one side of the page as if it were a component of the graphical dimension, gives an unexpected formal coherence to the whole, just as the entry hall at Strawberry Hill fused into a single conception a diversity of ornamental detail in the staircase, lantern, and armory. The house has an intentional, literary dimension: it was built for the mind. The book is more than an anthology of illustrated poems: it is, of its kind, a work of art.

Notes

1. *Blake's Illustrations to . . . Gray;* "Two Eighteenth-Century Illustrators"; "Bentley Bid the Pencil."

2. C. F. Bell, "Thomas Gray and the Fine Arts," *Essays and Studies by Members of the English Association*, xxx (1945), 80.

Appendix I: Designs for *The Bard*

ORIGINALLY, Gray wanted to finish *The Progress of Poesy* for inclusion in *Designs (Corr.* 14.60), but since this proved impossible, Walpole later decided to publish separately at his own Strawberry Hill Press two Pindaric odes with illustrations by Bentley. No drawings survive for *The Progress of Poesy*, if indeed they were ever made; however, three preliminary sketches and a final draft (figs. 39 to 42) do exist for *The Bard*, as well as an engraving (fig. 43) of a later drawing, now lost, that Bentley made in the mid-1760s after he had left Strawberry Hill. The draft shown in figure 42, which was completed under Walpole's roof in early 1757 yet never engraved, is surprisingly flat when compared with the illustrations for *Designs*. It fails for two related reasons, a lack of focus and unconvincing drama.

The central feature of the illustration is the invading army into Wales, with King Edward I at its head. But heavy emphasis is placed on a group of knights on high ground to the right; the predominance of this group is distracting and hard to explain since it has little bearing on the action. On the left the bard himself, standing on a ledge, is only lightly sketched. The sheer face of the cliff behind him should have emphasized his opposition to the king, but it does not convey his soaring emotion, his challenge to the invader, or his revenge against the world that has betrayed him; moreover, it does not show a downward movement that might have suggested his suicide. Below the poorly integrated landscape, the cataract appears less threatening and symbolic than one ought to expect from the eloquent description of it in stanza 2. In "*The Bard* of Thomas Gray, its Composition and its Use by Painters," F. I. McCarthy maintains that Bentley had never seen "the steep of Snowdon's shaggy side" and that the background of his picture was "manufactured . . . from the verbal suggestions of the poem."[1] In *The Figure in the Landscape*, John Dixon Hunt argues that Bentley's sense of scale is at fault and fails to capture the hero's vision and passionate intensity (146). The design does not communicate the spirit of the ode as we read it today.

Walpole's disappointment must have been great. He had written to the artist in Jersey, "Nothing but you or Salvator Rosa, and Nicolò Poussin, can paint up the expressive horror and dignity" of *The Bard* (18 Sept. 1755, *Corr.* 35.252), perhaps having in mind Rosa's *Morte di Empedocle Nella Voragine*, a painting he may have seen at the Pitti Palace in Florence in 1740–1741. Some of Bentley's landscapes generally influenced by Rosa and Poussin evoke an appropriate medievalism as, for example, in the Jersey scene showing Bentley himself in exile, in the attitude of Melancholy, about to be comforted by his wife and daughter (fig. 58), and in his brown wash drawing of a forest gorge and vaulted bridge (fig. 56). Clearly these pictures, many of which Bentley sent to Twickenham from Jersey, confirmed Walpole's enthusiasm, not to mention the earlier illustrations for the six odes that had so beautifully conveyed the expressive horror and gothic dignity of Gray's pervasive melancholy.

It seems as though the artist did not know how to respond to the stronger fare of Gray's new poem with its different kind of irony and cataclysmic setting or how to illustrate a violence of emotion when no Hogarthian dimension was called for. The poet-hero's pretension was of a different kind; he did not voice false sentiments in need of exposure; neither he nor King Edward required the satirical treatment Bentley had used so skillfully in the designs for the six odes, where his deceptively peaceful landscapes subtly but powerfully reflect quiescent submission to fate and where black melancholy borders on madness. Although the final draft for *The Bard* may share something of the horror and gothic gloom implicit in the designs for the earlier poems, it fails to dramatize the straightforwards anger of its protagonist or the energy of his incantation. Painful, purgative self-discovery is not the theme of *The Bard*; rather the spell the hero weaves has transformative power, and his suicide serves an avowed, redemptive purpose.

Whereas Bentley's draft remains mechanical, the three preliminary sketches (figs. 39 to 41)[2] are better; they are more fluid and provocative. They capture particular theatrical moments, show a superior sense of scale, and even suggest that the subject matter could be better treated in oils or washes than in the severe line of an engraving. They anticipate the different aesthetics of Benjamin West, Philip James de Loutherbourg, Thomas Jones, Henry Fuseli, William Blake, and John Martin, whose pictures of the Bard's rebellion succeed in fusing emotional strains into a single image expressive of the hero's predicament and challenge. All four drawings, however, reveal Bentley's skill in draftsmanship.

His portrait of the bard was undoubtedly influenced by Raphael's *Vision of Ezekial* and Parmigianino's *Moses*, as Hagstrum has speculated in *The Sister Arts*, two pictures that also influenced the poem.[3] But Bentley's figure with hair streaming "like a meteor to the troubled air" in the final draft is unlikely to evoke meteorological phenomena or recall Milton's image of rebellious Satan. This bard is not "robed in the sable garb of woe"; he is too small to be seen as haggard or frantic; and the careful balance struck between him and King Edward prevents the desolate and defiant prophet from standing out. Because our eye is not drawn immediately to the bard, we remain unconvinced that he would cause Gloucester to stand "aghast in speechless trance" or prompt Mortimer to cry "To arms!"—especially as the interminably long file of soldiers in the background winding over distant hills absorbs the energy of the landscape.

The spirits of the dead hovering above the hero hardly appear to be "avengers of their native land" about to weave with bloody fingers the tissue of Edward's line. Their shadows, incongruously graceful, recall the zephyrs in the headpiece to *Spring* and are in fact lifted straight from Kent's frontispiece to Thompson's *Seasons* (fig. 101), an unsuitable model for Gray's ode.[4] Bentley's failure to represent the details of the poem accurately or to use appropriate, pictorial analogues suggests either lack of interest or understanding.

There is, however, another possible reason for this failure: his interpretation of *The Bard* may have differed fundamentally from our post-Romantic reading of the ode. Gray's use of Miltonic imagery hints at an association between the bard and Satan; Bentley may not have shared our sympathy for the protagonist, for neither he nor Gray could have read or agreed that Milton was "of the Devil's party without knowing it," as Blake said in the *Marriage of Heaven and Hell* (1790). Indeed, had Gray intended the portrait of the hero to evoke an ambivalent response, then the same must surely apply to King Edward I, who might be seen not only as a cruel tyrant for whom the curse of the bards must come true but also as a leader who subdued the rebellious, satanic Welsh, practitioners of black magic, a conquest that ultimately led to a consolidation of the kingdom. This ambivalence over prophet and king might explain Bentley's balanced, antiheroic treatment of the theme. His artistic and intellectual sympathies were not Romantic; uninspired by Gray's Pindarics, he would have concurred with Walpole's and Montagu's derision of Gray (and Mason his imitator) as a man who "will cry and roar all night without the least provocation" (*Corr.* 9.238–239).

Gray expresses no opinion whatever on the sketches. His only mention of them in print is contained in his letter to Edward Bedingfield of 27 August 1756 (Toynbee and Whibley #222), in which he says only that he knows of them. There was probably no collaboration between poet and artist, another reason for failure. Walpole's dissatisfaction with the drawings is proved by his never having sent any of them to an engraver; between 16 July and 8 August 1757, he printed the odes at Strawberry Hill without illustrations.

When James Dodsley later reprinted *The Bard* in his fifth edition of *Designs* of 1766, which he expanded to include the two Pindaric odes, he must have asked Bentley for the tailpiece shown in figure 43, although no evidence of their transaction has come to light. The design succeeds where the others fail; it shows an engagement on Bentley's part which it seems he lacked for the earlier illustration. Grasping his harp, the bard raises his right arm in defiance as he leaps from a black and clearly defined promontory to his death in a roaring cataract. The picture was re-engraved and reprinted for the dramatic frontispiece in Sleater's edition of Gray's *Poems* in 1768 (fig. 44). It also inspired de Loutherbourg's design of ca. 1780–1784 (fig. 45).[5]

Notes

1. F. I. McCarthy, "*The Bard* of Thomas Gray, its Composition and its Use by Painters," in *National Library of Wales Journal*, vol. xiv, no. 1 (Summer 1965), 109.

2. Figures 40 and 41 are part of the collection at the Lewis Walpole Library, and figure 39 is at Harvard (Amy Lowell Collection). F. I. McCarthy suggested that the third figure mentioned in a note on one of the drawings was used for the tailpiece published in 1766 (fig. 43); this was a mistake for he did not know of the sketch at Harvard. The engraved print, published five years after Bentley had left Strawberry Hill, is completely different from the studies drawn for Walpole.

3. See Gray's letter to Edward Bedingfield in Toynbee and Whibley, #222, and Mason, *The Poems of Mr. Gray*, ii.91. Unfortunately, in *The Sister Arts* (308ff.), Hagstrum confused Philip de Loutherbourg's design (fig. 45) with Bentley's; he argues that the characters in this drawing (in fact by de Loutherbourg) are cramped and that King Edward's troops lack impressiveness. The fault is the reverse of Bentley's, a matter for which he, Bentley, compensated in his later illustration for Dodsley published in 1766.

4. A similar, incongruous effect occurs in Bentley's Jersey landscape that shows himself as Melancholy (fig. 58). On the ridge above the naked man, a tiny figure struts; perhaps he is wearing the garb of the satirist impertinently bemused by the theatricality of the scene below him.

5. F. I. McCarthy gives it this range of dates, arguing that its picturesque style, "both in landscape and in figure, . . . could not belong to a period in English art much before 1780" because "its dominant feeling is French" (109). It was first published in *Musical and Poetical Relicks of the Welsh Bards* (1784).

Appendix II: Identification of Engravers

Identification of engravers, either Johann Sebastian Müller or Charles Grignion, for *Designs by Mr. R. Bentley, for Six Poems by Mr. T. Gray.*

Title page fleuron, Müller
Ode on the Spring
frontispiece, Müller
headpiece and initial letter, Müller
tailpiece, Müller
Ode on the Death of a Favourite Cat
frontispiece, Grignion
headpiece and initial letter, Grignion
tailpiece, Grignion
Ode on a Distant Prospect of Eton College
frontispiece, Müller
headpiece and initial letter, Grignion
tailpiece, Grignion
A Long Story
frontispiece, Müller
headpiece and initial letter, Grignion
tailpiece, Grignion
Hymn to Adversity
frontispiece, Grignion
headpiece and initial letter, Müller
tailpiece, Grignion
Elegy Written in a Country Church-Yard
frontispiece, Grignion
headpiece and initial letter, Grignion
tailpiece, Grignion

Müller engraved 9 illustrations, including 1 fleuron, 3 frontispieces, 2 headpieces, 2 initial letters, and 1 tailpiece.

Grignion engraved 16 illustrations, including 3 frontispieces, 4 headpieces, 4 initial letters, and 5 tailpieces.

Given that Müller engraved the discarded frontispiece portrait of Gray, it would appear that the work was divided more or less evenly between the two men.

Appendix III: Illustrations

Unless otherwise noted, the designs are by Richard Bentley.

1. Drawing for title page fleuron
2. Drawing for the frontispiece, *Ode on the Spring*
3. Drawing for headpiece, *Ode on the Spring*
4. Drawing for initial letter, *Ode on the Spring*
5. Drawing for tailpiece, *Ode on the Spring*
6. Drawing for frontispiece, *Ode on the Death of a Favourite Cat*
7. Drawing of Chinese pagodas in a letter to Walpole, ca. 1752
8. Drawing for headpiece, *Ode on the Death of a Favourite Cat*
9. Drawing for initial letter, *Ode on the Death of a Favourite Cat*
10. Drawing for tailpiece, *Ode on the Death of a Favourite Cat*
11. Drawing for frontispiece, *Ode on a Distant Prospect of Eton College*
12. Drawing for headpiece, *Ode on a Distant Prospect of Eton College*
13. Draft for headpiece, *Ode on a Distant Prospect of Eton College*
14. Drawing for initial letter, *Ode on a Distant Prospect of Eton College*
15. Drawing for tailpiece, *Ode on a Distant Prospect of Eton College*
16. Drawing for frontispiece, *A Long Story*
17. Gray's sketch of Stoke Manor House
18. Drawing for headpiece, *A Long Story*
19. Drawing for initial letter, *A Long Story*
20. Drawing for tailpiece, *A Long Story*
21. Sketch of heads for tailpiece, *A Long Story*
22. Two drafts for tailpiece, *A Long Story*
23. Draft for tailpiece, *A Long Story*
24. Drawing for frontispiece, *Hymn to Adversity*
25. Frontispiece for *Hymn to Adversity* reproduced in *The London Magazine*, July 1753, xxii.332–333
26. Drawing for headpiece, *Hymn to Adversity*
27. Drawing for initial letter, *Hymn to Adversity*
28. Proof of Grignion's engraving for tailpiece, *Hymn to Adversity*
29. Drawing for tailpiece, *Hymn to Adversity*
30. Draft for tailpiece, *Hymn to Adversity*
31. Drawing for frontispiece, *Elegy Written in a Country Church-Yard*
32. Drawing for headpiece, *Elegy Written in a Country Church-Yard*

33. Drawing for initial letter, *Elegy Written in a Country Church-Yard*
34. Drawing for tailpiece, *Elegy Written in a Country Church-Yard*
35. Proofs of early drafts for tailpiece, *Elegy Written in a Country Church-Yard*
36. Proofs and engraving for tailpiece, *Elegy Written in a Country Church-Yard*
37. An engraving taken from Bentley's frontispiece for the *Elegy Written in a Country Church-Yard*, published in *Poems by Mr. Gray*, Dublin: William Sleater, 1768
38. An engraving taken from one of Bentley's drafts for the tailpiece, *Elegy Written in a Country Church-Yard*, published in *Poems by Mr. Gray*, Dublin: William Sleater, 1768. Compare figure 35.
39. A study for *The Bard*
40. A study for *The Bard*
41. A study of the ghosts for *The Bard*
42. The final draft for *The Bard*, completed at Strawberry Hill, 1757
43. Engraved tailpiece for *The Bard*, published by James Dodsley in *Designs...*, 5th edition (1766)
44. Re-engraving of figure 43 for *Poems by Mr. Gray*, Dublin: William Sleater, 1768
45. Design by Philip James de Loutherbourg for *The Bard*
46. Frontispiece and title page for *True and Faithful Account of the... Centaur*
47. Drawing for frontispiece, *Memoirs of King George II*
48. Drawings for headpiece and initial letter, *Memoirs of King George II*
49. Drawing for tailpiece, Book I, *Memoirs of King George II*
50. Drawing for tailpiece, Book II, *Memoirs of King George II*. Oval portrait of Archibald Campbell, 3rd Duke of Argyll, by Johann Heinrich Müntz
51. Drawing for tailpiece, Book III, *Memoirs of King George II*. Oval portrait of Henry Pelham by Johann Heinrich Müntz
52. Drawing for allegorical surround for headpiece of Henry Fox, Book V, *Memoirs of King George II*
53. Drawing for tailpiece, Book V, *Memoirs of King George II*. Oval portrait of William Pitt the elder by Johann Heinrich Müntz
54. Drawing for headpiece and initial letter, *The Judgment of Solomon*
55. Drawing for tailpiece, *The Judgment of Solomon*
56. Drawing of a vaulted bridge
57. Watercolor of a muzzled bear-like ape standing before Bentley's monogram
58. Scene in Jersey
59. Watercolor of the "Cave of Care" (Bentley's title) for Spenser's *Faerie Queene*, Book IV, canto v, stanzas 32–46
60. *The Temptation of St. Antony*
61. Watercolor, *Turkish Bath*
62. *A Prospect of Vapourland*

63. Watercolor drawing of the hall and staircase at Strawberry Hill
64. Drawing of a "view of the vestibule, with the armoury, going into the Library at Strawberry Hill, R. B. f. 1753"
65. Designs for calling cards for Lady Northumberland and Lady Ailesbury
66. Title page, vol. ii, Holinshed's *Chronicles* (1586), artist unknown
67. Frontispiece design by William Kent for Isaac Ware's *Four Books of Andrea Palladio's Architecture*... (1738), Peter Fourdrinier, *sculp.*
68. Antoine Watteau, *La Pèllerine Altérée*, Jacques-Gabriel Huquier, *sculp.*
69. Trade card for Mary Hooker
70. Trade card for Richard Lyford
71. Trade card for Edward Ashworth
72. Trade card for Benjamin Whitton
73. Pier Ghezzi, headpiece and initial letter for Tasso's *Della Gerusalemme Liberata* (1735), Francesco F. Aquila, *sculp.*
74. Giorgione, *The Three Philosophers*
75. Battista Dossi, *Flight into Egypt*
76. Jacques Callot, *Temptation of St. Anthony* (1635), engraving
77. Nicholas Poussin, *The Arcadian Shepherds*
78. Cesare Ripa, "Malinconia," *Nova Iconologia*, Part II (1624)
79. Giovanni Pietro Bellori, "Muta Poesis," *Le vite de' pittori, scultori et architetti moderni* (1692)
80. Louis Cheron, frontispiece for *The Works of Tibullus, Containing his four Books of Love-Elegies* (tr. John Dart, 1720), Gerard Vandergucht, *sculp.*
81. Salvator Rosa, etching of a seated woman
82. William Kent, illustration of Despair for Book I of *The Faerie Queene*
83. Albrecht Dürer, *Melencolia I*
84. Albrecht Dürer, *Penance of St. John Chrysostom*
85. Albrecht Dürer, *Joachim and Anna at the Golden Gate*
86. Albrecht Dürer, *Death of Orpheus*
87. Albrecht Dürer, *Der Hercules*
88. Albrecht Dürer, *Four Horsemen of the Apocalypse*
89. Hans Holbein the Younger, *The Dance of Death*, "Genesis III"
90. George Wither, *The Choice of Hercules*
91. George Wither, *Confined Magistrates*
92. P. Agustino Chesneav, *Orpheus Eucharisticus* (Paris, 1657)
93. Louis Cheron, headpiece for Prior's *Poems on Several Occasions* (1718), Nicholas-Dauphin de Beauvais, *sculp.*
94. Louis Cheron, headpiece and initial letter for prior's *Alma, or the Progress of the Mind*, in *Poems on Several Occasions* (1718), Nicholas-Dauphin de Beauvais, *sculp.*
95. Louis Cheron, tailpiece for Prior's *Alma, or the Progress of the Mind*, in *Poems on Several Occasions* (1718), Nicholas-Dauphin de Beauvais, *sculp.*

96. Frontispiece for Swift's *Battle of the Books* (1710), studio of Bernard Lens and John Sturt
97. Bernard Picart, *Monument Consacré à la Postérité en Mémoire de la Folie Incroyable XX. Année du XVIII. Siècle.*
98. Simon Gribelin, two tailpieces for Pope, *Works* (1717)
99. Anton Domenico Gabbiani, "Francesco Redi Crowned by the Muses," Redi, *Sonnetti* (Florence, 1702)
100. Frontispiece for Bolingbroke's *A Dissertation upon Parties*, artist unknown
101. William Kent, frontispiece for Thomson's *The Seasons* (1730), Nicolas-Henri Tardieu, *sculp.*
102. William Kent, frontispiece for "Summer," *The Seasons* (1730), Nicolas-Henri Tardieu, *sculp.*
103. William Kent, frontispiece for "Autumn," *The Seasons* (1730), Nicolas-Henri Tardieu, *sculp.*
104. William Kent, frontispiece for "Winter," *The Seasons* (1730), Nicolas-Henri Tardieu, *sculp.*
105. William Kent, headpiece for the "Introduction" to Gay's *Fables* (1727), Peter Fourdrinier, *sculp.*
106. John Wootton, headpiece for Fable XX, Gay's *Fables* (1727), Peter Fourdrinier, *sculp.*
107. William Kent, headpiece for Fable XXXIX, Gay's *Fables* (1727), Peter Fourdrinier, *sculp.*
108. William Kent, headpiece for Fable XLVII, Gay's *Fables* (1727), Bernard Baron, *sculp.*
109. William Kent, headpiece for Fable XLIX, Gay's *Fables* (1727), Benjamin de la Motte, *sculp.*
110. John Wootton, headpiece for Fable L, Gay's *Fables* (1727), Peter Fourdrinier, *sculp.*
111. Herbert-François Gravelot, frontispiece for Fable VII, Gay's *Fables* (1738), Gerard Scotin, *sculp.*
112. Herbert-François Gravelot, frontispiece for Fable XVI, Gay's *Fables* (1738), Gerard Scotin, *sculp.*
113. John Pine, headpiece, initial letter, and tailpiece for Horace, *Odes* I.ix (1733)
114. John Pine, headpiece, initial letter, and tailpiece for Horace, *Odes* I.xxv (1733)
115. John Pine, headpiece, initial letter, and tailpiece for Horace, *Odes* II.xiv (1733)
116. John Pine, headpiece and initial letter for Horace, *Odes* I.xxxv (1733)
117. William Hogarth, *Marriage à la Mode*, plate II
118. William Hogarth, *Marriage à la Mode*, plate V

1. Richard Bentley, drawing for title page fleuron. (Courtesy of The Lewis Walpole Library, Yale University.)

2. Richard Bentley, drawing for frontispiece, *Ode on the Spring*. (Courtesy of The Lewis Walpole Library, Yale University.)

3. Richard Bentley, drawing for headpiece, *Ode on the Spring.* (Courtesy of The Lewis Walpole Library, Yale University.)

4. Richard Bentley, drawing for initial letter, *Ode on the Spring*. (Courtesy of The Lewis Walpole Library, Yale University.)

5. Richard Bentley, drawing for tailpiece, *Ode on the Spring.* (Courtesy of The Lewis Walpole Library, Yale University.)

6. Richard Bentley, drawing for frontispiece, *Ode on the Death of a Favourite Cat.* (Courtesy of The Lewis Walpole Library, Yale University.)

7. Richard Bentley, drawing of Chinese pagodas in a letter to Walpole, ca. 1752. (By permission of the British Museum.)

8. Richard Bentley, drawing for headpiece, *Ode on the Death of a Favourite Cat.* (Courtesy of The Lewis Walpole Library, Yale University.)

9. Richard Bentley, drawing for initial letter, *Ode on the Death of a Favourite Cat.* (Courtesy of The Lewis Walpole Library, Yale University.)

10. Richard Bentley, drawing for tailpiece, *Ode on the Death of a Favourite Cat.* (Courtesy of The Lewis Walpole Library, Yale University.)

11. Richard Bentley, drawing for frontispiece, *Ode on a Distant Prospect of Eton College.* (Courtesy of The Lewis Walpole Library, Yale University.)

12. Richard Bentley, drawing for headpiece, *Ode on a Distant Prospect of Eton College.* (Courtesy of The Lewis Walpole Library, Yale University.)

13. Richard Bentley, draft for headpiece, *Ode on a Distant Prospect of Eton College.* (Courtesy of The Lewis Walpole Library, Yale University.)

14. Richard Bentley, drawing for initial letter, *Ode on a Distant Prospect of Eton College.* (Courtesy of The Lewis Walpole Library, Yale University.)

15. Richard Bentley, drawing for tailpiece, *Ode on a Distant Prospect of Eton College.* (Courtesy of The Lewis Walpole Library, Yale University.)

16. Richard Bentley, drawing for frontispiece, *A Long Story*. (Courtesy of The Lewis Walpole Library, Yale University.)

17. Thomas Gray, sketch of Stoke Manor House. (Courtesy of The Lewis Walpole Library, Yale University.)

18. Richard Bentley, drawing for headpiece, *A Long Story.* (Courtesy of The Lewis Walpole Library, Yale University.)

19. Richard Bentley, drawing for initial letter, *A Long Story.* (Courtesy of The Lewis Walpole Library, Yale University.)

20. Richard Bentley, drawing for tailpiece, *A Long Story.* (Courtesy of The Lewis Walpole Library, Yale University.)

21. Richard Bentley, sketch of heads for tailpiece, *A Long Story*. (Courtesy of The Lewis Walpole Library, Yale University.)

a

b

22. Richard Bentley, two drafts for tailpiece, *A Long Story.* (Courtesy of The Lewis Walpole Library, Yale University.)

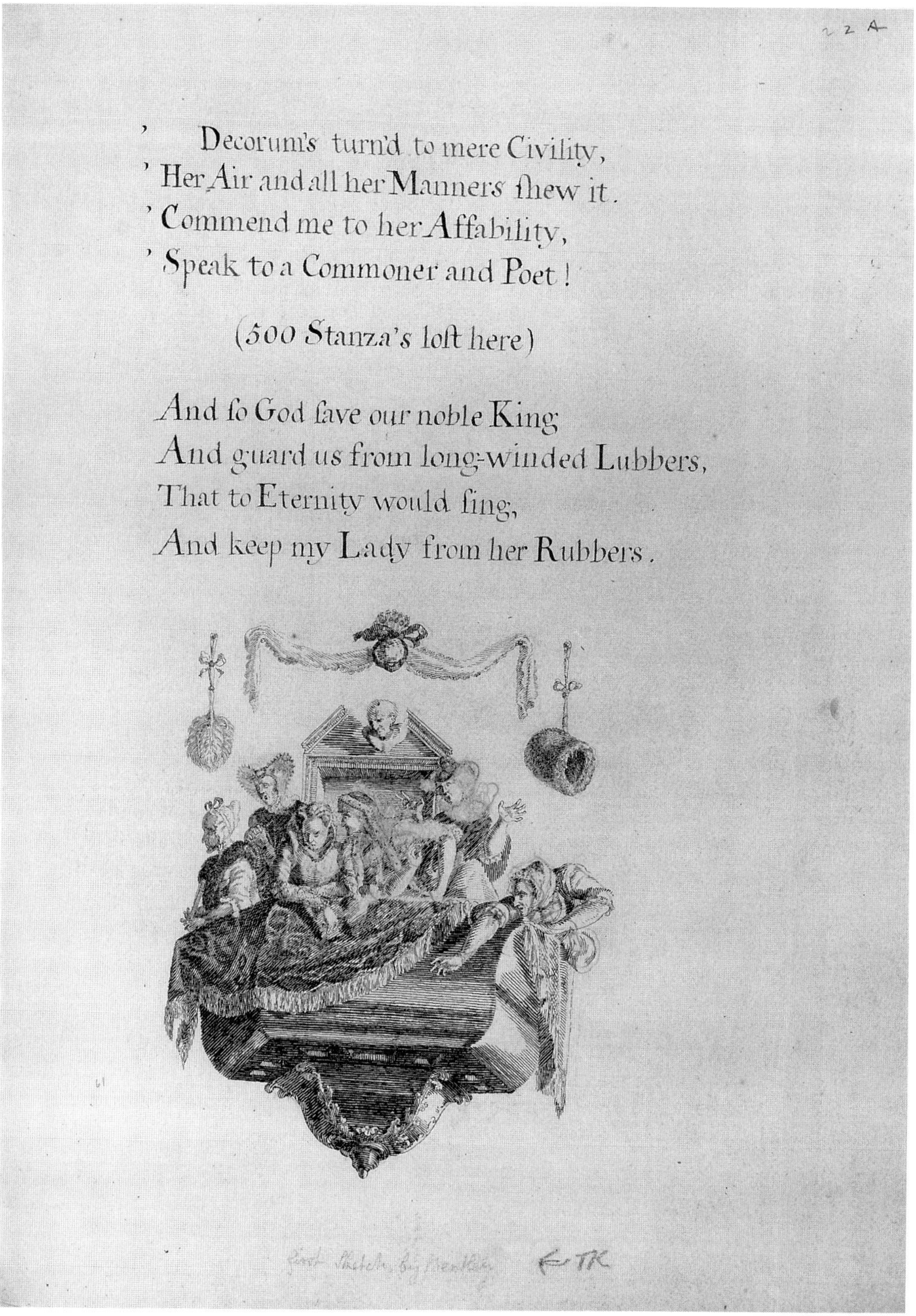
' Decorum's turn'd to mere Civility,
' Her Air and all her Manners ſhew it.
' Commend me to her Affability,
' Speak to a Commoner and Poet!

(500 Stanza's loſt here)

And ſo God ſave our noble King
And guard us from long-winded Lubbers,
That to Eternity would ſing,
And keep my Lady from her Rubbers.

23. Richard Bentley, draft for tailpiece, *A Long Story*. (Courtesy of The Lewis Walpole Library, Yale University.)

24. Richard Bentley, drawing for frontispiece, *Hymn to Adversity.* (Courtesy of The Lewis Walpole Library, Yale University.)

25. Frontispiece for *Hymn to Adversity* reproduced in *The London Magazine*, July 1753, xxii.333. (Courtesy of the Print Collection, Lewis Walpole Library, Yale University.)

26. Richard Bentley, drawing for headpiece, *Hymn to Adversity.* (Courtesy of The Lewis Walpole Library, Yale University.)

27. Richard Bentley, drawing for initial letter, *Hymn to Adversity.* (Courtesy of The Lewis Walpole Library, Yale University.)

28. Proof of Charles Grignion's engraving for tailpiece, *Hymn to Adversity.* (Courtesy of the Print Collection, Lewis Walpole Library, Yale University.)

29. Richard Bentley, drawing for tailpiece, *Hymn to Adversity*. (Courtesy of The Lewis Walpole Library, Yale University.)

30. Richard Bentley, draft for tailpiece, *Hymn to Adversity.* (Courtesy of The Lewis Walpole Library, Yale University.)

31. Richard Bentley, drawing for frontispiece, *Elegy Written in a Country Church-Yard.* (Courtesy of The Lewis Walpole Library, Yale University.)

32. Richard Bentley, drawing for headpiece, *Elegy Written in a Country Church-Yard.* (Courtesy of The Lewis Walpole Library, Yale University.)

33. Richard Bentley, drawing for initial letter, *Elegy Written in a Country Church-Yard.* (Courtesy of The Lewis Walpole Library, Yale University.)

34. Richard Bentley, drawing for tailpiece, *Elegy Written in a Country Church-Yard.* (Courtesy of The Lewis Walpole Library, Yale University.)

a

b

35. Proofs of early drafts for tailpiece, *Elegy Written in a Country Church-Yard.* (Courtesy of The Lewis Walpole Library, Yale University.)

a

b

36. Proof and engraving for tailpiece, *Elegy Written in a Country Church-Yard.* (Courtesy of The Lewis Walpole Library, Yale University.)

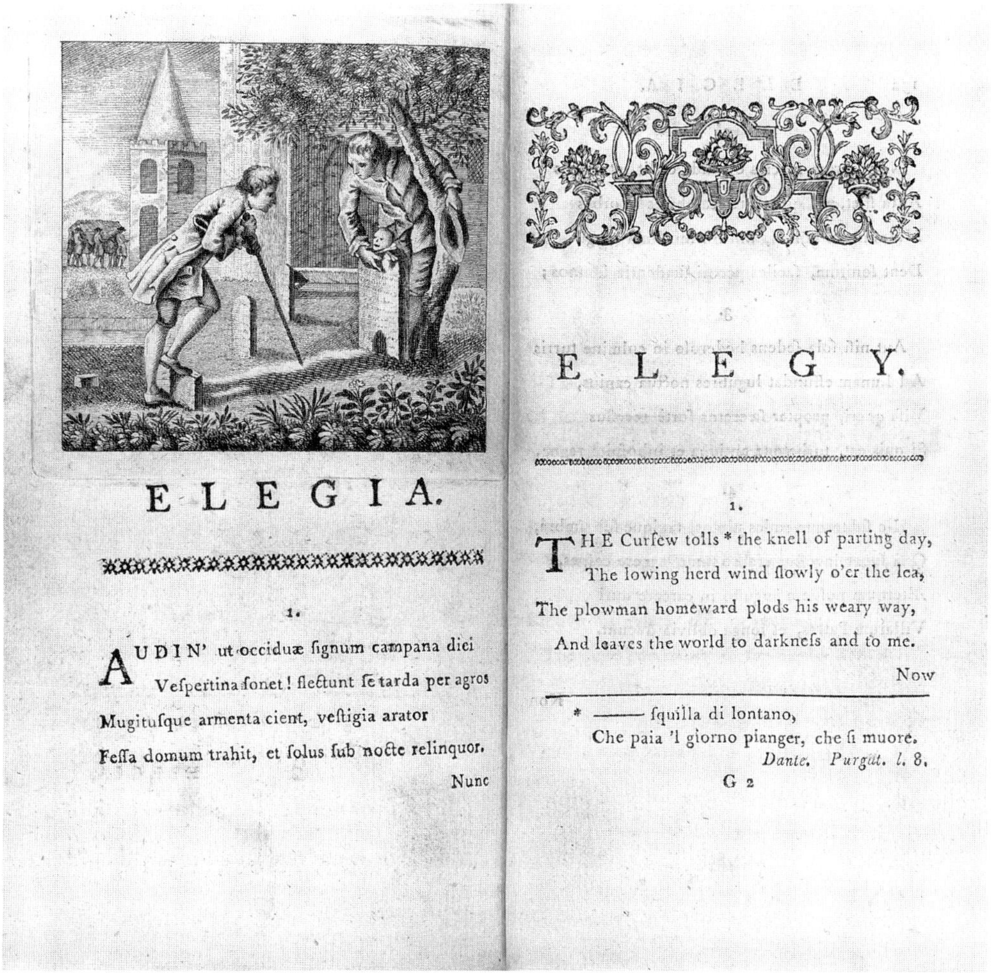

ELEGIA.

1.

AUDIN' ut occiduæ ſignum campana diei
Veſpertina ſonet! flectunt ſe tarda per agros
Mugituſque armenta cient, veſtigia arator
Feſſa domum trahit, et ſolus ſub nocte relinquor.
Nunc

ELEGY.

1.

THE Curfew tolls * the knell of parting day,
The lowing herd wind ſlowly o'er the lea,
The plowman homeward plods his weary way,
And leaves the world to darkneſs and to me.
Now

* —— ſquilla di lontano,
Che paia 'l giorno pianger, che ſi muore.
Dante. Purgat. l. 8.

G 2

37. An engraving taken from Bentley's frontispiece for the *Elegy Written in a Country Church-Yard,* published in *Poems by Mr. Gray,* Dublin: William Sleater, 1768. (Courtesy of the Print Collection, Lewis Walpole Library, Yale University.)

[151]

THE EPITAPH.

30.

HERE reſts his head upon the lap of Earth
A Youth to Fortune and to Fame unknown:
Fair Science frown'd not on his humble birth,
And Melancholy mark'd him for her own.

31.

Large was his bounty, and his ſoul ſincere,
Heav'n did a recompence as largely ſend:
He gave to Mis'ry all he had, a tear,
He gain'd from Heav'n ('twas all he wiſh'd) a friend.

32.

No farther ſeek his merits to diſcloſe,
Or draw his frailties from their dread abode,
(There they alike in trembling hope repoſe)*
The boſom of his Father and his God.

* —— paventoſa ſpeme. *Petrarch. Son.* 114.

38. An engraving taken from one of Bentley's drafts for the tailpiece, *Elegy Written in a Country Church-Yard,* published in *Poems by Mr. Gray,* Dublin: William Sleater, 1768. (Courtesy of the Print Collection, Lewis Walpole Library, Yale University.)

39. Richard Bentley, a study for *The Bard.* (By permission of the Houghton Library, Harvard University.)

40. Richard Bentley, a study for *The Bard.* (Courtesy of The Lewis Walpole Library, Yale University.)

41. Richard Bentley, a study of the ghosts for *The Bard*. (Courtesy of The Lewis Walpole Library, Yale University.)

42. Richard Bentley, final draft for *The Bard*, completed at Strawberry Hill, 1757. (Courtesy of The Lewis Walpole Library, Yale University.)

O D E S. 55

‘ Fond impious Man, think'ſt thou, yon ſanguine cloud,
‘ Rais'd by thy breath, has quench'd the Orb of day?
‘ To-morrow he repairs the golden flood,
‘ And warms the nations with redoubled ray.
‘ Enough for me: With joy I ſee
‘ The different doom our Fates aſſign.
‘ Be thine Deſpair, and ſceptred Care,
‘ To triumph, and to die, are mine.'
He ſpoke, and headlong from the mountain's height
Deep in the roaring tide he plung'd to endleſs night.

F I N I S.

43. Engraved tailpiece for *The Bard,* published by James Dodsley in *Designs* . . . , 5th edition (1766). (Courtesy of the Print Collection, Lewis Walpole Library, Yale University.)

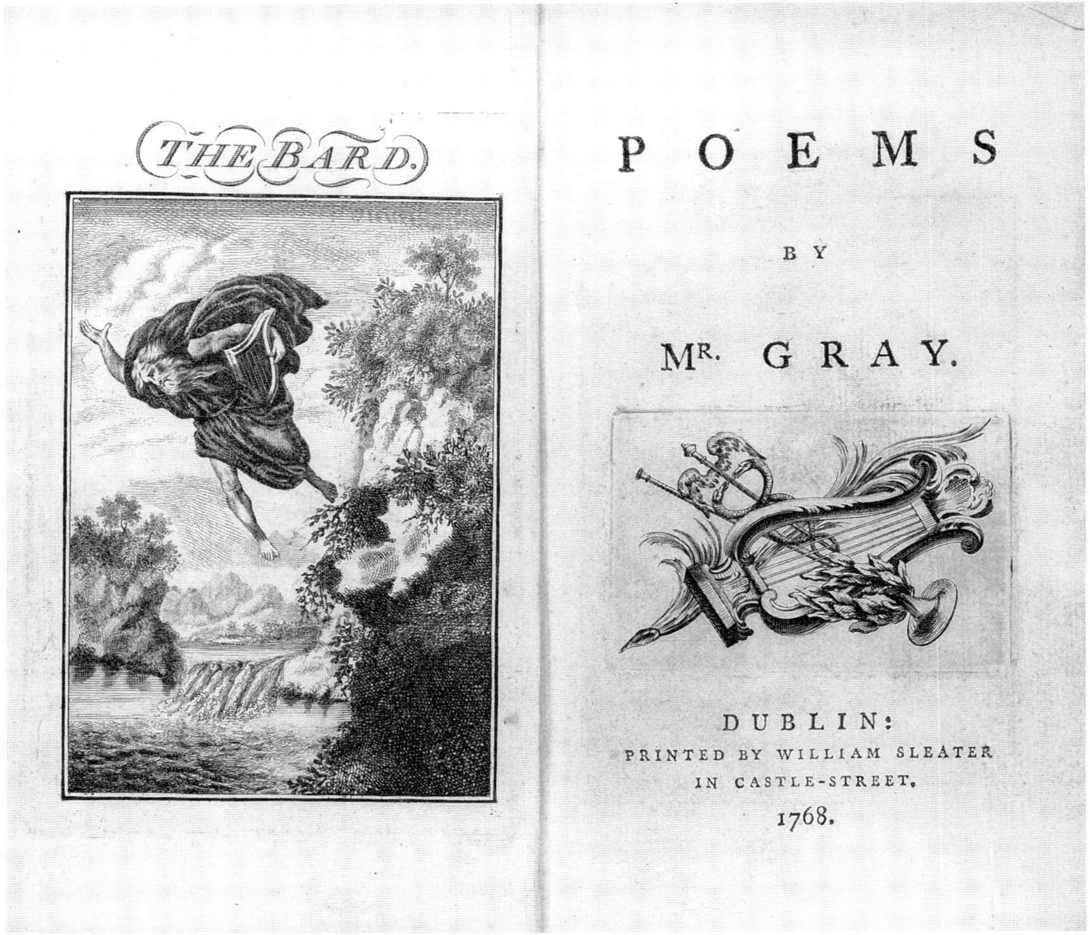

44. Re-engraving of figure 43 for *Poems by Mr. Gray*, Dublin: William Sleater, 1768. (Courtesy of the Print Collection, Lewis Walpole Library, Yale University.)

45. Philip James de Loutherbourg, design for *The Bard*. (Courtesy of The Lewis Walpole Library, Yale University.)

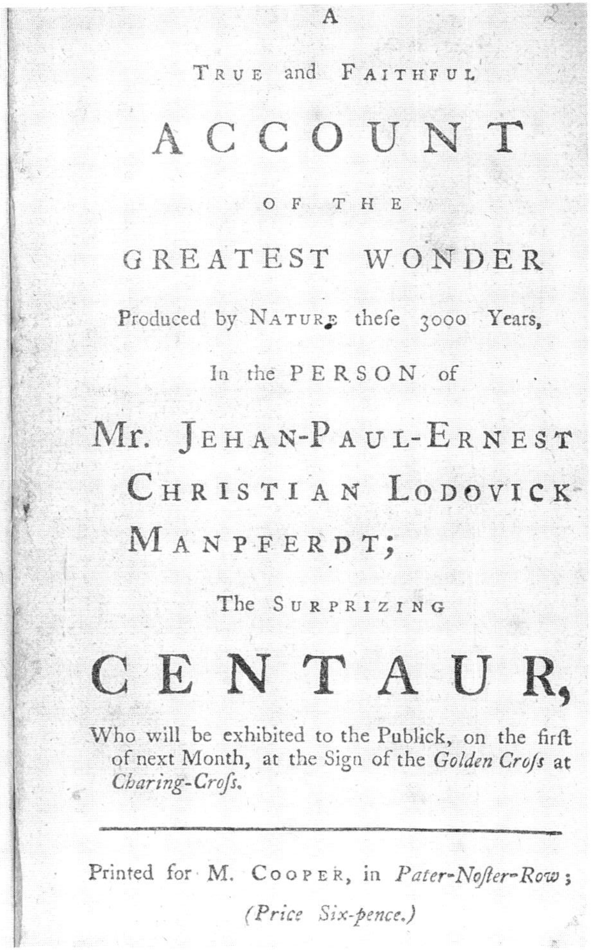

A

TRUE and FAITHFUL

ACCOUNT

OF THE

GREATEST WONDER

Produced by NATURE these 3000 Years,

In the PERSON of

Mr. JEHAN-PAUL-ERNEST CHRISTIAN LODOVICK MANPFERDT;

The SURPRIZING

CENTAUR,

Who will be exhibited to the Publick, on the first of next Month, at the Sign of the *Golden Cross* at *Charing-Cross.*

Printed for M. COOPER, in *Pater-Noster-Row;*

(Price Six-pence.)

46. Richard Bentley, frontispiece and title page for *True and Faithful Account of the . . . Centaur.* (Courtesy of the Print Collection, Lewis Walpole Library, Yale University.)

47. Richard Bentley, drawing for frontispiece, *Memoirs of King George II*. (Courtesy of The Lewis Walpole Library, Yale University.)

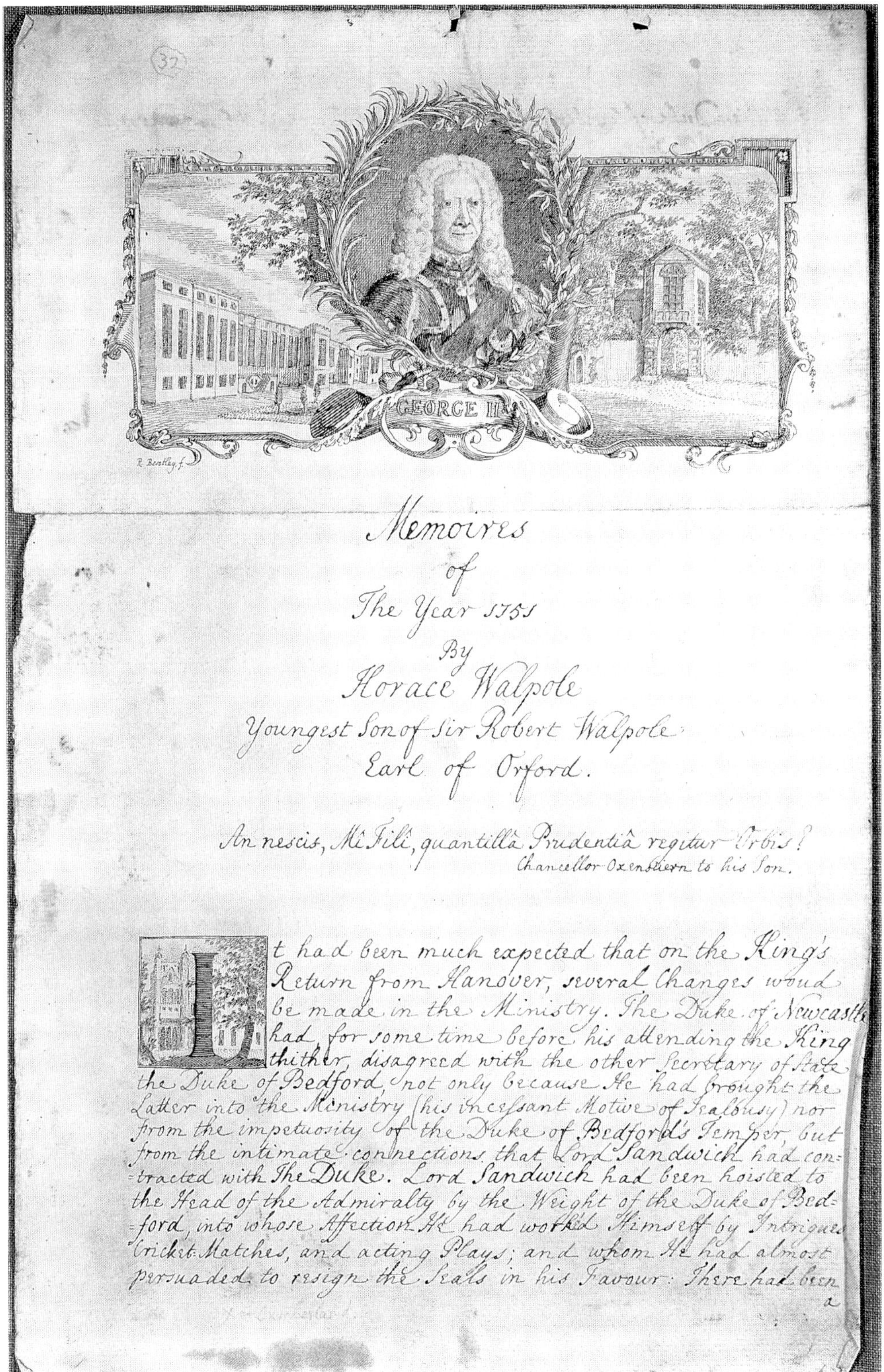

GEORGE II

R. Bentley f.

Memoires
of
The Year 1751
By
Horace Walpole
Youngest Son of Sir Robert Walpole
Earl of Orford.

An nescis, Mi Fili, quantillâ Prudentiâ regitur Orbis?
Chancellor Oxenstiern to his Son.

It had been much expected that on the King's Return from Hanover, several Changes woud be made in the Ministry. The Duke of Newcastle had for some time before his attending the King thither, disagreed with the other Secretary of State the Duke of Bedford, not only because He had brought the Latter into the Ministry (his incessant Motive of Jealousy) nor from the impetuosity of the Duke of Bedford's Temper, but from the intimate connections that Lord Sandwich had contracted with The Duke. Lord Sandwich had been hoisted to the Head of the Admiralty by the Weight of the Duke of Bedford, into whose Affection He had worked Himself by Intrigues Cricket Matches, and acting Plays; and whom He had almost persuaded to resign the Seals in his Favour. There had been a

48. Richard Bentley, drawings for headpiece and initial letter, *Memoirs of King George II*. (Courtesy of The Lewis Walpole Library, Yale University.)

95.

from his extravagant Bounty to his Enemies and Antagonists. Indifferent People were too indifferent to Him; and for Intelligence, It was one of the greatest Ble=mishes of his Administration, He wanted it so entirely—not Resolution more! Sr Robert Walpole's Friendships were chiefly confined to persons much below Him; Mr Pelham's were almost all founded on Birth and Rank. The One was too familiar, the Other never so. Sr R. Walpole was forgiving to a Fault, ; Mr Pelham never forgave, but when He durst not resent. Sr R. Walpole met with much Ingratitude; Mr Pelham was guilty of much. Both were frequently betrayed; Sr R. Walpole without being Deceived; Mr Pelham not half so often as He suspected it. The One was most depreciated while He was Minister: the Other will be most when He ceases to be Minister. All Men thought Mr Pelham honest till He was in Power; the Other never was thought so till He was out.

Both were fortunate in Themselves, Unhappy in their Brothers. With unbounded Thirst for Politics, the Duke of Newcastle and Horace Walpole were wretched Politicians: Each inferior to their Brothers in every thing Laudable; Each assuming and jealous of their own Credit, tho the Duke nor Horace coud ever have been considerable, but by the Fortune of their Brothers. The One childish and extravagant; the Other a Buffoon and Avaricious; Horace sunk into Contempt when His Brother fell with honour; The Duke was often on the point of dragging his Brother down, and was the Object of all Contempt, even where his Brother had still Power and Honour. Mr Pelham maintained his Inferiority to Sr Robert Walpole even in the Worthlessness of his Brother.

J'aye dict le Mot, pour ne frustrer la Posterité.

H. Etienne, Apologie d'Herodote.

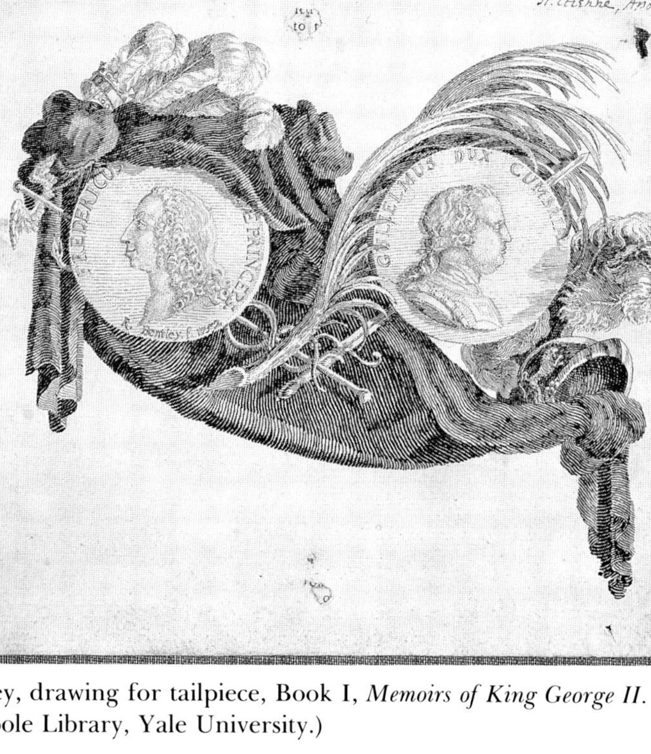

49. Richard Bentley, drawing for tailpiece, Book I, *Memoirs of King George II.* (Courtesy of The Lewis Walpole Library, Yale University.)

25

ster was not fixed till the beginning of the new year, but I shall include promotion here, not to interrupt the thread of the narration: it was Thomas, who during the first civil war of Leicester-house, had read ayers to the present King: it was not till within two years of this period at the King had found an opportunity of preferring him, & then made im Bishop of Peterborough. He was a Man of a fair character, esteemed rather a Tory in his principles. It may not be unentertaining to mention another instance of the King's good fortune in being able to promote an old friend. General Ligonier one day went & offerred his Majesty the nomination to a living in his gift. The King expressed the greatest joy & gratitude, & said, "there is one I have long tried to make a prebendary, but my Ministers never would give me an opportunity; I am much obliged to you, I will give the Living to him."

End of the second book.

50. Richard Bentley, drawing for tailpiece, Book II, *Memoirs of King George II.* Oval Portrait of Archibald Campbell, 3rd Duke of Argyll, by Johann Heinrich Müntz. (Courtesy of The Lewis Walpole Library, Yale University.)

51. Richard Bentley, drawing for tailpiece, Book III, *Memoirs of King George II.* Oval portrait of Henry Pelham by Johann Heinrich Müntz. (Courtesy of The Lewis Walpole Library, Yale University.)

52. Richard Bentley, drawing for allegorical surround for headpiece of Henry Fox, Book V, *Memoirs of King George II.* Oval portrait of Fox by Johann Heinrich Müntz. (Courtesy of The Lewis Walpole Library, Yale University.)

53. Richard Bentley, drawing for tailpiece, Book V, *Memoirs of King George II.* Oval portrait of William Pitt the elder by Johann Heinrich Müntz. (Courtesy of The Lewis Walpole Library, Yale University.)

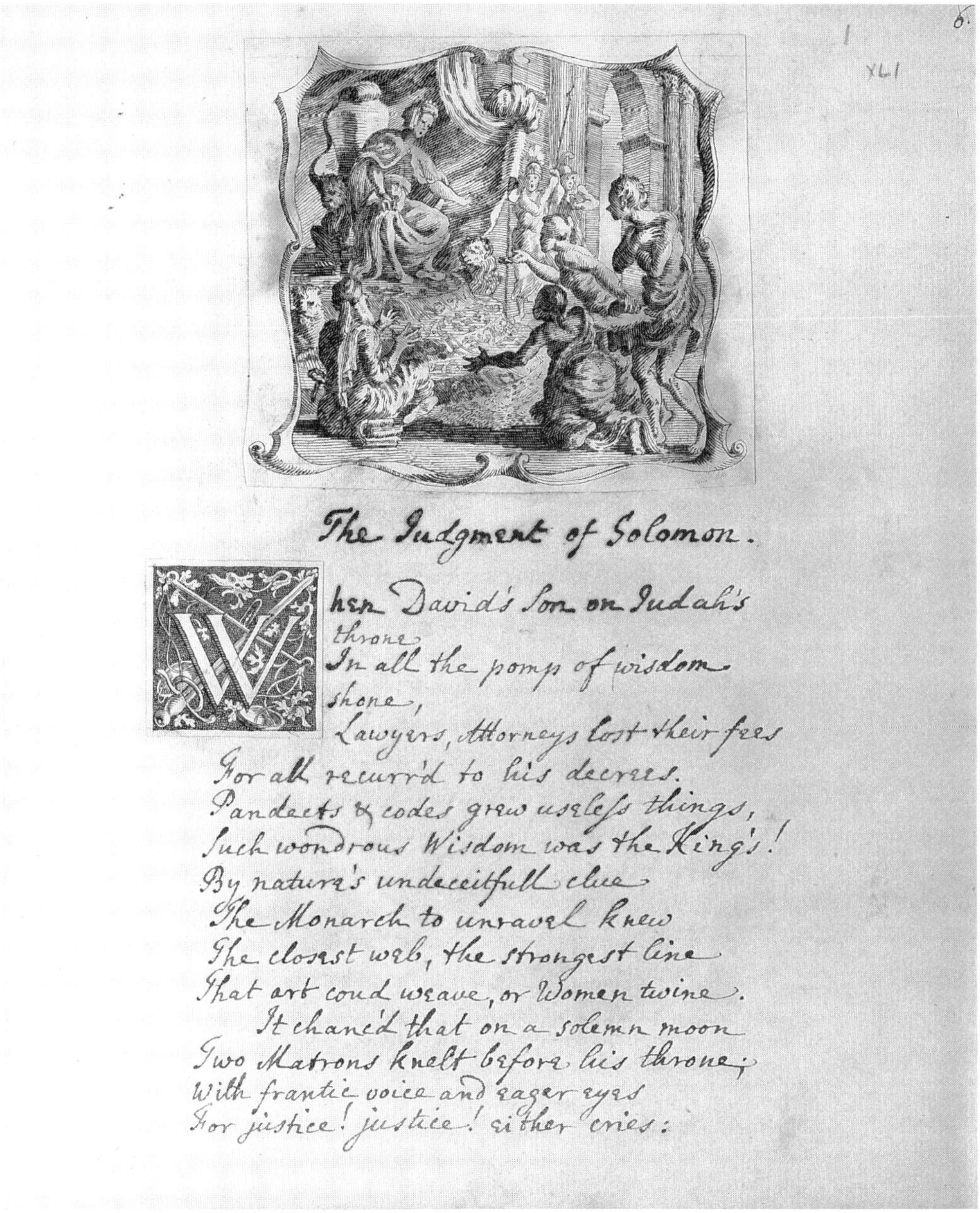

The Judgment of Solomon.

When David's Son on Judah's throne
In all the pomp of wisdom shone,
Lawyers, Attorneys lost their fees
For all recurr'd to his decrees.
Pandects & codes grew useless things,
Such wondrous Wisdom was the King's!
By nature's undeceitfull clue
The Monarch to unravel knew
The closest web, the strongest line
That art coud weave, or Women twine.
It chanc'd that on a solemn moon
Two Matrons knelt before his throne;
With frantic voice and eager eyes
For justice! justice! either cries:

54. Richard Bentley, drawing for headpiece and initial letter, *The Judgment of Solomon.* (Courtesy of The Lewis Walpole Library, Yale University.)

55. Richard Bentley, drawing for tailpiece, *The Judgment of Solomon.* (Courtesy of The Lewis Walpole Library, Yale University.)

56. Richard Bentley, drawing of a vaulted bridge. (Courtesy of The Lewis Walpole Library, Yale University.)

57. Richard Bentley, watercolor of a muzzled bear-like ape standing before Bentley's monogram. (Courtesy of The Lewis Walpole Library, Yale University.)

58. Richard Bentley, scene in Jersey. (Courtesy of The Lewis Walpole Library, Yale University.)

59. Richard Bentley, watercolor of the "Cave of Care" (Bentley's title) for Spenser's *Faerie Queene*, Book IV, canto v, stanzas 32–46. (Courtesy of The Lewis Walpole Library, Yale University.)

60. Richard Bentley, *The Temptation of St. Antony.* (Courtesy of The Lewis Walpole Library, Yale University.)

61. Richard Bentley, watercolor, *Turkish Bath.* (Courtesy of The Lewis Walpole Library, Yale University.)

62. Richard Bentley, *A Prospect of Vapourland.* (Courtesy of the Yale Center for British Art, Paul Mellon Collection.)

63. Richard Bentley, watercolor drawing of the hall and staircase at Strawberry Hill. (Courtesy of The Lewis Walpole Library, Yale University.)

64. Richard Bentley, drawing of a "view of the vestibule, with the armoury, going into the Library at Strawberry Hill, R. B. f. 1753." (Courtesy of The Lewis Walpole Library, Yale University.)

a b c d

65. Richard Bentley, designs for calling cards for Lady Northumberland and Lady Ailesbury. (Courtesy of The Lewis Walpole Library, Yale University.)

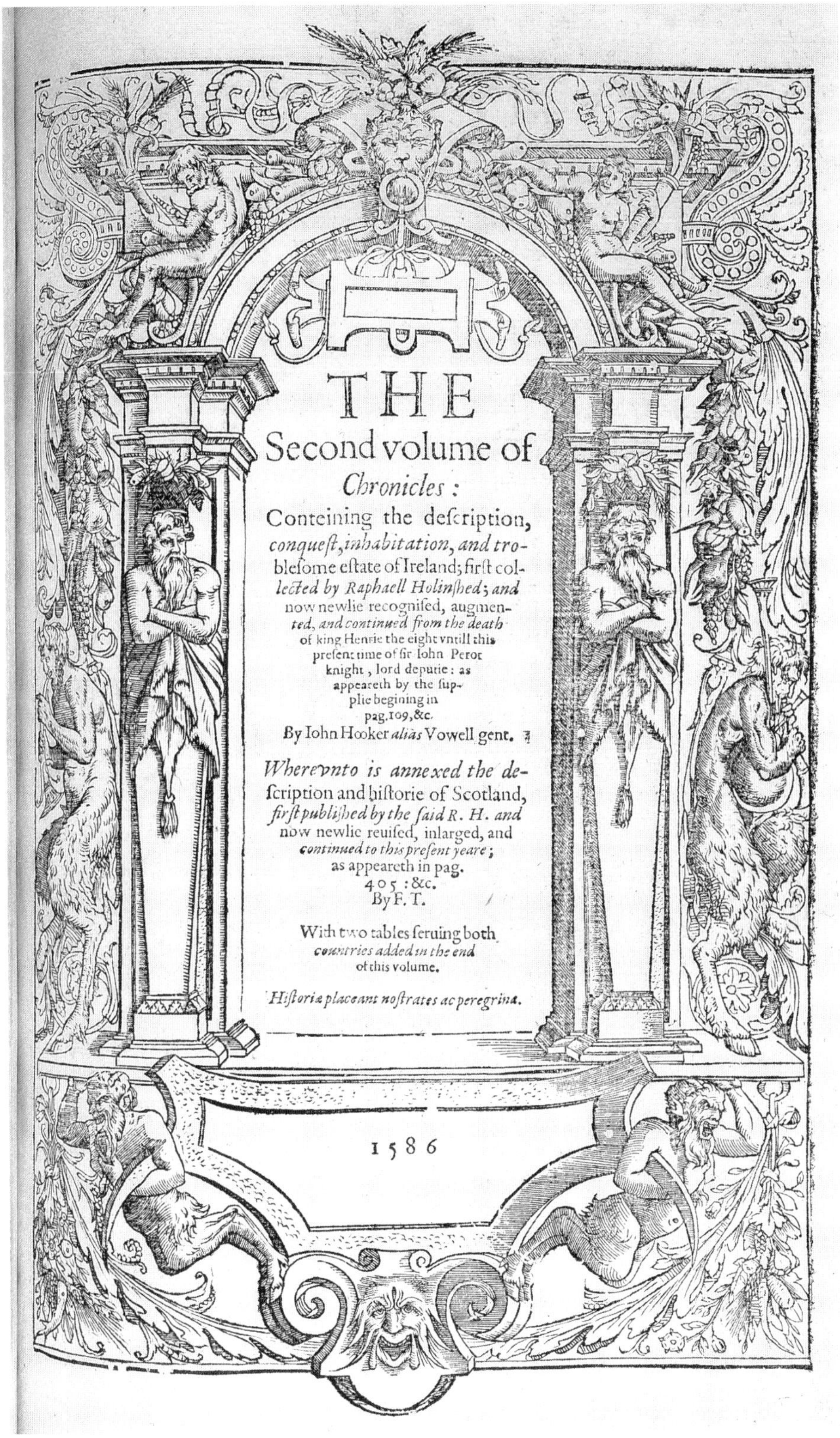

THE
Second volume of
Chronicles:
Conteining the deſcription, *conqueſt, inhabitation, and trobleſome* eſtate of Ireland; firſt col-*lected by Raphaell Holinſhed; and* now newlie recogniſed, augmen-*ted, and continued from the death* of king Henrie the eight vntill this preſent time of ſir Iohn Perot knight, lord deputie: as appeareth by the ſup-plie begining in pag. 109, &c.
By Iohn Hooker *alias* Vowell gent.

*Wherevnto is annexed the de-*ſcription and hiſtorie of Scotland, *firſt publiſhed by the ſaid R. H. and* now newlie reuiſed, inlarged, and *continued to this preſent yeare;* as appeareth in pag. 405: &c.
By F. T.

With two tables ſeruing both *countries added in the end* of this volume.

Hiſtoriæ placeant noſtrates ac peregrinæ.

1586

66. Title page, vol. ii, Holinshed's *Chronicles* (1586), artist unknown. (Courtesy of the Beinecke Rare Book and Manuscript Library, Yale University.)

67. William Kent, frontispiece design for Isaac Ware's *Four Books of Andrea Palladio's Architecture*... (1738), Peter Fourdrinier, *sculp.* (Courtesy of the Art and Architecture Library, Yale University.)

68. Antoine Watteau, *La Pèllerine Altérée,* Jacques-Gabriel Huquier, *sculp.* (Courtesy of the Sterling Memorial Library, Yale University.)

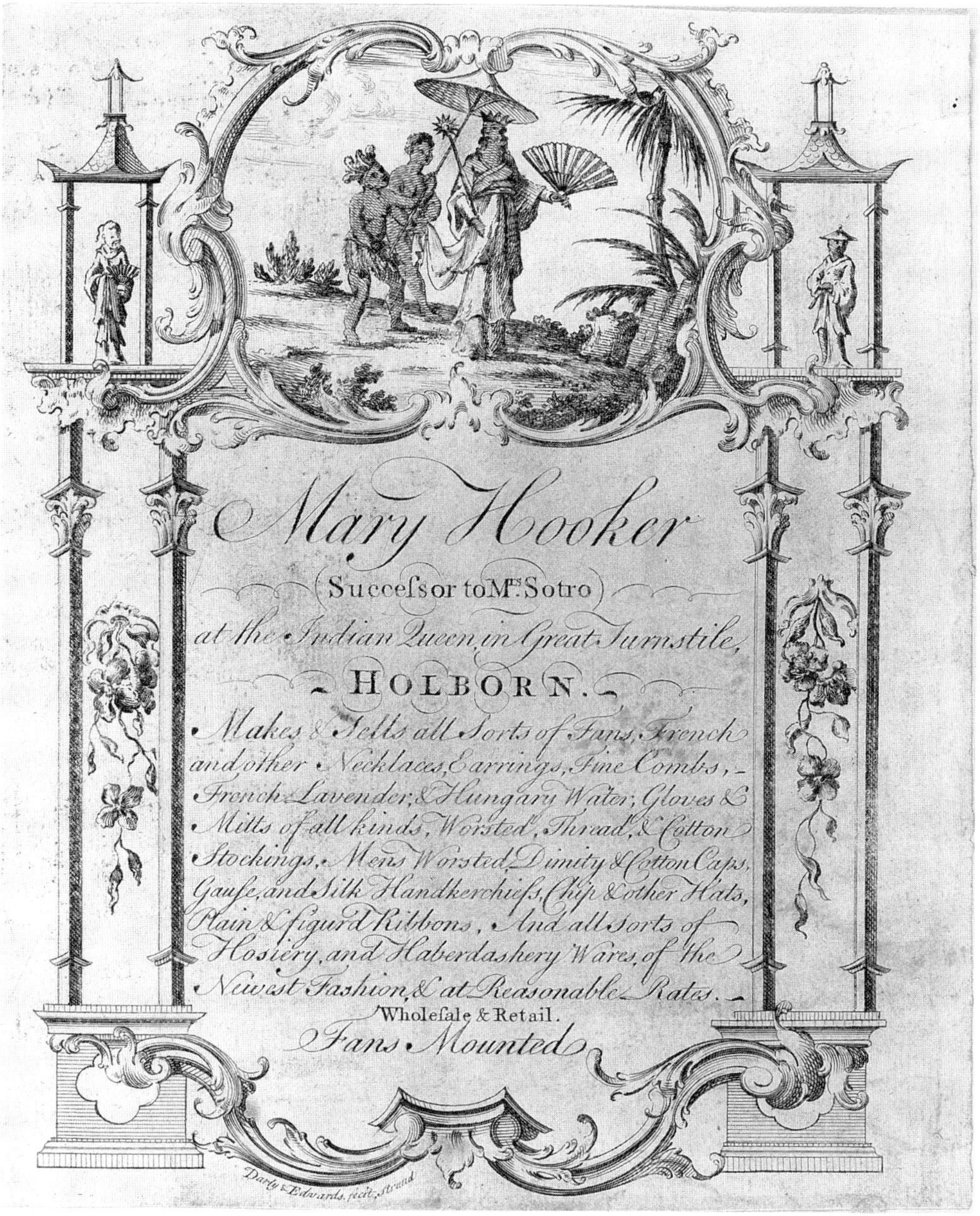

69. Trade card for Mary Hooker. (Courtesy of The Lewis Walpole Library, Yale University.)

70. Trade card for Richard Lyford. (Courtesy of The Lewis Walpole Library, Yale University.)

71. Trade card for Edward Ashworth. (Courtesy of The Lewis Walpole Library, Yale University.)

72. Trade card for Benjamin Whitton. (Courtesy of The Lewis Walpole Library, Yale University.)

1

DELLA GERUSALEMME LIBERATA DI TORQUATO TASSO.

CANTO PRIMO.

1

CANTO l' Armi pietose, e 'l Capitano,
Che 'l gran Sepolcro liberò di CRISTO:
Molto egli oprò col senno, e con la mano;
Molto soffrì nel glorioso acquisto:
E in van l'Inferno a lui s'oppose; e in vano
S'armò d' Asia, e di Libia il popol misto;
Che favorillo il Cielo, e sotto a i santi
Segni ridusse i suoi Compagni erranti.

2

O Musa tu, che di caduchi Allori
Non circondi la fronte in Elicona;
Ma su nel Cielo infra i beati Cori
Hai di stelle immortali aurea corona;
Tu spira al petto mio celesti ardori;
Tu rischiara il mio canto; e tu perdona,
S' intesso fregi al ver, s' adorno in parte
D' altri diletti, che de' tuoi, le carte.

3

Sai, che là corre il Mondo, ove più versi
Di sue dolcezze il lusinghier Parnaso,
E che 'l vero condito in molli versi
I più schivi allettando ha persuaso.
Così all' egro fanciul porgiamo aspersi
Di soave licor gli orli del vaso:
Succhi amari, ingannato, intanto ei beve,
E dall' inganno suo vita riceve.

A Tu

73. Pier Ghezzi, headpiece and initial letter for Tasso's *Della Gerusalemme Liberata* (1735), Francesco F. Aquila, *sculp.* (Courtesy of the Print Collection, Lewis Walpole Library, Yale University.)

74. Giorgione, *The Three Philosophers.* (Courtesy of the Kunsthistorisches Museum, Vienna.)

75. Battista Dossi, *Flight into Egypt.* (Courtesy of the Lowe Art Museum, University of Miami, The Samuel H. Kress Foundation.)

76. Jacques Callot, *Temptation of St. Anthony* (1635), engraving. (Courtesy of the Yale University Art Gallery.)

77. Nicholas Poussin, *The Arcadian Shepherds.* (Courtesy of the Musée du Louvre.)

Parte Seconda. 407

nido, oue ella si pone, così il maligno, non cessa mai con la pessima sua natura di danneggiare ogn'opera lodeuole, & virtuosa.

La coturnice nella guisa che dicemo, significa Malignità, perche come narra Pierio Valeriano nel lib. 24. de' suoi Geroglifici, volendo gl'Egittij mostrare la Malignità, dipingeuano vna coturnice, perciòche è di così pessima, & maligna natura, ch'hauendo beuuto, con le zampe, & con il becco intorbida il resto dell'acqua, acciò che niun'altro animale ne possi bere, & a questo fine Ezechiele Profeta nel cap. 34. rimprouerando la Malignità degli Hebrei dice: *Et cum purissimam aquam biberitis reliquam pedibus vestris turbatis.*

MALINCONIA.

DONNA vecchia, mesta, & dogliosa, di brutti panni vestita, senza alcun'ornamento, starà a sedere sopra vn sasso, con gomiti posati sopra i ginocchi, & ambe le mani sotto il mento, & vi sarà a canto vn'albero senza fronde, & frà i sassi. Fà la malinconia nell'huomo quegli effetti istessi che fà la forza del verno ne gl'alberi, & nelle piante, liquali agitati da diuersi venti, tormentati dal freddo, & ricoperti dalle neui, appariscono secchi, sterili, nudi, & di vilissimo prezzo, però non è alcuno, che non fugga, come cosa dispiaceuole la conuersatione de gl'huomini malinconici, vanno essi sempre col pensiero nelle cose difficili, le quali se gli fingono presenti, & reali, il che mostrano i segni della mestitia, è del dolore.

Vecchia si dipinge, perciòche gl'è ordinario de' giouani stare allegri, & i vecchi malenconici, però ben disse Virg. nel 6.

Pallentes habitant morbi, tristisque senectus.

E mal vestita senza ornamento, per la conformità de gl'alberi senza foglie, & senza frutti, non alzando mai tanto l'animo il malenconico, che pensi a procurarsi le commodità per stare in continua cura di sfuggire, ò proueder a mali, che s'imagini esser vicini.

Il sasso

78. Cesare Ripa, "Malinconia," *Nova Iconologia,* Part II (1624). (Courtesy of the Beinecke Rare Book and Manuscript Library, Yale University.)

79. Giovanni Pietro Bellori, "Muta Poesis," *Le vite de' pittori, scultori et architetti moderni* (1692). (Courtesy of the Beinecke Rare Book and Manuscript Library, Yale University.)

80. Louis Cheron, frontispiece for *The Works of Tibullus, Containing his four Books of Love-Elegies* (tr. John Dart, 1720), Gerard Vandergucht, *sculp.* (Author's copy.)

81. Salvator Rosa, etching of a seated woman. (Courtesy of the Print Collection, Lewis Walpole Library, Yale University.)

82. William Kent, illustration of Despair for Book I of *The Faerie Queene*. (Author's copy.)

83. Albrecht Dürer, *Melencolia I.* (Courtesy of the Yale University Art Gallery.)

84. Albrecht Dürer, *Penance of St. John Chrysostom.* (Courtesy of the Yale University Art Gallery.)

85. Albrecht Dürer, *Joachim and Anna at the Golden Gate.* (Courtesy of Marie Antoinette Evans Fund, Museum of Fine Arts, Boston.)

86. Albrecht Dürer, *Death of Orpheus.* (Courtesy of the Kunsthalle Museum, Hamburg.)

87. Albrecht Dürer, *Der Hercules.* (Courtesy of the Yale University Art Gallery.)

88. Albrecht Dürer, *Four Horsemen of the Apocalypse.* (Courtesy of the Yale University Art Gallery.)

ADAM, & HEVA cognito peccato ſuffugiunt faciem DEI, ac morti obiiciuntur. Cherubim ante paradiſum uoluptatis cũ flammeo gladio collocatur.

GENESIS III.

Pour le peché qu'ilz feirent contre Dieu,
Furent maudictz chaſcum ſelon l'offenſe:
Puis Cherubim les met hors de ce lieu,
Et contre mort n'eurent plus de defenſe.

B

89. Hans Holbein the Younger, *The Dance of Death,* "Genesis III." (Courtesy of the Print Collection, Lewis Walpole Library, Yale University.)

22

When Vice *and* Vertue *Youth ſhall wooe,*
Tis hard to ſay, which way 't will goe.

14

ILLVSTR. XXII. Book. I.

MY hopefull *Friends* at thrice five yeares and three,
Without a *Guide* (into the World alone)
To ſeeke my *Fortune*, did adventure mee;
And, many hazards, I alighted on.
Firſt, *Englands* greateſt *Rendevouz* I ſought,
Where VICE and VERTVE at the higheſt ſit;
And, thither, both a *Minde* and *Bodie* brought,
For neither of their Services unfit.
Both, woo'd my *Youth*: And, both perſwaded ſo,
That (like the *Young man* in our *Emblem* here)
I ſtood, and cry'd, *Ah! which way ſhall I goe?*
To me ſo pleaſing both their Offers were.
VICE, *Pleaſures* beſt Contentments promiſt mee,
And what the wanton *Fleſh* deſires to have:
Quoth VERTVE, *I will Wiſdome give to thee,*
And thoſe brave things, which nobleſt Mindes doe crave.
Serve me ſaid VICE, *and thou ſhalt ſoone acquire*
All thoſe Atchievements which my Service brings:
Serve me ſaid VERTVE, *and Ile raiſe thee higher,*
Then VICES *can, and teach thee better things.*
Whil'ſt thus they ſtrove to gaine me, I eſpyde
Grim *Death* attending VICE; and, that her Face
Was but a painted *Vizard*, which did hide
The foul'ſt Deformity that ever was.
LORD, *grant me grace for evermore to view*
Her Vglineſſe: And, that I viewing it,
Her Falſehoods and allurements may eſchew;
And on faire VERTVE *my Affection ſet;*
Her Beauties contemplate, her Love embrace,
And by her ſafe Direction, runne my Race.

I pine

90. George Wither, *The Choice of Hercules.* (Courtesy of the Print Collection, Lewis Walpole Library, Yale University.)

When Magiſtrates *confined are*,
They revell, who were kept in feare.

ILLVSTR. VII. Book. 4

A Tyrannous, or wicked *Magiſtrat*,
Is fitly repreſented by a *Catt:*
For, though the *Mice* a harmfull vermine bee,
And, *Cats* the remedie; yet, oft wee ſee,
That, by the *Mice*, far leſſe, ſome houſe-wives leeſe,
Then when they ſet the *Catt* to keepe the *Cheeſe*.
A ravenous *Cat*, will puniſh in the *Mouſe*,
The very ſame Offences, in the houſe,
Which hee himſelfe commits; yea, for that *Vice*,
Which was his owne (with praiſe) he kils the *Mice*;
And, ſpoyleth not anothers life alone,
Ev'n for that very *fault* which was his *owne*,
But *feeds*, and *fattens*, in the ſpoyle of them,
Whom hee, without compaſſion did condemne.
Nay, worſe than ſo; hee cannot bee content,
To ſlaughter them, who are as innocent,
As hee *himſelfe*; but, hee muſt alſo play,
And ſport his wofull *Pris'ners* lives away;
More torturing them, 'twixt fruitleſſe *hopes* and *feares*,
Than when their bowels, with his teeth he teares:
For, by much terrour, and much crueltie,
Hee kills them, ten times over, e're they die.
When, ſuch like *Magiſtrates* have rule obtain'd,
The beſt men wiſh their powre might be reſtrain'd:
But, they who ſhun enormities, through *Feare*,
Are glad when *good-men* out of Office are.
Yea, whether *Governours* bee good or bad,
Of their diſplacings *wicked-men* are glad;
And, when they ſee them brought into diſgraces,
They boldly play the *Knaves* before their faces.

Loe,

91. George Wither, *Confined Magistrates.* (Courtesy of the Print Collection, Lewis Walpole Library, Yale University.)

ORPHEVS
EVCHARISTICVS
PRIMVM EMBLEMA.
TOTIVS OPERIS IDEA
ORPHEVS ILLVSTRIORES NATVRÆ
PARTES LYRÆ MODVLIS PELLICENS.

Vltro veniunt, quod amore trahantur.

L'attraict de l'amour est si fort,
Qu'elles le suiuent sans effort.

1

ORpheus ut primum vocales pollice neruos
Impulit, & dulces edidit ore sonos:

92. P. Agustino Chesneav, *Orpheus Eucharisticus* (Paris, 1657). (Courtesy of the Print Collection, Lewis Walpole Library, Yale University.)

93. Louis Cheron, headpiece for Prior's *Poems on Several Occasions* (1718), Nicholas-Dauphin de Beauvais, *sculp.* (Author's copy.)

THE

FIRST CANTO.

ATTHEW met RICHARD; when
or where
From Story is not mighty clear:
Of many knotty Points They ſpoke;
And *Pro* and *Con* by turns They took.
Ratts half the Manuſcript have eat:
Dire Hunger! which We ſtill regret:
O! may they ne'er again digeſt
The Horrors of ſo ſad a Feaſt.
Yet leſs our Grief, if what remains,
Dear JACOB, by thy Care and Pains
Shall be to future Times convey'd.
It thus begins:
* * * * Here MATTHEW ſaid:

Mmmm2 ALMA

94. Louis Cheron, headpiece and initial letter for Prior's *Alma, or the Progress of the Mind,* in *Poems on Several Occasions* (1718), Nicholas-Dauphin de Beauvais, *sculp.* (Author's copy.)

POEMS *on ſeveral* OCCASIONS. 381

If to be ſad is to be wiſe;
I do moſt heartily deſpiſe
Whatever SOCRATES has ſaid,
Or TULLY writ, or WANLEY read.

Dear DRIFT, to ſet our Matters right,
Remove theſe Papers from my Sight;
Burn MAT'S DES-CART', and ARISTOTLE:
Here, JONATHAN, Your Maſter's Bottle.

95. Louis Cheron, tailpiece for Prior's *Alma, or the Progress of the Mind,* in *Poems on Several Occasions* (1718), Nichols-Dauphin de Beauvais, *sculp.* (Author's copy.)

96. Frontispiece for Swift's *Battle of the Books* (1710), studio of Bernard Lens and John Sturt. (Courtesy of the Beinecke Rare Book and Manuscript Library, Yale University.)

97. Bernard Picart, *Monument Consacré à la Postérité en Mémoire de la Folie Incroyable XX. Année du XVIII. Siècle.* (Courtesy of the Print Collection, Lewis Walpole Library, Yale University.)

a

b

98. Simon Gribelin, two tailpieces for Pope, *Works* (1717). (Author's copy.)

99. Anton Domenico Gabbiani, "Francesco Redi Crowned by the Muses," Redi, *Sonnetti* (Florence, 1702). (Courtesy of the Yale Medical Historical Library.)

100. Frontispiece for Bolingbroke's *A Dissertation upon Parties,* artist unknown. (Courtesy of The Seeley Mudd Library, Yale University.)

101. William Kent, frontispiece for Thomson's *The Seasons* (1730), Nicolas-Henri Tardieu, *sculp.* (Author's copy.)

102. William Kent, frontispiece for "Summer," *The Seasons* (1730), Nicolas-Henri Tardieu, *sculp.* (Author's copy.)

103. William Kent, frontispiece for "Autumn," *The Seasons* (1730), Nicolas-Henri Tardieu, *sculp.* (Author's copy.)

104. William Kent, frontispiece for "Winter," *The Seasons* (1730), Nicolas-Henri Tardieu, *sculp.* (Author's copy.)

W. Kent inv. P. Fourdrinier sculp.

INTRODUCTION
TO THE
FABLES.

The SHEPHERD *and the* PHILOSOPHER.

REMOTE from cities liv'd a Swain,
Unvex'd with all the cares of gain,
His head was ſilver'd o'er with age,
And long experience made him ſage;

B In

105. William Kent, headpiece for the "Introduction" to Gay's *Fables* (1727), Peter Fourdrinier, *sculp.* (Courtesy of the Print Collection, Lewis Walpole Library, Yale University.)

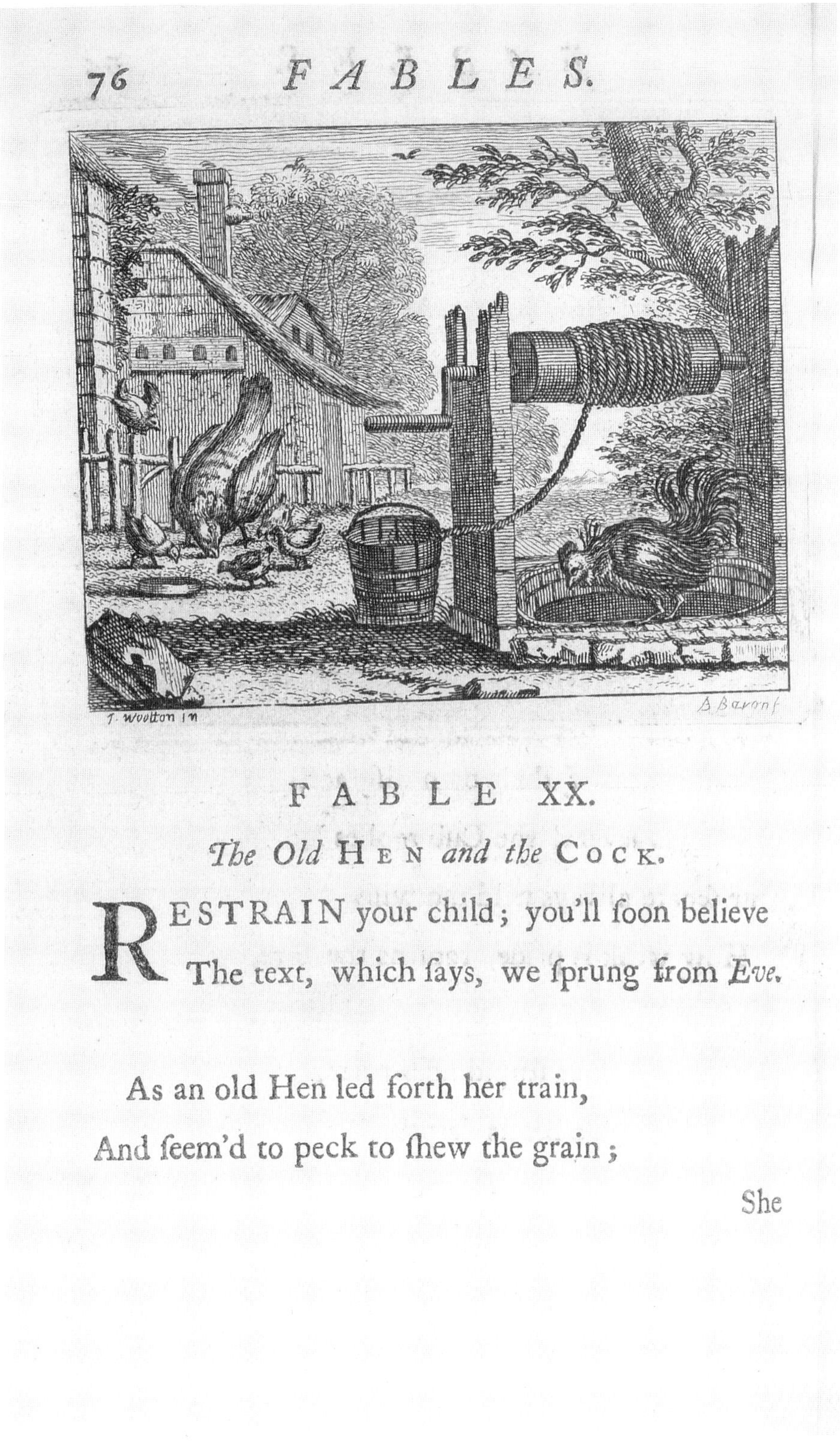

76 *FABLES.*

J. Wootton in A Baron f

FABLE XX.

The Old HEN *and the* COCK.

RESTRAIN your child; you'll ſoon believe
The text, which ſays, we ſprung from *Eve.*

As an old Hen led forth her train,
And ſeem'd to peck to ſhew the grain;

She

106. John Wootton, headpiece for Fable XX, Gay's *Fables* (1727), Peter Fourdrinier, *sculp.* (Courtesy of the Print Collection, Lewis Walpole Library, Yale University.)

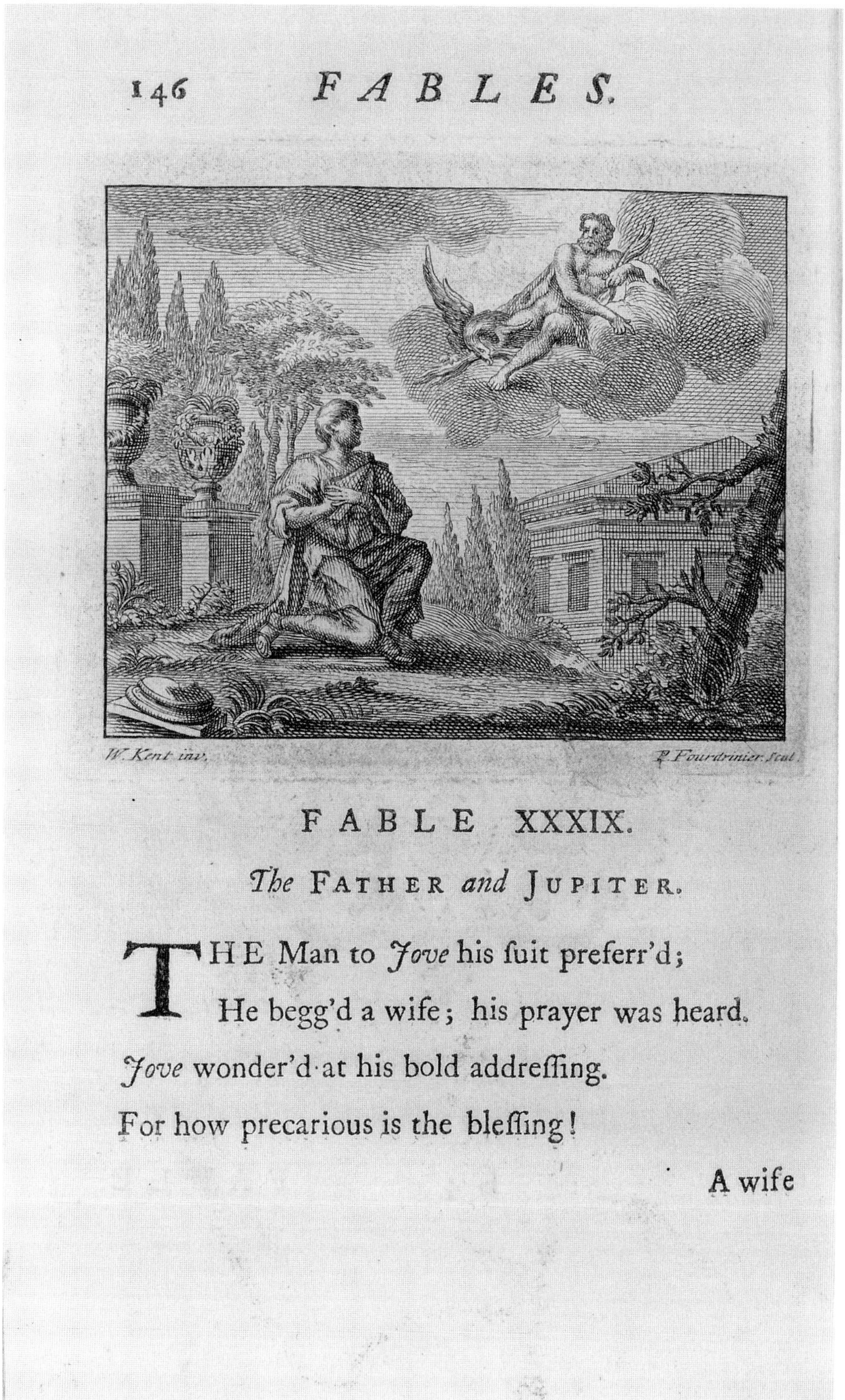
146 FABLES.

W. Kent inv. P. Fourdrinier Sculp.

FABLE XXXIX.

The FATHER *and* JUPITER.

THE Man to *Jove* his ſuit preferr'd;
He begg'd a wife; his prayer was heard.
Jove wonder'd at his bold addreſſing.
For how precarious is the bleſſing!

A wife

107. William Kent, headpiece for Fable XXXIX, Gay's *Fables* (1727), Peter Fourdrinier, *sculp.* (Courtesy of the Print Collection, Lewis Walpole Library, Yale University.)

178 *FABLES.*

Wm Kent in. B. Baron f.

FABLE XLVII.

The COURT *of* DEATH.

DEATH, on a ſolemn night of ſtate,
In all his pomp of terrors ſate:
Th' attendants of his gloomy reign,
Diſeaſes dire, a ghaſtly train,

Croud

108. William Kent, headpiece for Fable XLVII, Gay's *Fables* (1727), Bernard Baron, *sculp.* (Courtesy of the Print Collection, Lewis Walpole Library, Yale University.)

186 *FABLES.*

FABLE XLIX.

The MAN *and the* FLEA.

WHETHER on earth, in air, or main,
Sure ev'ry thing alive is vain!
Does not the hawk all fowls ſurvey,
As deſtin'd only for his prey?

And

109. William Kent, headpiece for Fable XLIX, Gay's *Fables* (1727), Benjamin de la Motte, *sculp.* (Courtesy of the Print Collection, Lewis Walpole Library, Yale University.)

190 FABLES.

J. Wootton inv. P. Fourdrinier. sculp.

FABLE L.

The HARE *and many* FRIENDS.

FRIENDSHIP, like love, is but a name,
Unlefs to one you ftint the flame.
The child, whom many fathers fhare,
Hath feldom known a father's care;

'Tis

110. John Wootton, headpiece for Fable L, Gay's *Fables* (1727), Peter Fourdrinier, *sculp.* (Courtesy of the Print Collection, Lewis Walpole Library, Yale University.)

111. Herbert-François Gravelot, frontispiece for Fable VII, Gay's *Fables* (1738), Gerard Scotin, *sculp.* (Courtesy of the Print Collection, Lewis Walpole Library, Yale University.)

112. Herbert-François Gravelot, frontispiece for Fable XVI, Gay's *Fables* (1738), Gerard Scotin, *sculp.* (Courtesy of the Print Collection, Lewis Walpole Library, Yale University.)

16 Q. HORATII FLACCI

ODE IX.

AD THALIARCHVM.

VIDES, ut alta ſtet nive candidum
Soracte; nec jam ſuſtineant onus
Silvae laborantes; geluque
Flumina conſtiterint acuto?
Diſſolve frigus, ligna ſuper foco
Large reponens; atque benignius
Deprome quadrimum Sabina,
O Thaliarche, merum diota.
Permitte Divis caetera: qui ſimul
Stravere ventos aequore fervido
Deproeliantes; nec cupreſſi,
Nec veteres agitantur orni.
Quid ſit futurum cras, fuge quaerere; et
Quem fors dierum cunque dabit, lucro
Appone: nec dulces amores
Sperne puer, neque tu choreas;

CARMINVM LIBER I. 17

Donec virenti canities abeſt
Moroſa. nunc et Campus, et areae,
Leneſque ſub noctem ſuſurri
Compoſita repetantur hora;
Nunc et latentis proditor intimo
Gratus puellae riſus ab angulo,
Pignuſque dereptum lacertis,
Aut digito male pertinaci.

E

113. John Pine, headpiece, initial letter, and tailpiece for Horace, *Odes* I.ix (1733). (Courtesy of the Print Collection, Lewis Walpole Library, Yale University.)

46 Q. HORATII FLACCI

ODE XXV.

AD LYDIAM.

PARCIVS junctas quatiunt fenestras
Ictibus crebris juvenes protervi,
Nec tibi somnos adimunt: amatque
Ianua limen,
Quae prius multum faciles movebat
Cardines. audis minus et minus jam,
Me tuo longas pereunte noctes,
Lydia, dormis?
Invicem moechos anus arrogantes
Flebis in solo levis angiportu,
Thracio bacchante magis sub inter-
lunia vento:
Cum tibi flagrans amor, et libido,
Quae solet matres furiare equorum,

CARMINVM LIBER I. 47

Saeviet circa jecur ulcerosum;
Non sine questu,
Laeta quod pubes edera virenti
Gaudeat, pulla magis atque myrto;
Aridas frondes hiemis sodali
Dedicet Hebro.

114. John Pine, headpiece, initial letter, and tailpiece for Horace, *Odes* I.xxv (1733). (Courtesy of the Print Collection, Lewis Walpole Library, Yale University.)

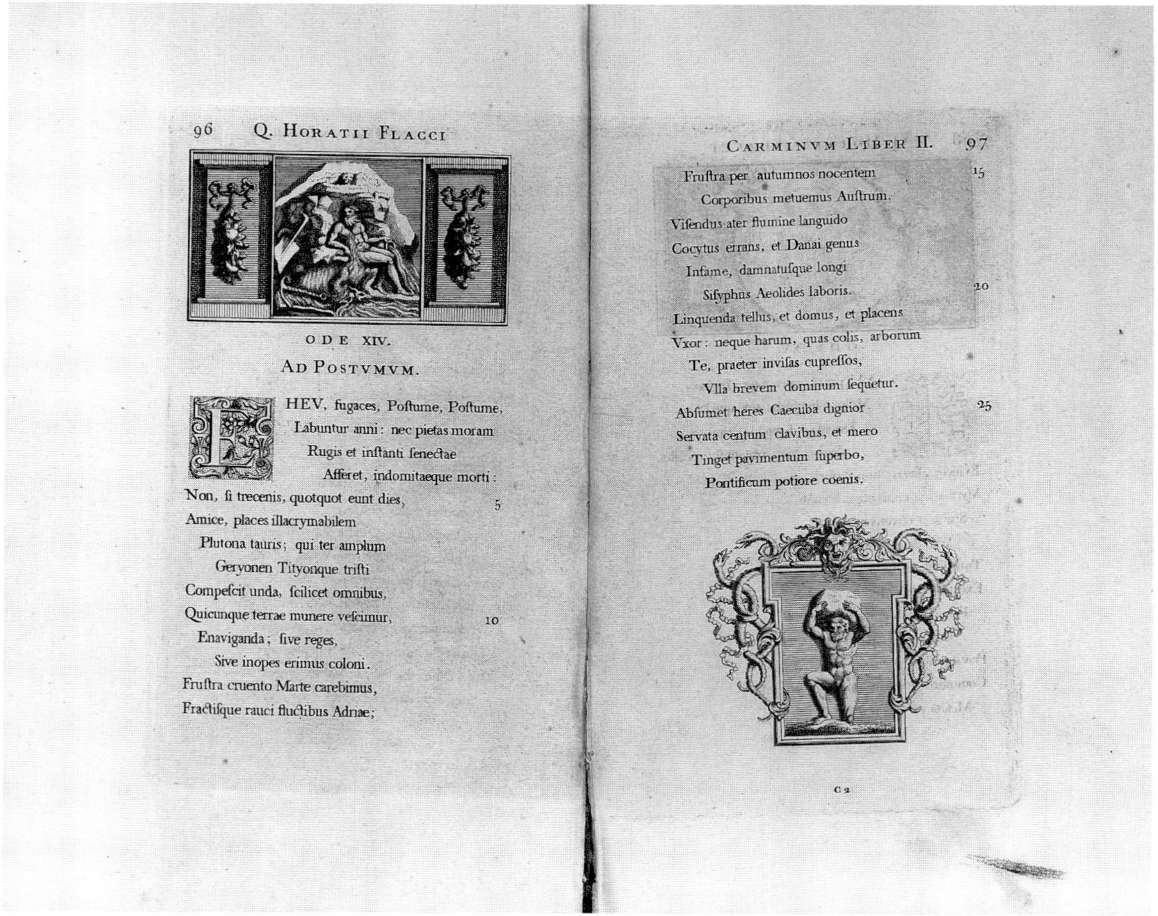
96 Q. HORATII FLACCI

ODE XIV.

AD POSTVMVM.

EHEV, fugaces, Poftume, Poftume,
Labuntur anni: nec pietas moram
Rugis et inftanti fenectae
Afferet, indomitaeque morti:
Non, fi trecenis, quotquot eunt dies,
Amice, places illacrymabilem
Plutona tauris; qui ter amplum
Geryonen Tityonque trifti
Compefcit unda, fcilicet omnibus,
Quicunque terrae munere vefcimur,
Enaviganda; five reges,
Sive inopes erimus coloni.
Fruftra cruento Marte carebimus,
Fractifque rauci fluctibus Adriae;

CARMINVM LIBER II. 97

Fruftra per autumnos nocentem
Corporibus metuemus Auftrum.
Vifendus ater flumine languido
Cocytus errans, et Danai genus
Infame, damnatufque longi
Sifyphus Aeolides laboris.
Linquenda tellus, et domus, et placens
Vxor: neque harum, quas colis, arborum
Te, praeter invifas cupreffos,
Vlla brevem dominum fequetur.
Abfumet heres Caecuba dignior
Servata centum clavibus, et mero
Tinget pavimentum fuperbo,
Pontificum potiore coenis.

C2

115. John Pine, headpiece, initial letter, and tailpiece for Horace, *Odes* II.xiv (1733). (Courtesy of the Print Collection, Lewis Walpole Library, Yale University.)

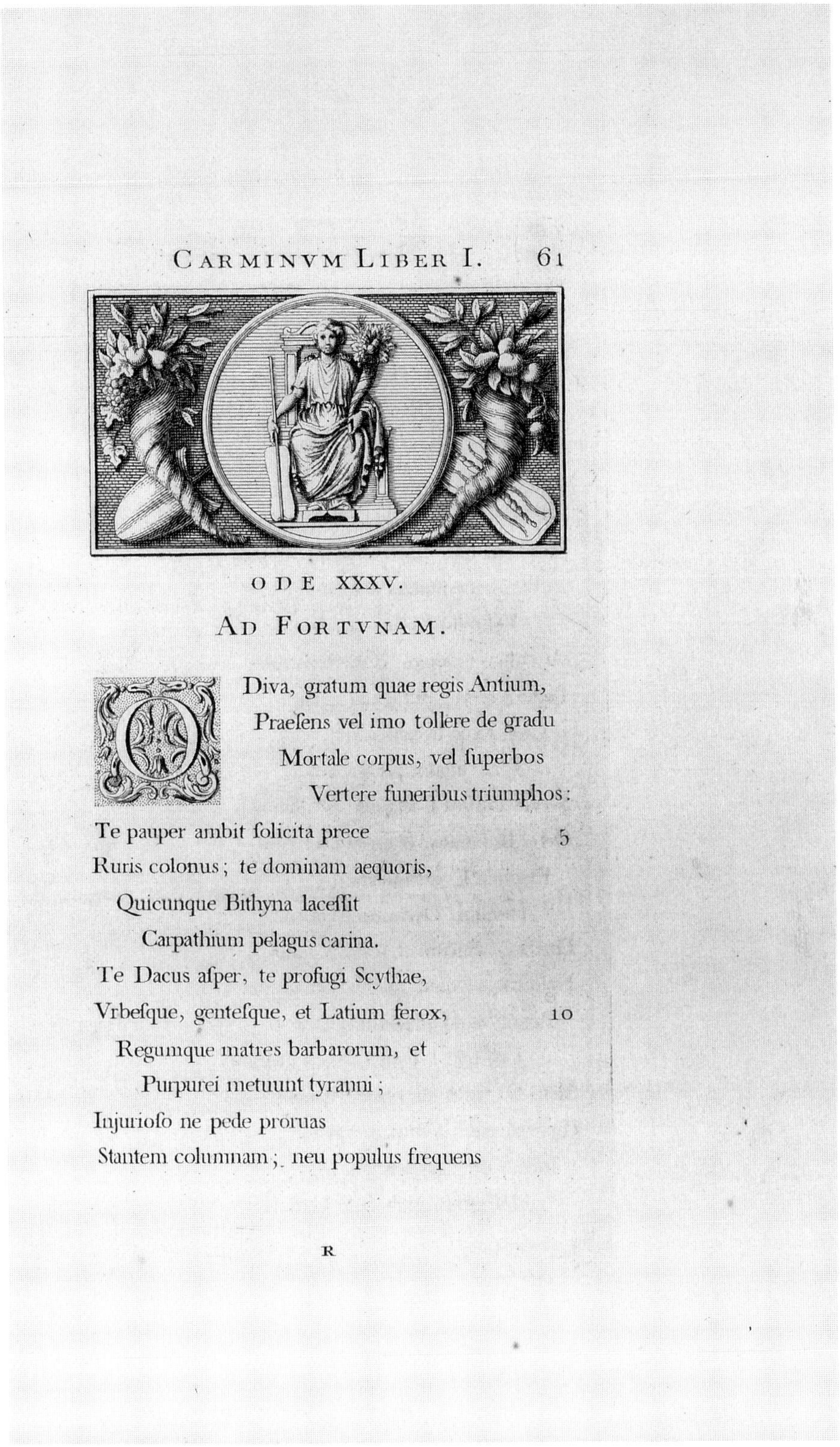
CARMINVM LIBER I. 61

ODE XXXV.

AD FORTVNAM.

O Diva, gratum quae regis Antium,
Praeſens vel imo tollere de gradu
Mortale corpus, vel ſuperbos
Vertere funeribus triumphos:
Te pauper ambit ſolicita prece
Ruris colonus; te dominam aequoris,
Quicunque Bithyna laceſſit
Carpathium pelagus carina.
Te Dacus aſper, te profugi Scythae,
Vrbeſque, genteſque, et Latium ferox,
Regumque matres barbarorum, et
Purpurei metuunt tyranni;
Injurioſo ne pede proruas
Stantem columnam; neu populus frequens

R

116. John Pine, headpiece and initial letter for Horace, *Odes* I.xxxv (1733). (Courtesy of the Print Collection, Lewis Walpole Library, Yale University.)

117. William Hogarth, *Marriage à la Mode*, plate II. (Courtesy of the Print Collection, Lewis Walpole Library, Yale University.)

118. William Hogarth, *Marriage à la Mode*, plate V. (Courtesy of the Print Collection, Lewis Walpole Library, Yale University.)

Index

Academy, St. Martin's Lane, 107–8, 115, 119
Actaeon, representations of or allusions to, 116–17, 128n.23
Addison, Joseph, 119, 133, 159n.3, 168, 174n.7, 200, 209, 215
Aeschylus, 106, 189
Aesculapius, 216
Aesop's Fables, 109, 115, 153, 159n.2, 174n.10
Ailesbury, Caroline Campbell, Lady: Bentley's calling card for, 126
Albrizzi (publisher). *See* Tasso, Torquato
Alkon, Paul, 89n.8
Allen, B. Sprague, 159n.7
Allen, Brian, 184n.4
Antal, Frederick, 107, 127n.8, 158–59
Apollo: Apollonian themes, 91, 127n.3, 132–33, 134, 135–37, 139, 141, 142, 143, 153, 154, 158, 173n.5, 181
Aquila, Francesco F. (engraver). *See* Tasso, Torquato
Argyle, Archibald Campbell, Duke of, 107
Arion, 141, 142, 143, 153
Ashburnham House. *See* King's Library at
Ashton, Thomas, 160, 173
Athena, 121, 187, 188, 189, 190, 192, 199n.4, 203
Atropos. *See* Fates

Barbari, Jocopo de', 195
The Bard, 85, 100, 127n.3, 148, 186, 211, 214, 218–21; Bentley's published tailpiece for, 100, 101, 218, 220–21; Bentley's unpublished designs for, 218–21
Barlow, Francis (painter), 109
Baron, Bernard (engraver), 108, 128n.19
Beattie, James, 101
Beauvais, Nicholas-Dauphin de (engraver), 128n.19
Bedingfield, Edward, 213, 220, 221n.3
Bell, C. F., 85, 89n.5, 213–14, 217n.2
Bellori, Giovanni Pietro: *Muta Poesis*, 133, 137, 162, 193, 195, 197, 200
Bentley, Richard: aesthetic innovations of, 85, 87–88, 98, 99–100, 105–6, 112–26, 131, 133, 139, 150, 155, 158–59, 176, 201, 207–9, 211–12, 214–17 (*see also* Sister Arts, interplay of; Strawberry Hill; Walpole, Horace); bibliography of written work, 88n.4; children of, 210n.5; compared with William Kent by Walpole, 91, 92, 93; with Nicolas Poussin and Salvator Rosa, 87, 148, 218; death and burial of, 84–85; early life, 83–84; exile in Jersey, 84, 102n.7, 109, 111, 123, 130n.42, 218; fiscal irresponsibility of, 84, 102n.7; penchant for grotesques, animals, and pictorial metamorphoses, 107, 108, 109–12, 114, 131, 134, 136, 141, 158, 166, 176; for puns, 110, 116, 120, 125–26, 132–33, 134, 135, 139, 150, 157, 163, 176, 179, 183, 188, 190, 194, 197, 200–201, 204, 207–8, 216; pictorial satire, methodology for, 107, 108, 111–18, 120–26, 128n.11, 131–39, 140nn. 10 and 12, 142, 149–50, 153–54, 156, 157, 161–63, 169, 175, 177–81, 187, 188, 200–201, 204–6, 211–17, 219; pictorial strategies, in complement to Gray's literary ones, 94, 96, 98–101, 115–18, 120–21, 131, 134, 136–38, 141–42, 144–46, 148, 150, 153–56, 158, 160–65, 175, 179–80, 182–83, 186–90, 193, 200–201, 204, 206, 212–17, 219; portrait of, by Eccardt, 99, 103n.22, 196; relationship with Walpole, 84, 86, 91–94, 100, 102nn. 8 and 10, 104–18, 121–26, 131–32, 139n.2, 156, 165, 184, 186, 212, 214–17; with Gray, 85, 92–101, 106, 131–32, 134, 165, 214–17; temperament, compared with Gray's, 165–66; Walpole's assessment of, 91, 109 (*see also* Walpole, Horace). WORKS: architectural designs for Strawberry Hill (*see* Committee on Taste; Strawberry Hill); design for the chapel at The Vyne, 93, 130n.39; design for "The Cöhue or Town House at St. Helier in Jersey," 140n.7; designs for Chinese summer houses, 92, 156–57,

159n.8; designs for greeting cards, 126; drawing for Spenser's "Cave of Care," 109, 113–14; for Walpole's *Fugitive Pieces*, 84; for Walpole's "Judgment of Solomon," 129n.26, 149, 151n.12, 181–82; for Walpole's *Memoirs of King George II* (see *Memoirs of King George II*); of "two lovers... looking at the tombs of Abelard and Eloisa," 194; "Muzzled ape" and arms of Jersey, 109; "Prospect of Vapourland," 108, 110, 149, 196–98, 199n.7, 215, 216; "Scene in Jersey," 109, 219, 221n.4; "Temptation of St. Antony," 109, 134, 167, 169, 181; "Turkish Bath," 108, 109; "a vaulted bridge," 109, 219 (see also *Drawings and Designs by Richd. Bentley*); illustrations for Gray's poems and architecture, 106, 126, 186–87, 200–206, 208, 214, 216–17; for Gray's poems and theater, 126–27, 159, 166, 188, 200, 205; for Gray's poems and tradesmen cards, 126 (see also *The Bard; Designs by Mr. R. Bentley, for Six Poems by Mr. T. Gray; Elegy Written in a Country Church-Yard; Hymn to Adversity; Ode on the Death of a Favourite Cat; Ode on a Distant Prospect of Eton College; Ode on the Spring; Progress of Poesy*); literary satires, pamphlets, plays, and poetry in general, 84; *Apology for his R*[oyal] *H*[ighness] *the D*[uke], 88n.4, 122; *The Centaur*, 88n.4, 110–12, 128nn. 13 and 14, 135, 162, 176, 213; *James Maclean*, 88n.4, 185n.6; *Patriotism*, 84, 88n.4, 102n.8; *Philodamus*, 84, 88n.4; *The Wishes*, 84, 88n.4, 101, 199n.9
Bentley, Richard (Master of Trinity College), 83–84, 88n.1, 91, 93, 102n.8, 128n.15, 147, 177–78
Berain, Jean (artist), 106, 175, 213
Bernard, J. F. *See* Picart, Bernard
Bethlehem (Bedlam) Hospital. *See* Madness
Bickham, George (engraver), 157
Bindman, David, 88, 90n.14
Birch, Thomas, 91
Blair, Robert: *The Grave*, 104
Blake, William (artist), 85, 88, 154, 161, 162, 189, 191, 192–93, 211, 214, 219, 220
Boccaccio, Giovanni, 196
Bolingbroke, Henry St. John, Viscount, 186, 188, 189
Botticelli, Sandro (artist), 196, 199n.6
Boucher, François (artist), 107, 116, 169
Bracelli, Giovanni Battista (artist): *Bizarie di varie figure*, 109
Bronson, Bertrand H., 99, 103n.20
Brooke, John, 129nn. 31, 34 and 35
Brown, Sir Thomas: *Pseudodoxia Epidemica*, 155, 153n.5
Buckingham, John Sheffield, Duke of, 210n.7
Burlington, Richard Boyle, 3rd Earl of, 91, 104, 115–16, 117, 127n.3, 129nn. 23 and 30, 132, 212
Burnet, Thomas, 111
Bute, John Stuart, 3rd Earl of, 84, 132

Callot, Jacques (artist), 167
Cambridge University, 92, 171; King's College, 172, 174n.11
Caravaggio, Michelangelo Merisi da (artist), 147, 183
Carretta, Vincent, 128n.14, 198n.1
Cebes: *Tabula Cebetis*, 128n.18, 168, 169, 170, 174n.6, 188, 203
Centaur, True and Faithful Account of the.... *See* Bentley, Richard
Cérémonies et coutumes religieuses de tous les peuples du monde. See Picart, Bernard
Chapin, Chester F., 173n.4
Charon, 158, 159, 203
Chaucer, Geoffrey, 176
Chenevix, Mrs. (toy-shop keeper), 105, 127n.2
Cheron, Louis (engraver), 128nn. 19 and 21; engravings for Prior, 114–15, 132, 170, 184, 184n.3, 190; for Tibullus, 128n.22, 137, 198
Chesneav, P. Agustino. See *Orpheus Eucharisticus*
Chesterfield, Philip Dormer Stanhope, 4th Earl of, 160
Chinoiserie, 126, 154–57
Chiswick House, 117; compared with Strawberry Hill, 91, 104, 117
Chute, John, 84, 91, 93, 104, 130n.39
Cibber, Caius-Gabriel (sculptor), 166
Cibber, Colley, 112, 166
Clark, Kenneth, 85, 87, 89n.5
Cleyn, Francis (painter), 109, 128n.12
Cobham, Anne Halsey Temple, Viscountess, 178, 179
Codex Alexandrinus, 83
Cohen, Ralph, 116–17

Collins, William: *Ode on the Poetical Character*, 95
Committee on Taste, 84, 91, 104
Congreve, William, 135
Conway, Henry Seymour, 127n.2
Cottonian Library. *See* King's Library at Ashburnham House
"Course-a-park," 118, 148, 177
Coypel, C. A. (artist), 119
The Craftsman, 186, 188, 189
Cross, Wilbur L., 174n.8
Culloden, Battle of, 122
Cumberland, Richard, 131–32, 139n.2
Cumberland, William Augustus, Duke of, 111, 122–23, 125, 151n.3; addressed by Bentley, 122; visit to Strawberry Hill, 105

The Daily Advertiser, 100, 103n.18
Dante Alighieri, 166, 173n.5
Dart, Reverend John, 104, 127n.1, 128n.22, 198
Day, Thomas, 160
Deacon, James (artist): miniature portrait of George II, 121, 129n.29
Democritus, 123–25
Designs by Mr. R. Bentley, for Six Poems by Mr. T. Gray: biographical themes in, 85, 87, 96–97, 106, 108, 109, 117–18, 121, 131, 138, 141, 146–48, 150, 151n.9, 161–62, 165, 171, 173, 175, 176–84, 186, 190–91, 193–94, 201, 206, 207; as a coherent work of art, 85, 96, 99–100, 116–18, 126, 144–45, 152, 153, 207–9, 211–12, 214–17; comparison between engravings and original drawings for, 86–87, 97, 100, 114, 132–33, 134, 141, 146, 147, 161, 162, 164, 165, 169, 171, 184, 186, 195, 205, 206–7, 209, 213; cost to purchasers, 98, 100, 103n.18; critical appraisal of, 85, 86, 87–88, 89n.6, 97, 100, 110, 213; editions of, 83, 89n.7, 100, 101, 103n.27, 177, 183, 220, 221n.3; European graphic art, influence of, 106–9, 112, 115, 120, 135, 138–39, 140n.12, 142, 150, 175–76, 186–87, 190, 201, 212; format, 99–100, 126, 211, 212, 216–17; genesis of, 83, 88, 91–94, 97–100; Gray's reaction to, 92–94, 97, 98–101, 177; half-title for, 100, 103n.23, 217; Dr. Johnson's reference to, 85–86; Thomas Kirgate's extra-illustrated edition of, 86, 100, 123, 184, 195, 206; pictorial methodology of, 85–86, 105–6, 113, 115, 116, 117–18, 120–21, 125, 126–27, 131–37, 139, 141–42, 145, 146, 148, 150, 153–54, 157, 158–59, 160–61, 175, 176–78, 179–80, 194, 200, 201, 206, 211–17; rejected frontispiece portrait of Gray for, 98, 141–42, 146; relationship of designs to text, 98, 99–100, 106, 115, 117–18, 120–21, 126, 142, 158, 211, 217; title of, Gray's anxiety about, 94, 98, 100; titlepage of, 100, 103nn. 24 and 29; titlepage fleuron for, 109, 131–40, 141, 143, 154, 163, 165, 198, 208, 214, 215; Walpole's copy of with original drawings, 87; Walpole's initiation and sponsorship of, 86, 91–92, 212. *See also* Bentley, Richard; Gray, Thomas; Grignion, Charles; Müller, Johann Sebastian; Sister Arts, interplay of, Strawberry Hill; Walpole, Horace
Diogenes, 167
Dodsley, James, 101, 103n.27, 220, 221n.3
Dodsley, Robert, 83, 86, 98, 99, 100, 204
Doherty, F., 150n.1
Dorigny, Nicholas (engraver), 124
Dossi, Battista (artist): *Flight into Egypt*, 124
Drawings and Designs by Richd. Bentley, only son of Dr. Bentley, Master of Trinity-College Cambridge, 91, 102n.3
Dryden, John, 95, 96, 97, 109, 119; *Alexander's Feast*, 152, 153; *Epistle to Kneller*, 95, 102n.14; *Theodore and Honoria*, 93, 196
Du Fresnoy, Charles: *De Arte Graphica*, 95, 119
Dugdale, Sir William, 104, 127n.1
Dürer, Albrecht (artist), 85, 140n.12, 150, 198, 204; *Death of Orpheus*, 138–39, 150, 157, 180, 190; *Four Horsemen of the Apocalypse*, 167; *Der Hercules*, 139, 190; *Knight, Death and Devil*, 195; *Meeting of Joachim and Ann at the Golden Gate*, 203, 204; *Melencolia I*, 93, 147, 195, 215; *The Nativity*, 204; *Penance of St. John Chrysostom*, 195; *St. Jerome in his Study*, 195
D'Urfey, Thomas, 182

Eccardt, John Giles (artist), 98, 99, 103n.22, 141, 196
Edward I (king of England), 218, 219, 220, 221n.3
Elegy Written in a Country Church-Yard, 83, 96, 104, 114, 116, 134, 135, 137, 141, 144–45, 146, 147, 150, 151n.2, 178, 183, 184, 194, 200–210, 214, 216; frontispiece for, 101,

126, 134, 162, 167, 200–205, 208–9, 210n.8, 214, 216, 222; headpiece for, 169, 205–6, 222; initial letter for, 127, 206, 210n.7, 222; tailpiece for, 93, 97, 101, 102n.6, 106, 116, 142–43, 150, 151n.9, 203, 206–9, 214, 222
El Greco (Domenico Teotocopulo) (artist): *Laocoön*, 113
Elizabeth I (queen of England), 175, 178, 179
Emblem books, 99, 103nn. 19 and 21, 112–13, 212, 214. *See also* Freeman, Rosemary; Quarles, Francis; Ripa, Cesare; Whitney, Geoffrey; Wither, George
Emblems: Bentley's use of, 113, 120, 132, 133, 136, 138, 141–43, 146–47, 148, 149, 153, 155, 157, 160, 164, 166, 168, 172, 176–78, 187, 193, 196, 200, 206, 208–9; Walpole's advice concerning, 113, 120, 206. *See also* Apollo; Athena; Charon; Dürer, Albrecht; Emblem books; Fates; Graces, The Three; Hercules; Hogarth, William; Madness; Melancholy; Orpheus; Ripa, Cesare; River gods; Shaftesbury, Anthony Ashley Cooper, 3rd Earl of; Venus; Zephyrs; Zeus
Empson, William, 159n.1
Eton College, 160, 163, 171–72, 174n.12, 178, 190
European graphic art in illustrated texts. See *Designs by Mr. R. Bentley, for Six Poems by Mr. T. Gray*

Fates, 154, 155, 157, 159, 166, 180, 203
Fielding, Henry, 160
Fincino, Marsilio, 148
Fiori, Mario di (artist): *A Concert of Birds*, 188
Folkenflik, Robert, 89n.8
Foulis, R. and A. (publishers), 101
Fourdrinier, Peter (engraver), 112
Fox, Henry, 107, 123
Frederick, Prince of Wales, 121–23, 125–26, 129nn. 30 and 34
Freeman, Rosemary, 103n.21, 112–13, 128n.18
Furniture makers: pattern books, 126
Fuseli, Henry (artist), 219

Gabbiani, Anton Domenico (artist), 162, 168, 170, 173n.5
Gainsborough, Thomas (artist), 206
Gay, John: *Beggar's Opera*, 126, 182, 185n.6; *Dione. A Pastoral Tragedy*, 210n.2, 212; *Fables*, 115, 119, 134, 135, 146, 153, 156, 162, 182, 186, 201–2, 207, 210n.5, 212, 216; *Shepherd's Week*, 120, 169, 205
The Gentleman's Magazine, 88n.2, 111
George I (king of England), 121
George II (king of England), 121–22, 188
George III (king of England), 84
Ghezzi, Pier (illustrator). *See* Tasso, Torquato
Gibbon, Edward, 160
Gillot, Claude (artist), 174n.10
Giordamo, Luca (artist): *The Cyclops at their Forge*, 113
Giorgione (Giorgio Barbarelli) (artist): *The Three Philosophers*, 124–25
Gleckner, Robert F., 90n.14
Goldsmith, Oliver, 164
Gothic architecture: Bentley's use of in book illustrations, 124, 125, 162, 169, 172, 173, 175, 200, 201–5, 206, 208, 214, 216, 217; opposed to Palladian architecture, 91, 104, 156; revival of by Bentley and Walpole, 91, 104–6, 109, 131, 174n.11, 205, 206, 214, 219; Walpole's passion for, 104, 214. *See also* Committee on Taste; Strawberry Hill
Graces, The Three, 148–49, 151nn. 3 and 11, 179
Granville, John Carteret, 1st Earl of, 110
Gravelot, Hubert (artist), 115, 119, 120, 212, 214, 216; illustrations for *Cérémonies Religieuses*, 119; Gay's *Fables* (1738), 115, 186, 201–2, 203, 204
Gray, Mrs. Philip (poet's mother), 86, 93, 94
Gray, Thomas: appreciation of Bentley's drawings, 87, 94–100, 102n.11; association with Bentley and Walpole, 83, 85, 92–100, 131–32, 212; with James Dodsley, 101, 103n.27; with Robert Dodsley, 98, 99, 100; Commonplace Book of, 97; concern over publication, 94, 98–101, 106, 177; dislike of "explanations," 99, 103n.19, 106, 127n.4; drawing of Stoke Manor House, 93, 182, 183; hesitancy about collaboration with Bentley, 92, 94, 98, 101; insecurity of, 92, 94, 95–97, 98, 101, 165; literary strategies in poems, 85, 94, 95–97, 115, 120–21, 136–37, 139, 141, 142, 144, 145–46, 148, 152–53, 156, 158, 159n.3, 161, 162–63, 166, 172, 177, 178, 179, 186, 187, 189, 190–91, 195, 197, 211, 214, 215, 216,

219; pictorial allusions in poetry, 186, 201, 219; pictorial arts, attraction to, 95, 186–87, 196, 199n.6; portrait of, by Eccardt, 98, 99, 103n.22, 141; quarrel with Walpole on Grand Tour, 94, 102n.9; ridicule of in *Designs*, 97, 131–33, 134–35, 149–50, 175–81, 183–84; teased by Bentley and Walpole, 85, 92–94, 108, 132, 149–50, 151n.9, 175–81, 183–84, 196, 212, 217; temperament, compared with Bentley's, 165–66. WORKS: see *The Bard; Elegy Written in a Country Church-Yard; Hymn to Adversity; Ode on the Death of a Favourite Cat; Ode on a Distant Prospect of Eton College; Ode on the Pleasure arising from Vicissitude; Ode on the Spring; Progress of Poesy; Sonnet on the Death of Richard West; Stanzas to Mr. Richard Bentley. See also* Bentley, Richard; *Designs by Mr. R. Bentley, for Six Poems by Mr. T. Gray*; Eton College; Madness; Melancholy; Sister Arts, interplay of; Walpole Horace

Green, Matthew: Gray's echo of in *Ode on the Spring*, 146

Greeting cards, 126

Gribelin, Simon (engraver): illustrations for Pope's *Works* (1717), 114, 170

Griffiths, Ralph. See *The Monthly Review*

Grignion, Charles (engraver), 86, 97, 100, 119, 184, 186, 196, 197, 205, 209, 213, 222–23

Guernier, Louis du (engraver), 120, 128n.21

Hagstrum, Jean H., 88, 89n.12, 90n.14, 95, 103n.21, 186–87, 199n.6, 201, 209n.1, 219, 221n.3

Halifax, George Montagu Dunk, 2nd Earl of, 84

Halsband, Robert, 86, 88, 90n.12, 120, 129n.27, 132

Hammer, Thomas, 119

Hardinge, George, 102n.10

Hardwicke, Margaret Cocks, Lady, 111

Harvey, J. H., 90n.14

Hatton, Sir Christopher, 142, 151n.5, 175, 178–79, 180, 183, 203

Hayman, Francis (artist), 119, 120, 137, 184n.4, 186

Hazen, Allen T., 89nn. 6 and 11, 100, 102n.3, 103n.18, 107, 108, 129n.36, 151n.5, 174n.10, 179, 200

Helmstadler, Thomas H., 90n.14

Hendrickson, J. R. *See* Starr, H. W.

Henry VI (king of England), 171–72

Hentzner, Paul: *Itinerarium... Angliae*, 84

Heraclitus, 123–25, 130n.39

Hercules, 111, 121, 138–39, 182, 188, 189, 199n.4, 203, 216; Choice or Judgment of, 113, 128n.23, 139, 168, 172, 191; contrasted with Orpheus, 138–39

Hesiod, 140n.8

Highmore, Joseph (artist), 186

Hogarth, William (artist), 88, 106, 107, 115, 118, 119–20, 129n.26, 188, 211, 212, 219; influence on Bentley, 119–21, 125, 126, 140n.10, 176. WORKS: *The Beggar's Opera*, 126, 214; *Characters and Caricaturas*, 197; *Four Times of the Day*, 130n.40; *The Gate of Calais*, 120; *George Augustus, Prince of Wales*, 121; *The Harlot's Progress*, 119, 130n.40, 135, 174n.9; *Hudibras*, illustrations for, 119; *Laughing Audience*, 197; *March to Finchley*, 167; *Marriage à la Mode*, 156, 182, 183; *Moses brought to Pharoah's Daughter*, 186; *Paul Pleading Against His Accuser Tertullus*, 140n.10; *Turkish Bath*, 108

Holbein, Hans, the Younger (artist), 139, 191

Holinshed, Raphael, 108–9, 128n.11, 162

Holland, Henry Vassall Fox, 3rd Lord, 123, 129n.35

Hollar, Wenceslaus (engraver), 109, 119, 183

Horace, 95, 113, 114, 118–19, 128n.20, 129n.24, 147, 148, 150, 170, 173, 177, 186, 189, 191, 193, 198, 212, 215. *See also* Pine, John

Houghton Hall, 113, 187, 188

Howard, Hugh (artist), 128n.21

Hume, David, 136

Humphries, A. R., 150n.1

Hunt, John Dixon, 88, 90n.12, 218

Huquier, Gabriel (engraver), 107; *La Pèllerine Altérée*, 107

Hurd, Richard, 136

Hymn to Adversity, 83, 92, 135, 141, 144–45, 147, 150, 164, 186–99, 208, 214, 216; frontispiece for, 146, 147, 186–90, 191, 193, 203, 222; headpiece for, 116, 146, 147, 149, 189, 190–91, 193, 222; initial letter for, 147, 191, 193, 197, 222; tailpiece for, 93, 97, 99, 113, 146–47, 149, 189, 190, 191–98, 200, 208, 209, 214–15, 222

James, G. Ingli, 90n.14
Jarrett, Derek, 129n.32, 173n.3, 199n.5
Jealousy. *See* Madness
Jersey, Island of. *See* Bentley, Richard
Johnson, Samuel, 86, 89n.8, 174n.6, 194, 195, 197; *Lives of the Poets*, "Gray," 85–86, 98, 152–53, 200
Jones, Thomas (artist), 219
Joue, Jacques de la (artist): *Livre nouveau de divers morceaux de fantaisie*, 107
Judgment of Hercules. *See* Hercules
Julienne, Chevalier Jean de: *Oeuvre gravé d'Antoine Watteau*, 107

Kent, William (artist), 85, 93, 106, 115–18, 126, 132, 139n.3; as architect and decorator, 91, 156, 162; compared with Bentley by Walpole, 91, 92, 93, 132; connection with Burlington, 91, 132, 212; illustrations for Gay, 115, 128n.17, 134–35, 146, 162, 182, 201–2, 204, 210n.2, 212, 216; for Pope, 112, 115, 128n.17, 212; for Spenser, 91, 102n.4, 114, 119, 128n.16, 184n.4, 198, 211, 212; for Thomson, 116–17, 119, 128n.17, 129n.23, 149, 162, 169, 206, 208, 212, 220; his monument for Congreve, 135; his murals for Houghton Hall, 187
Ketton-Cremer, R. W., 85, 88, 89nn. 5, 9, and 12, 102n.9, 160, 171, 173nn. 1 and 2
King's Library at Ashburnham House: fire at, 83–84
Kirgate, Thomas (printer), 86, 100, 103n.26, 123, 184, 195, 206. See also *Designs by Mr. R. Bentley, for Six Poems by Mr. T. Gray*

Law, John. *See* Picart, Bernard
Lens, Bernard (artist), 128n.15, 142, 151n.3, 177
Lewis Walpole Library, 86, 103n.26, 129n.33, 130n.43, 151n.12, 221n.2
Lewis, Wilmarth Sheldon, 86, 88, 89nn. 6 and 12
Lies, theme of in the *Centaur*, 111; play on lyre, 136–37, 140n.8, 141, 164, 175, 197, 214; source of irony and sentimentality in *Designs*, 96, 115, 121, 135–37, 139, 140n.8, 143, 144–46, 147, 150, 152, 155, 163, 168, 169, 172, 178, 193, 202, 203, 205, 208, 213, 214, 215–16
Locke, John, 133, 160, 215
The London Magazine, 186
A Long Story, 83, 97, 98, 101, 135, 141, 142, 143, 144–45, 147, 148, 150, 175–85, 200–201, 208, 214, 216; frontispiece for, 106, 107, 108, 116, 125, 175–83, 190, 203, 213–14, 222; headpiece for, 93, 97, 183, 222; initial letter for, 109, 183, 222; tailpiece for, 101, 103n.26, 123, 127, 178, 183–84, 193, 208, 222
Lorrain, Claude (artist), 123, 142, 150
Loutherbourg, Philip James de (artist), 219, 221, 221nn. 3 and 5
Lucan: *Pharsalia*, 84

Mack, Maynard, 146, 151n.7
Maclean, James (highwayman), 180, 184, 185n.6. *See also* Bentley, Richard
Madness, 147, 149, 164–66, 170, 183, 187, 189, 190, 191, 197, 214; Bethlehem (Bedlam) Hospital, 166, 167, 203; and Jealousy, 161, 162, 164–66, 167, 168, 180, 203, 204; and Melancholy ("vultures of the mind"), 147, 149, 161, 165, 166, 170, 183, 190, 191–98, 199nn. 5 and 9, 214, 216, 219; and Science, 173
Mainardi, Girolama (printer). *See* Tasso, Torquato
Mann, Horace, 91, 92, 127n.2
Mantegna, Andrea (artist), 137
Marolles, Michel de: *Tableux du Temple des Muses*, 129n.23, 169
Martin, John (artist), 219
Mason, William, 95, 97, 102nn. 11 and 14, 110, 137, 151n.2, 208, 213, 220, 221n.3
Masucci, Agostino (artist): *The Holy Family*, 130n.39
Mathieu, Jean (engraver), 209n.1
Mayor, A. Hyatt, 127n.7
McCarthy, F. I., 218, 221nn. 1, 2, and 5
McCarthy, Michael J., 88, 89n.6, 90n.12
Meissonier, Juste Aurèle (artist): *Livre d'ornemens*, 107
Melancholy: Bentley's self-portrait as, 134, 138, 219; emblematic use of by Bentley, 93, 113, 114, 133, 139n.4, 146–47, 148, 170, 191–98, 199n.8, 200, 209, 214; fashionable subject in the arts, 104, 124, 162, 194, 214; Gray portrayed as, 114, 134, 138, 147, 148, 149, 170; Gray's obsession with, 93–94, 147, 161, 192–98, 200, 206, 207, 214–16; as Lydia in Pine's *Horace*, 146–47, 191, 194, 195, 196, 198; as "Muta Poesis," 133, 137; portrayed by Dürer, 93, 147, 195, 215; by Ripa, 93, 133, 137,

139n.4, 199n.8. See also *Hymn to Adversity*, tailpiece for; Madness
Melcombe, George Bubb Dodington, Baron, 84
Memoirs of King George II, 84, 92, 107, 121–26, 127, 129nn. 26, 28, 35, and 36, 130n.42; Bentley's designs for frontispiece, 123–26, 129n.28, 132; for headpiece, Book I, 121; for initial letter, Book I, 121–22; for tailpiece, Book I, 122–23, 125, 129n.28; for headpiece showing the Duke of Argyle, 107; for headpiece showing Henry Fox, 107, 123; for headpiece showing Henry Pelham, 107; for headpiece showing William Pitt, 107; edition of 1822, 123, 129n.35
Mengel, Elias, 112, 115
Miller, Norbert, 88, 90n.12
Milton, John, 85, 95, 96, 119, 137, 143, 146, 149, 150, 153, 159n.4, 165, 166, 167, 168, 214, 219, 220
Minerva. *See* Athena
Mitchell, W. J. T., 90n.14
Mitford, Reverend J., 102n.14, 187, 199n.6
Molière: *Oeuvres* illustrated by Boucher, 107
Montagu, George, 84, 91, 92, 99, 104, 105, 160, 196, 220
The Monthly Review, 100
Monument Consacré à la Postérité en Mémoire de la Folie Incroyable XX. Année du XVIII. Siècle. See Picart, Bernard
Müller, Johann Sebastian (engraver), 86, 97, 98, 100, 114, 119, 133, 134, 137, 141, 147, 161, 162, 164, 165, 169, 213, 222–23
Müntz, Johann Heinrich (artist), 130n.42
Murray, Alexander, 110
Murray, John (publisher), 123
Muta Poesis. See Bellori, Giovanni Pietro
Mythology: in Bentley, 154, 158–59, 173n.5, 186–90. *See also* Apollo; Arion; Athena; Charon; Fates; Hercules; Madness; Narcissus; Orpheus; Persephone; River gods; Sisyphus; Venus; Zephyrs; Zeus

Narcissus, narcissism, 138, 153, 155, 159n.4
Newcastle, Thomas Hollis, Duke of, 123
Niquet, Claude (engraver), 209n.1
Northumberland, Lady Elizabeth Seymour: Bentley's calling card for, 126

Ode to Adversity. See *Hymn to Adversity*
Ode on the Death of a Favourite Cat, 83, 135, 138, 141, 143, 144–45, 147, 150, 152–58, 181, 183, 184, 201, 208, 214, 216; frontispiece for, 93, 107, 115, 126–27, 152–57, 160, 166, 176, 180, 181, 203, 222; headpiece for, 153, 157–58, 222; initial letter for, 153, 158, 222; tailpiece for, 153, 158–59, 170, 173, 183, 193, 208, 222
Ode on a Distant Prospect of Eton College, 83, 99, 135, 141, 144–45, 147, 149, 150, 160–74, 177, 193, 195, 200–201, 208, 214, 216; frontispiece for, 108, 116, 147, 149–50, 160–70, 172, 173, 174nn. 10 and 12, 176, 177, 180, 181, 184, 188, 189, 190, 191, 193, 197, 198, 198n.1, 201, 203, 204, 209, 214, 222; headpiece for, 170–72, 222; initial letter for, 170, 172–73, 222; tailpiece for, 173, 174n.12, 208, 222
Ode on the Pleasure arising from Vicissitude, 208
Ode on the Spring, 83, 114, 116, 134, 135, 136, 137, 138, 141–51, 152, 153, 193, 207, 208, 214, 216; frontispiece for, 113, 114, 126–27, 131, 141–48, 150, 152, 154, 158, 160, 162–63, 166, 170, 177, 184, 188, 193, 194, 198, 202, 203, 207–8, 209, 215, 222; headpiece for, 114, 116, 148–50, 179, 220, 222; initial letter for, 150, 222; tailpiece for, 120, 148, 150, 151n.13, 207, 208, 222
Ogilby, John (translator), 109
Ogilvie, Vivien, 173n.3
Orpheus: Orphean themes, 137–39, 147, 157, 191, 193, 214, 216. *See also* Hercules
Orpheus Eucharisticus, 137
Ovid, 137, 138, 154, 159n.4, 169

Palladian architecture, 91, 104, 156
Panofsky, Erwin, 138, 139, 140n.11, 195, 203
Parker, Matthew (Archbishop of Canterbury), 127n.3
Parmigianino (Girolamo F. M. Mazzuoli) (artist), 219
Paulson, Ronald, 88, 90n.13, 102n.13, 103n.21, 119, 120, 127nn. 6 and 9, 129n.23, 135, 139, 140n.6, 156, 159n.6, 174n.6, 199n.3, 210n.6, 212
Pelham, Henry, 107, 123
Persephone, 153
Philip II (king of Spain), 179
Piazzetta (illustrator). *See* Tasso, Torquato
Picart, Bernard (engraver and illustrator), 107, 112, 118, 119, 175, 201; *Cérémonies et coutumes religieuses de tous les peuples du*

monde, 107–8; *Monument Consacré à la Postérité en Mémoire de la Folie Incroyable XX. Année du XVIII. Siècle,* 108, 127n.10, 177–78
Pine, John (artist), 106, 115, 118–19, 174n.12, 183, 191, 199n.8, 211; *Quinti Horatii Flacci Opera,* 118, 212; illustrations for "Ad Fortunam," 195; for "Ad Lydiam," 146–47, 191, 193, 194, 195, 196, 198, 215; for "Ad Postumum," 170; for "Ad Thaliarchum," 118–19, 148, 177
Pitt, William (the elder), 107
Pius V, 175, 178, 179
Polonius, Thomas. *See* Vincidor, Tommaso di Andrea
Pope, Alexander, 94, 96, 97, 114, 212; *The Dunciad,* 112, 115, 128n.15, 166; *Eloisa to Abelard,* 104, 105, 194, 195, 215; *Epistle to Mr. Jervas,* 95, 102n.14, 134; *Essay on Criticism,* 120, 129n.25, 132, 133, 212; *Essay on Man,* 159n.3, 164; *Pastorals,* 118–19, 137, 141, 177; *Rape of the Lock,* 112, 179, 197, 215; *Windsor Forest,* 154–55, 167–68, 169, 170, 177
Poussin, Nicolas (artist), 85, 87, 134, 148, 162, 201, 202, 203, 204, 205, 206, 208, 209n.1, 210n.2, 214, 216, 218
Prior, Matthew: *Alma, or the Progress of the Mind,* 114–15, 184, 190; *Poems on Several Occasions,* 114, 128nn. 20 and 21, 132, 184n.3. *See also* Cheron, Louis
Prodicus. *See* Hercules, Choice of
The Progress of Poesy, 98, 100, 103nn. 16 and 19, 106, 127n.4, 151n.13, 188–89, 192–93, 199n.6, 204, 218
Public schools. *See* Eton College
Purt, Reverend Robert, 175, 178, 180

Quadruple Alliance, 160, 163
Quarles, Francis, 112–13
Quarrie, Paul R., 174n.12

Raphael (Raffaello Santi) (artist), 124–25, 170, 186, 219
Redi, Francesco, 162, 168, 173n.5
Reindel, Albert (engraver), 209n.1
Renaissance woodcuts and engravings, 108–9, 128n.11, 162, 212. *See also* Dürer, Albrecht; Holbein, Hans; Holinshed, Raphael; Hollar, Wenceslaus
Reni, Guido (artist), 186, 187
Richardson, Jonathan, 95, 119, 135
Richardson, Samuel, 119, 120
Ripa, Cesare, 85, 93, 133, 137, 139n.4, 195, 199n.8, 215
River gods, 154, 166, 169, 180; Father Nile, 170; Father Thames, 151n.3, 154, 163, 167, 169–70; Father Tiber, 169–70
Robsart, Sir Terry, 105
Rococo design, 86, 105, 115, 119, 120–21, 126, 155–57, 162, 175, 177, 181–82, 190, 203, 212, 213; pattern books, 107
Rogers, Pat, 85, 89n.5
Romano, Giulio (architect), 135, 140n.7
Rosa, Salvator (artist), 87, 148, 162, 170, 195, 218–19

Sambrook, James, 128n.17
Sandford, Francis, 104, 105, 127n.1
Schaub, Marguerite de Ligonier du Buisson, Lady, 151n.3, 176–81, 182–83, 203
Shaftesbury, Anthony Ashley Cooper, 3rd Earl of, 113, 114, 120, 128nn. 18 and 23, 140n.10, 168
Shakespeare, William, 95, 116, 117, 119, 135, 146, 153, 193, 197, 198, 209
Shenstone, William, 184n.5
Silvester, R. (engraver), 174n.12
Simonides, 95, 133
Sister Arts, interplay of: Bentley's and Gray's corresponding or conflicting methodologies, 85, 87, 94–101, 115, 120–21, 131–39, 141–42, 145, 150, 153, 154, 165–66, 175–78, 183, 186–87, 207–8, 211–12; Bentley's innovative approach toward, 85, 87–88, 96, 99, 106, 111–15, 120–21, 126, 132–35, 139, 150, 157, 158, 159, 161, 175, 183, 207–9, 211–12; commemorated in poems, 85, 94–97, 134; subject of critical discussion, 88, 95, 102n.13; *ut pictura poesis,* 95, 113, 126; Walpole's attitude toward, 95, 120–21. *See also* Bellori, Giovanni Pietro; Blake, William; Cheron, Louis; Gravelot, Hubert; Gribelin, Simon; Hogarth, William; Kent, William; Pine, John
Sisyphus, 170
Sitter, John, 144, 151n.6, 162, 200
Sleater, William (publisher), 101, 206–7, 210n.8, 221
Smart, Christopher, 129n.24, 148, 151n.8, 174n.13, 177
Smollett, Tobias, 160
Snodin, Michael, 127n.6

Sonnet on the Death of Richard West, 95–96
Spacks, Patricia Meyer, 96, 103n.15, 141, 150n.1, 173n.4
Speed, Henrietta Jane, 151n.3, 176–81, 182–83, 196, 203
Spence, Joseph: *Polymetis*, 151n.11, 169–70, 199n.4
Spenser, Edmund, 104, 109, 113–14, 128n.16, 137, 166, 167, 168, 175, 187, 198, 211
Spike, John T., 173n.5, 184n.4, 212
Stanzas to Mr. Richard Bentley, 85, 87, 94–97, 102n.11, 103n.16
Starr, H. W., 102n.11, 127n.4, 198n.2
Steele, Sir Richard, 119, 124, 160, 174n.7
Stoke Manor House, 93, 97, 183. See also *A Long Story*
Stoke Poges, 93, 204, 210n.8
Stowe, Buckinghamshire, 135
Strawberry Hill, 84, 86, 91, 92, 104, 105–6, 110, 117, 121, 123–24, 129n.28, 131, 156–57, 188, 212, 213, 221n.2; allusive in a literary manner, 104–6, 121, 217; Bentley's designs for, 84, 92, 99, 104–6, 129n.28, 131, 194; for armory at, 105, 205, 217; for a Chinese summer house at, 92, 156–57, 159n.8; for lantern in hall, 105, 217; for shell bench at, 128n.12; for staircase and hall at, 91, 92, 105, 217; connection with *Designs*, 104, 105–6, 117, 121, 126, 131, 135, 205, 217; embodiment of Walpole's visions, 104, 105–6, 127n.2, 135, 156–57; the hall called the Paraclete at, 105, 194; as a stage set, 104–6, 123–24, 127n.3, 217; Walpole's methodology for and polemical purpose of, 104–6, 117; as Walpole's "monastery," 109, 124, 127n.3, 135. *See also* Bentley, Richard; Committee on Taste; Gothic architecture; Walpole, Horace
Strawberry Hill Press, 86, 127n.3, 131, 139n.1, 218, 220
Stuart, Bonnie Prince Charles, 111
Stubbs, George (artist), 206
Sturt, John (engraver), 128n.15, 177
Suckling, Sir John, 118
Summerson, John, 106, 127n.5
Swift, Jonathan, 181, 193, 211; *Battle of the Books*, 112, 128n.15, 177–78; *Gulliver's Travels*, 167; "The Lady's Dressing Room," 176; *A Tale of a Tub*, 167, 193, 197

Tabula Cebetis. See Cebes
Tasso, Torquato: *Gerusalemme Liberata*, 107
Tayler, Irene, 88, 89n.6, 90n.12, 103n.24, 106, 126, 127n.7, 130n.44, 132, 134, 146–47, 156, 159n.1, 161–62, 165, 173n.4, 176–77, 182–83, 189, 191, 192–93, 211, 217n.1
Teddington, 84, 85
Temple, Richard Grenville, 135
Theodore and Honoria. See Dryden, John
Thomson, James (engraver), 123
Thomson, James (poet), 117, 212, 220; *The Seasons*, 116–17, 119, 128n.17, 129n.23, 149, 162, 169
Thornhill, Sir James (artist), 186, 188
Tibaldi, Pellegrino (artist), 158
Tibullus. *See* Cheron, Louis
Tiepolo, Giovanni Battista (artist), 116, 175, 186
Tillotson, Geoffrey, 150n.1
Topsell, Edward: *History of the Four Footed Beasts*, 134, 135, 138, 140n.5
Townshend, Etheldreda Harrison, Viscountess, 111
Toynbee, Paget, 127n.3; and Leonard Whibley, 92, 98, 101, 102n.5, 192, 213, 220, 221n.3
Tradesmen cards, 126
Tuberville, A. S., 174n.12
Turner, A. Richard, 130n.38

Ut pictura poesis. See Sister Arts, interplay of

Vandeput, Sir George, 111
Venus, 116, 145, 148, 154
Vernon, P. F., 148, 151n.1
Verrio, Antonio (artist), 184n.4
Vinci, Leonardo da (artist): *St. Jerome*, 124
Vincidor, Tommaso di Andrea (Polonius) (artist), 198
Virgil, 85, 96, 109, 113, 145, 146, 150, 152, 159, 166, 167, 168, 203, 214

Walpole, Horace: aesthetic innovations of, 85, 86, 99, 104–6, 117–18, 120–21, 214–15, 217; approached Robert Dodsley as publisher for *Designs*, 83; armorials of, 105, 123–24, 126, 186; *The Bard*, reaction to, 220; character of, 93–94, 102n.10; choice and encouragement of Bentley as illustrator, 84, 92, 94, 97, 109, 131–32, 148, 165, 212, 218; coaching of Bentley as artist, 106–10, 111–16, 117–18, 119–21, 132, 151n.3, 166, 212–13; as architect, 104; compares himself with Burlington, 91, 104, 115–16, 117, 127n.3, 132, 212; correspondence with Bentley, 93, 105, 109, 112, 132, 148, 156, 159n.8, 212; with Gray, 92, 93, 98–99, 101, 103n.27, 106, 146, 149, 151nn. 9 and 11, 160, 196, 206, 213, 218; with Mann, 91, 105, 127n.2; with Montague, 84, 91, 92, 93, 99, 104, 156, 160, 196, 220; *Designs*, explanations and annotations for poems in, 99, 106, 141, 144, 154, 157, 161, 171, 175, 179, 183, 187–88, 189, 190, 191, 200, 203; friendship with Gray, 83, 99, 102nn. 9 and 10, 103n.27, 160, 214–15 (*see also* Eton College); indulges in "Vasari-hood," 109, 212; opinion of Bentley, 84, 87, 91, 218; of Kent, 91–92, 93, 102n.4, 112, 116, 128n.16, 139n.3; opposes Bentley to Gray, 87, 93–94; as patron, critic, and collector of the arts, 91, 107–9, 112–13, 114–21, 128nn. 11 and 19, 129nn. 26 and 29, 132, 137, 140nn. 10 and 12, 151n.11, 158, 166, 174n.10, 188, 196, 212–14; pornography of, 129n.26, 149, 181–82; portrait of, by Eccardt, 99, 103n.22; as "priest" at his "monastery," 91, 106, 127n.3, 135; quarrel with Bentley, 100, 132, 139n.2; with Gray on Grand Tour, 94, 102n.9, 199n.6, 218; teasing of Gray, 92–94, 99, 106, 132, 149–50, 151n.9, 196, 212, 217, 220. WORKS: *Anecdotes of Painting*, 91, 102nn. 2 and 4, 104, 109, 119–20, 128nn. 12, 16, and 19, 129n.29, 166; *Book of Materials*, 129n.29; *Castle of Otranto*, 105; *Catalogue of Engravers*, 109, 114, 118, 119; *Description of... Strawberry-Hill*, 99, 101n.1, 104, 106, 129n.29, 188, 194; *Fugitive Pieces*, 151n.12, 171, 181; "The Beauties. An Epistle to Mr. Eckhardt the Painter," 95; "The Funeral of the Lioness," 92; "In Memory of King Henry the Sixth," 171–72, 173n.11; *Journal of the Printing Office*, 127n.3; "Judgment of Solomon," 129n.26, 149, 151n.12, 181–82; *Memoirs of King George II* (see *Memoirs of King George II*); *On Modern Gardening*, 139n.3, 142, 151n.4; "Short Notes" of his life, 151n.3; *The World*, essays in, 125, 139n.3. *See also* Bentley, Richard; Committee on Taste; Gothic architecture; Gray, Thomas; Sister Arts, interplay of; Strawberry Hill

Walpole, Horace of Wolverton, 123, 129n.34

Walpole, Sir Robert, 102n.8, 122, 123, 188, 198n.1

Warburton, William, 111

Ward-Jackson, Peter, 127n.6

Ware, Isaac: *Four Books of Andrea Palladio's Architecture*, 126

Wasserman, Earl, 213

Watteau, Jean Antoine (artist), 107, 119, 135, 142, 150, 175, 213

West, Benjamin (artist), 219

West, Richard, 95–96, 160, 173, 192

Whibley, Leonard. *See* Toynbee, Paget

Whiston, William, 111

Whitefield, Reverend George, 110

Whitney, Geoffrey, 173

Williams, Iolo A., 89n.6

Williamson, John: *The British Angler*, 157

Wimsatt, W. K., 128n.17

Wind, Edgar, 151n.10, 184n.2

Wither, George, 139, 157

Wittkower, Rudolf, 124, 129n.37

Wittreich, Joseph Anthony, Jr., 88, 90n.14, 213

Wootton, John (artist): illustrations for Gay's *Fables* (1727), 115, 153, 156, 206

The World, 125, 130n.41, 139n.3

Wren, Christopher, 174n.11

Zephyrs, 114, 116, 149–50, 190, 220

Zeus (Jove, Jupiter), 187, 188, 189, 190, 191, 199n.4